INTERVIEWING CHILDREN
The Science of Conversation in Forensic Contexts

DEBRA ANN POOLE

American Psychological Association
Washington, DC

Second Printing, February 2017

Published by
American Psychological Association
750 First Street, NE
Washington, DC 20002
www.apa.org

To order
APA Order Department
P.O. Box 92984
Washington, DC 20090-2984
Tel: (800) 374-2721; Direct: (202) 336-5510
Fax: (202) 336-5502; TDD/TTY: (202) 336-6123
Online: www.apa.org/pubs/books
E-mail: order@apa.org

In the U.K., Europe, Africa, and the Middle East, copies may be ordered from
American Psychological Association
3 Henrietta Street
Covent Garden, London
WC2E 8LU England

Typeset in Goudy by Circle Graphics, Inc., Columbia, MD

Printer: Sheridan Books, Inc., Chelsea, MI
Cover Designer: Beth Schlenoff Design, Bethesda, MD

The opinions and statements published are the responsibility of the authors, and such opinions and statements do not necessarily represent the policies of the American Psychological Association.

Library of Congress Cataloging-in-Publication Data

Names: Poole, Debra Ann, author.
Title: Interviewing children : the science of conversation in forensic
   contexts / Debra Ann Poole.
Description: Washington, DC : American Psychological Association, [2016] |
   Includes bibliographical references and index.
Identifiers: LCCN 2015046378 | ISBN 9781433822155 | ISBN 1433822156
Subjects: LCSH: Interviewing in law enforcement. | Child witnesses. |
   Conversation. | Forensic child psychology.
Classification: LCC HV8073.3 .P66 2016 | DDC 363.25/4083—dc23 LC record available at
   http://lccn.loc.gov/2015046378

British Library Cataloguing-in-Publication Data
A CIP record is available from the British Library.

Printed in the United States of America
First Edition

http://dx.doi.org/10.1037/14941-000

For Jack and John.
Nonna's still listening.

CONTENTS

Acknowledgments .... *ix*

Introduction 3

Chapter 1.   The Science of Interviewing Children 7

Chapter 2.   The Forensic Perspective 29

Chapter 3.   Conversational Habits 49

Chapter 4.   Conventional Content: Early Interview Phases 79

Chapter 5.   Conventional Content: Case Issues Phases 109

Chapter 6.   Case-Specific Decisions and Exploration...................... 141

Chapter 7.   Protocols and Interviewer Training............................... 169

References 191

Index 219

About the Author... 233

ACKNOWLEDGMENTS

Primary credit for this book goes to the many investigators who meticulously produced the evidence underlying interviewing guidelines. I am personally indebted to the colleagues who agreed to work and write with me over the years, including Larry White, Steve Lindsay, Amina Memon, Ray Bull, Amye Warren, Narina Nunez, Laura Melnyk, Chuck Brainerd, Valerie Reyna, Maggie Bruck, Michael Lamb, Kami London, Jason Dickinson, and Sonja Brubacher, along with the numerous students who served as co-authors and research assistants. The National Institute of Mental Health and the National Science Foundation generously supported my studies, which could not have been completed without the parents and children who volunteered time to help us learn more about the best ways to talk to children. Many people answered questions or offered feedback to improve the manuscript, and for this valuable input I thank Martine Powell, Kami London,

---

Any opinions, findings, and conclusions or recommendations in this book that are based on my grant-funded work are mine and do not necessarily reflect the views of the funding agencies named here.

Deb Connolly, David Thompson, Sonja Brubacher, Michael Lamb, Tom Lyon, Dayna Woiwod, and Jason Dickinson. Beth Hatch, development editor in APA Books, deserves special thanks for gently pointing out sections where I became bogged down in detail or forgot to tell readers where the story was heading. Finally, to Bret, Lin, and their families, my love and appreciation for your support.

INTERVIEWING CHILDREN

INTRODUCTION

Some of my favorite research in developmental psychology explored children's ability to explain something to another person. In a typical study, children looked at a drawing of four geometric shapes and tried to describe it so a listener could draw it accurately. Because the shapes had different sizes, colors, and locations relative to other shapes, children had to explain many pieces of information to succeed. This usually did not happen. In one sample, third graders mentioned only six features of the drawing, on average, which simply was not enough to cue listeners to the true state of affairs. Transcripts of children explaining a game to a blindfolded listener were charming. For example, one second grader said, "This side is red and you're supposed to put it, um, go on these. This side is blue and you're supposed to go on these. You put these in your hand, um, you choose, um, which pig you want. Told ya!" (Flavell, Botkin, Fry, Wright, & Jarvis, 1975, p. 98).

We would laugh less at children if we contemplated our own inexpert (and sometimes embarrassing) directions and e-mails. The truth is that children

http://dx.doi.org/10.1037/14941-001
Interviewing Children: The Science of Conversation in Forensic Contexts, by D. A. Poole
Copyright © 2016 by the American Psychological Association. All rights reserved.

do not have a monopoly on ambiguous communication. Put children and adults together and you have the question that has fascinated me for decades: Of all the possible things a conversation could have meant, what is the best explanation for what it actually did mean?

This question gripped my heart in the 1980s, when researchers around the globe read about day care abuse cases in which numerous youngsters made inconsistent and sometimes bizarre allegations. At the time, I was a directionless academic—bored with the basic research I had been trained to design and busy watching my babies grow. But after I learned what investigators were asking child witnesses and how the children responded, I found a purpose for my peculiar set of skills: I was not sure why children said what they said during criminal investigations, but I knew how to test some ideas.

That testing took a two-pronged approach. Because a developmental psychologist's home is an impromptu laboratory, for years I frequently squatted down, delivered questions to my son and daughter, and listened to the result. (Later, they trained research assistants and, eventually, produced a new generation of homegrown demonstration children.) My second strategy was to work with talented colleagues who were also interested in bringing legions of children into the laboratory. Those legions usually proved us wrong. Until recently, I never predicted the results of a study and often marveled at what drove other investigators to try their unlikely ideas. These discrepancies between what I thought children would do and what they actually did motivated this book, which is my way of sharing how evidence-based practice can reduce the ambiguities that permeate adult–child conversations in forensic contexts.

Because the science of conversation is broad, the range of topics covered in this book is also broad. Chapter 1 explains how adults usually talk to children, why this style impedes forensic goals, and the types of studies researchers conduct to look for solutions. Chapter 2 introduces the overarching characteristics of the forensic perspective, explains the differences between forensic and clinical roles, and discusses the benefits and limitations of blind versus informed interviewing. Chapters 3 to 6 translate the forensic perspective into three "C" skills: conversational habits (discussed in Chapter 3), conventional content (Chapters 4 and 5), and case-specific decisions and exploration (Chapter 6). *Conversational habits* are general skills, such as the nonverbal behaviors that put children at ease and the crafting of questions that children understand. *Conventional content* refers to the instructions and interview phases in protocols, whereas *case-specific decisions and exploration* involves the moves interviewers make to customize interviews. Dividing skills into these groups establishes general skills before introducing skills that are more difficult to master and more context dependent. Finally, Chapter 7 discusses interview protocols and the characteristics of effective training programs.

These chapters were designed for busy professionals who will put down this book and either do what they just read or analyze what someone else has done. To be useful for forensic interviewers, clinicians, attorneys, and the many other professionals who rely on children's testimony, the narrative is action oriented. Research-based practice recommendations are illustrated with example dialogue, summarized in chapter recaps, and reviewed in periodic Quick Guide sections that synthesize core ideas and skills. Each chapter also contains a Principles to Practice section, which presents a question about child interviewing and my response. Throughout, the goal is to illustrate evidence-based practice, not to imply that a single approach is best for every situation.

This focus on practice dictated a number of difficult decisions. Because some readers would not be interviewers, I violated a well-known tenet of training materials (see Chapter 7) by writing chapter subheadings that function as nouns rather than action statements (e.g., "Introducing the Topic" rather than "Introduce the Topic"). I also limited research reviews to illustrative examples, thereby omitting many classic and recent studies that deserved to be mentioned. I apologize for these omissions and refer readers to cited books and chapters for more in-depth reviews. Although I mentioned technical terms when doing so would help readers find other resources on a topic, I avoided unnecessary jargon.

It is also important to mention what is not in this book. Obviously absent is the enormous body of knowledge that professionals need to fulfill their roles as child protection workers, advocacy center interviewers, arson investigators, prosecutors, defense attorneys, judges, mental health workers, physicians, or mandated reporters in schools. And although it is true that general principles of talking to children apply across a wide variety of situations, conversational skill is only one component of the training needed for effective practice in these fields.

Also absent are topics that have not attracted enough research to support evidence-based guidelines. For example, interviewers should treat children and adolescents differently, but what this entails is still largely based on common sense rather than systematic research. Similarly, many widely distributed techniques have not been adequately studied and, for that reason, are not discussed in this book. I hope that these gaps will be filled in the years to come, which will give interviewers a wider range of techniques to choose from and a better foundation for tailoring practice to the needs of individual cases.

As guidelines continue to evolve, the primary goal of conversations with child witnesses will remain the same: to help children describe events in their lives as completely, accurately, and unambiguously as they can. The obstacles blocking this goal, and the techniques that overcome those obstacles, make up the science of conversation in forensic contexts.

1

THE SCIENCE OF INTERVIEWING CHILDREN

As Officer Matt Sonders drove to meet his students in an abandoned school, he mentally reviewed how the skills he was about to demonstrate could one day save lives.[1] After the Columbine High School massacre, U.S. law enforcement officials abandoned the practice of waiting for SWAT teams to confront active shooters and began training local police and sheriff's departments to respond in a coordinated effort. Matt's simulated munitions class included law enforcement representatives from several communities, and he had one goal: to teach them to react in ways that were radically different from how they would naturally react.

The challenges Matt faced are fascinating. It is unnatural to move toward threats, and police officers are often accustomed to planting their feet on the gun range. As a result, they may pause at "fatal funnels": structures

---

[1]Throughout this book, I changed the names of professionals, parents, and children who provided stories and conversation examples.

http://dx.doi.org/10.1037/14941-002
Interviewing Children: The Science of Conversation in Forensic Contexts, by D. A. Poole

such as doorways that look like protective barriers but actually stack responders into a line that makes them more vulnerable. Once they plow through, responders tend to collectively engage a hostile target instead of maintaining responsibility for their separate sectors of fire. During an interview that I conducted with him, Matt explained why these natural responses put them at greater risk of death, where new guidelines came from, why experienced officers sometimes resist new approaches, and the characteristics of effective training. Repeatedly, I muttered, "It is the same for us . . . this is why interviewing is so hard."

What does a task requiring unparalleled bravery have in common with interviewing? Consider how Matt's primary challenge—helping experienced professionals set aside their default ways of thinking and acting—is also a challenge in other professions. Emergency room physicians must temporarily ignore alarming injuries to resolve subtle yet life-threatening ones, trial attorneys must inhibit the urge to object when doing so would be nonstrategic, and financial experts must not overreact to short-term market fluctuations. Interviewing children also requires exceptional *effortful control*, which is the ability to suppress a dominant response and substitute another response. Professionals who excel at forensic interviewing regularly set aside how they usually speak because the conversational habits of everyday life can undermine a fact-finding process.

Just as the guidelines Matt trained were designed to address a set of problems, the conversational style we call *forensic interviewing* is a collection of techniques that mitigate problems—in this case, the problems that sometimes occur when adults talk with children. You will read more about Matt's story at the end of this book, where he shares his experiences as a trainer. This chapter explains why interviewing children is a specialized skill by reviewing how adults usually structure conversations with children—and the surprising ways some children respond.

THE CURIOUS ADULT: TELL ME WHAT I WANT TO KNOW, AND TELL ME NOW

Melissa and her 6-year-old daughter, Claire, had just participated in a research project when I asked whether I could record them talking to each other for a few minutes. After they agreed, I asked Melissa to find out what Claire had done during a recent activity. Here is the start of their conversation:

Melissa: OK, so what did you do at school Friday?

Claire: I was getting a pumpkin and playing.

Melissa:	At the pumpkin patch?
Claire:	And then Papa took me for a ride in a hayride.
Melissa:	A hayride? What did you ride in?
Claire:	Hay, I mean a trailer.
Melissa:	It was a trailer? Did it have a horse pulling it, or . . .
Claire:	There was a tractor pulling it.
Melissa:	A tractor? How many kids were on that?
Claire:	I don't quite know.
Melissa:	Was there like, just a few, or . . .
Claire:	There was three lanes and the teacher said, umm, only the teachers could be on the, on the middle lane.
Melissa:	Oh, teachers had to be in the middle. Kids had to be on the outside?
Claire:	Yeah, but, umm, kids went in the middle.
Melissa:	How come?
Claire:	I don't know. Because . . . they just wanted, I guess.
Melissa:	Oh. So what else did you guys do? Did you guys, like, eat apples? Or anything?
Claire:	We had donuts, and apples, and cider.
Melissa:	You did?
Claire:	Yes.
Melissa:	Is that when Papa was talking?
Claire:	No.
Melissa:	Oh, that was afterwards?
Claire:	Yes, it was before. It was after the hayride.
Melissa:	Was that the first thing you did?
Claire:	Umm-hmm.
Melissa:	It was?
Claire:	The hayride.
Melissa:	Oh, cool. Was it too cold?
Claire:	Well, not really.

Notice that after Melissa established the topic ("OK, so what did you do at school Friday?"), she constructed her understanding of the event piece by piece using questions that asked for specific details. Instead of inviting Claire to tell what happened on Friday, most of Melissa's conversational turns were comments such as "Did it have a horse pulling it?" and "Is that when Papa was talking?"—yes/no questions containing information Claire had not yet mentioned. Perhaps because Melissa was guessing what had happened (based on sketchy knowledge of a typical visit to this community favorite), much of the information embedded in her questions was, in fact, wrong.

What this transcript cannot convey is the pressured way Melissa spoke to Claire. Whenever Claire stopped speaking, Melissa waited less than a second before asking another question, and she often asked multiple questions without waiting for a response (i.e., "So what else did you guys do? Did you guys, like, eat apples?"). In turn, Claire usually said only a few words and then waited for Melissa to speak again.

It is not startling news that parents direct conversations with children. Most children do not produce extended narratives about the past until 3 to 5 years of age, and even then their parents provide questions and information that give children's stories their structure and content (Wang, 2013). At home, this process teaches children how to organize stories and what types of information make a good story. It is rarely a problem that parents control the storytelling process because they usually are not trying to learn from children. Instead, conversations about shared and emotionally charged experiences are vehicles for teaching children how to reminisce with others, how to cope with emotional events, and how to express emotions in culturally appropriate ways (Fivush, Berlin, Sales, Mennuti-Washburn, & Cassidy, 2003).

The problem is that this directive style of conversation infiltrates professionals' behavior at work, as a well-known study by Amye Warren and her colleagues illustrated (Warren, Woodall, Hunt, & Perry, 1996). These researchers analyzed dozens of sexual abuse interviews to find out how child protective services personnel elicited information. Mirroring Melissa's behavior, the interviewers dominated conversation. For example, they talked three times as much as the children did during initial rapport building, populated interviews with questions focused on specific details, and were often the first ones to mention critical information (including names and actions). Furthermore, there were hundreds of series of multiple questions in a subset of only 20 interviews, and interviewers failed to clarify over half of the ambiguous names that children provided. Subsequent studies found that teachers and police officers also direct conversations by asking children numerous specific questions (Brubacher, Powell, Skouteris, & Guadagno, 2014; R. M. Smith, Powell, & Lum, 2009).

Of course, a directive style of conversation does not always prevent interviewers from finding out what happened. When Melissa spoke to Claire, for example, the target event was known (Claire actually went to the pumpkin patch), Claire was eager to talk about her experiences, and she readily said "I don't know" and corrected Melissa's mistakes. In this low-stress situation, Claire was a reliable witness despite Melissa's inexpert interviewing. But Melissa's techniques do not always work well in more challenging situations, such as this next example from my laboratory.

One fall, a college student named Lindsey[2] asked some children to play an "opposites" game by pointing to one dot on a card whenever two dots appeared on a computer screen and vice versa. Next she said, "I want to ask you a few questions, but we have a rule about answering questions. The rule is don't guess. If I ask a question and you don't know the answer, just say, 'I don't know.'" Lindsey then asked 10 simple questions, such as "What is your favorite color?" including five questions asking for information the children did not know. This is how Paige (4 years old) answered the tricky questions:

Lindsey: What is my favorite color?

Paige: White.

Lindsey: I like a game called Silly Seven [a nonexistent game]. Do you like Silly Seven?

Paige: No.

Lindsey: We keep games in that box. What is one of the games in that box?

Paige: Mickey Mouse.

Lindsey: How many games are in that box?

Paige: Ten.

Lindsey: This picture [a simple house with a dog in front] is from this morning. Did I draw this?

Paige: Yes.

Lindsey: What's the dog's name?

Paige: Poodle.

Paige's answers are not an anomaly. Alex (4 years old) told us there were 50 games in the box, and Sam (6 years old) said the assistant had not drawn the picture. Also, more than one child integrated information embedded in

---

[2]Lindsey Schiller conducted this study for her undergraduate honors thesis at Central Michigan University in 2013.

questions into their subsequent answers. For example, Maggie (4 years old) said that Silly Seven was the game in the box and ended by saying, "I'll name it [the dog] Silly Seven." Children who invented wrong answers had difficulty playing the opposites game, revealing brain systems for effortful control that were still under construction.

Jean Piaget (1928), a famous developmental psychologist, once said that a striking characteristic of young children is their "extreme assurance on all subjects" (p. 202). This tendency to answer focused questions in the absence of knowledge diminishes as children mature, but it never entirely disappears (Pratt, 1990). For instance, one research team embedded an unanswerable question in an interview about a scuffle that had occurred between a man and a woman (Poole & White, 1991). When interviewers asked, "What does the man do for a living—what is his job?" over a quarter of the 4- and 6-year-olds offered speculations during their first interview, such as "He works with my father" and "He works at the lumber yard." Fewer 8-year-olds guessed, but, remarkably, over half the adults did. Thus even older witnesses, when they believe they might know the answer, sometimes just guess.

It is well known that some forms of questions/prompts encourage speculation more often than others. (The term *prompts* refers to questions and other behaviors intended to elicit information from children, including statements that function as questions, such as "Tell me about ___.") Because there is no uniform system for categorizing interviewer prompts, Quick Guide 1.1 includes some of the terms Michael Lamb, Martine Powell, and their colleagues have used while noting alternative terms (e.g., D. A. Brown et al., 2013; Powell & Snow, 2007, Sternberg, Lamb, Orbach, Esplin, & Mitchell, 2001).[3] Facilitators (also called *minimal encouragers*) include utterances such as "OK" and "umm-hmm," along with repetition of a few words children just said, which interviewers interject to show they are listening and to encourage children to continue talking. As discussed in Chapter 3, these utterances do not explicitly ask for information but nonetheless serve an important function during interviews.

Open-ended recall prompts (also called *open prompts, open-ended questions,* and *invitations*) are statements that invite children to talk about a topic. These utterances include invitations such as "Tell me everything that happened" (an open-ended broad question), "What happened next?" (an open-ended breadth question), and "Tell me more about the part where [action the child mentioned]" (an open-ended depth question). These types of prompts invite

---

[3]In this book, I use the term *recall-detail* to label questions such as "When did that happen?" Such questions are often called *specific* questions. Martine Powell and her colleagues use *specific cued-recall* questions (e.g., C. H. Jones & Powell, 2005), and Lamb and his colleagues use *directives* (e.g., Andrews, Lamb, & Lyon, 2015).

QUICK GUIDE 1.1
Types of Prompts

Interviewing prompts include behaviors that merely encourage children to talk (facilitators), prompts that allow children to choose which details to report (open-ended recall prompts), and prompts that ask about specific details (focused prompts). Prompts that suggest information children have not yet mentioned in the current interview (suggestive prompts) are discouraged. (See Quick Guide 5.2 for terms that describe some specific functions of comments/prompts in interviews.)

Facilitators (also called minimal encouragers)

Utterances like "Okay" and "Umm hmm," and restatements of something children just said, which interviewers interject to show they are listening and to encourage children to continue talking. Silence and head nodding are nonverbal encouragers.

Open-Ended Recall Prompts (also called open prompts, open-ended questions, invitations, and free-narrative prompts)

Requests that encourage an elaborated response by allowing children to decide which details to report. These prompts include initial *invitations* to talk about a topic, such as "Tell me everything that happened" (*open-ended broad questions*); invitations to tell more about a sequence of activities, such as "Then what happened?" (*open-ended breadth questions*); and *cued invitations* that ask children to discuss something they already mentioned, such as "Tell me more about the part where [action the child mentioned]" (*open-ended depth questions*).

Focused Questions

Questions that prompt children to provide specific details of interest to interviewers.

Recall-Detail Questions (also called *Wh*-questions, directives, and specific questions)

Questions that ask children to recall a specific detail about people, objects, or events they have already mentioned. These questions typically contain the letters *W* and/or *H*, such as "When did that happen?" and "Where did he touch you?"

Option-Posing Questions (also called closed and forced-choice questions)

Questions that engage recognition memory by providing information for children to accept or reject. *Multiple-choice questions* (e.g., "Where you at your mom's house, your dad's house, or somewhere else last weekend?") and *yes/no questions* (e.g., "Did you start the fire?") are option-posing.

Suggestive Prompts

Prompts suggesting information children have not yet mentioned in the current interview (e.g., "Tell me about the computer pictures"), including *explicitly leading questions* (e.g., "You were playing with matches, weren't you?").

Note. The terms *facilitators, invitations, cued invitations, focused questions*, and *suggestive questions* reflect usage by Michael Lamb and his colleagues; e.g., Sternberg et al. (2001). Martine Powell and her colleagues have divided open-ended questions into broad, breadth, and depth questions; e.g., Powell and Snow (2007).

children to talk about a broad topic, say more about a sequence of activities, or elaborate on something they already mentioned, respectively (Powell & Snow, 2007). The type of memory retrieval required to answer open-ended recall prompts is called *free recall* because witnesses search memory without help from targeted memory cues.

Because free recall develops later than more primitive forms of memory retrieval (Newcombe, Lloyd, & Ratliff, 2007), young children typically recall only a few pieces of information in response to each open-ended prompt. To draw out more information, laypeople often deliver a large number of *focused prompts*, which are utterances that cue children to remember specific details of an event. One type of focused prompt is a *recall-detail question* ("Wh-"), which often contains the letters W and/or H, such as "When did that happen?" "Where did he touch you?" and "How do you think he got away with this so long?" ("Why" questions are avoided in forensic interviewing; see Chapter 5.) Recall-detail questions cue memory retrieval by focusing children's attention on some aspect of a person, object, or event. Partly because cued-recall is an easier mental task than free recall, asking these questions after children have stopped responding to open-ended prompts increases the amount of information reported.

Children engage in recognition memory when interviewers mention a detail and ask whether that detail was previously encountered. *Option-posing questions*, such as multiple-choice questions (e.g., "Did he take your picture one time or more than one time?") and yes/no questions (e.g., "Did he tell you not to tell?"), test recognition memory. Finally, *suggestive questions/prompts* include explicitly leading questions (e.g., "You were playing with matches, weren't you?") and comments containing details children have not yet mentioned in the current interview. For example, it is suggestive to say, "Tell me about the computer pictures" if the child has not reported anything about computers or pictures. (Because *leading question* means different things to attorneys and memory researchers, *suggestive question* is the more general term for questions that suggest information.)

More so than open-ended prompts, focused questions encourage children to speculate and to remember information that did not originate from the matters under investigation. There are a number of reasons why focused questions tend to reduce children's eyewitness accuracy, including the following five.

Cooperative Behavior

Many children have a deeply engrained habit to answer any question an authority figure asks. The desire to cooperate by answering questions is so strong that children (and adults) frequently answer bizarre questions such as "Is a cup sadder than an orange?" even though they readily recognize that such questions are silly (Pratt, 1990, p. 170). We know that children sometimes realize they are speculating because they occasionally tell us so. For instance, after Lindsey asked one boy what the dog's name was, he said, "I don't know, so I'm going to guess Mr. Poodle." The challenge for forensic interviewers is that children usually fail to flag when they are uncertain. Open-ended prompts are less likely than focused questions to invite speculation because open prompts allow children to take a conversational turn by reporting only what they remember best.

Language Confusions

Many errors children make during interviews occur automatically and without awareness that answers are wrong. This is the case when children misinterpret questions because of insufficient attention or fragile language skills. For example, it is unclear whether Paige, the girl mentioned earlier, actually named the dog or thought the question was asking about the dog's breed. Misunderstandings were transparent in another study when several children responded to "What's my dog's name?" by saying, "I don't have a dog," thereby revealing confusion between "my" and "your" (Dickinson, Brubacher, & Poole, 2015). Unlike open-ended prompts, such as "Tell me what happened," focused questions more often include concepts, words, and grammatical structures that flummox children, causing them to respond to different questions than the ones interviewers asked.

Memory Intrusions

Rather than storing event memories as discrete and permanent traces, our brains construct memories by linking different aspects of experiences together through binding processes (Newcombe, Lloyd, & Balcomb, 2012; Raj & Bell, 2010). Findings from brain-imaging and other evidence suggest that a particular part of the brain, the hippocampus, plays an important role in specifying which subsets of brain cells comprise each event memory, making this structure critical for laying down new autobiographical memories and retrieving old ones. Our memories are far from static, however. Through a process called *reconsolidation*, memories can be updated each time we access them as related memories blend together and our minds fill in missing details with information from general knowledge. In other words, memory "may be less like a library and more like Wikipedia, where each entry is open to editing anytime it's pulled up" (Miller, 2012, p. 31).

Research on memory-updating processes has helped explain why focused questions are simultaneously a blessing and a curse: People remember more when memory tests provide cues that match their original experiences, but these cues can increase *intrusions*, which are false memories that are conceptually related to original experiences (Hupbach, Gomez, Hardt, & Nadel, 2007; St. Jacques & Schacter, 2013). In other words, simply directing children's recall by cuing them to recall specific details can cause their memory systems to alter recollections in ways that introduce inaccurate information.

Source-Monitoring Errors

Source monitoring is the process of knowing when, where, and how something was learned (Johnson, Hashtroudi, & Lindsay, 1993). You engage in source monitoring when you worry about whether you locked the car or only thought about locking it, whether you or your friend suggested a particular restaurant, and whether you saw a plane crash on television or only read about it in the newspaper. People remember where knowledge came from when they recall the contextual details that specify the source of that knowledge and then make good decisions about what those details mean. For example, you might think, "I remember hearing the beep, so I must have locked the car." The ability to recall event details and make accurate source decisions develops gradually during childhood as the brain regions that support source judgments, including the hippocampus and the prefrontal cortex, mature (Foley, 2014; Ghetti & Angelini, 2008).

Children arrive at interviews with knowledge from many sources, including images from television, information from books, and things they have heard others say. Interviewers want them to share what they actually experienced, but filtering out the irrelevant information is a difficult task. To understand why, consider a girl who has multiple representations of a visit to Disney World, some from her trip to Disney World and others from listening to people talk about Disney World. A number of developments must be in place before she can sort out memories of what she actually experienced, including the ability to recall sufficient details about these representations to support accurate decisions. This decision process requires a sophisticated understanding of how memory works. For example, children may not realize that detailed memories of how something looked or tasted are more likely than sketchy memories to be based on personal experience (Poole, Brubacher, & Dickinson, 2015).

Because the skills involved in source-monitoring judgments take time to develop, children do not always accurately report the source of their knowledge. In fact, young children sometimes misreport where they learned something even minutes after learning it. One research team illustrated this phenomenon by reading stories to 4- and 5-year-olds that contained novel facts (M. Taylor, Esbensen, & Bennett, 1994). Immediately afterward, they asked each child to confirm this new knowledge (e.g., "What do cats use their whiskers for?") and then asked, "OK, I want to know how long you have known that [experimenter repeats child's answer]. Have you known this for a long time or did you just learn this today?" (p. 1584). (Half the time, the order of these questions was reversed.) The children tended to say they always knew what they had just learned and that other children also knew this information (see also Drummey & Newcombe, 2002). This lack of awareness for when and how information was learned is useful in early development, when children need to rapidly acquire general information about the world (Bjorklund, 2007).

Because of source-monitoring difficulties, children sometimes describe information they acquired from sources other than the event of interest. In one study, for example, over a quarter of 7-year-olds and 9% of 8-year-olds reported during free recall that a male assistant had touched them, even though this touching had only been described in a story they had heard (Poole & Lindsay, 2001). When interviewers then asked yes/no questions about the suggested touching, about a third of the children erroneously said that touching had occurred. Furthermore, many went on to describe these fictitious events, showing remarkable memory for a few sentences of the story. Today, it is well known that young children's error rates soar during interviews when words embedded in focused questions trigger memories acquired from sources other than target events, such as conversations with parents or peers (Principe, Greenhoot, & Ceci, 2014).

Source-monitoring difficulties also come into play when children experience repeated instances of a similar event. Compared with memory narratives from children who experienced something once, the narratives of those with repeated experiences seem more inconsistent because they sometimes import details from one episode into narratives describing other episodes (H. L. Price, Connolly, & Gordon, 2015). This type of mix-up, which experts call an *internal intrusion*, occurs more often when children answer focused questions (Gomes, Sheahan, Fitzgerald, Connolly, & Price, 2015).

Confabulation

Throughout life, damage to the frontal lobe of the brain can cause a variety of memory disturbances, including an unusual behavior, *confabulation*, in which individuals make up answers to questions and tell fantastically false stories (mostly about their own lives; Borsutzky, Fujiwara, Brand, & Markowitsch, 2008). Wild tales from confabulating patients are believed to be memory based because these fictitious reports often consist of bits of true memories displaced in time and place (Nahum, Bouzerda-Wahlen, Guggisberg, Ptak, & Schnider, 2012; Schnider, 2003). Apparently, environmental cues continually activate memories that are irrelevant to current tasks and goals, but a healthy adult brain usually keeps unwanted memories from intruding into awareness. In contrast, the brains of confabulators have malfunctioning filters (Ciaramelli, Ghetti, & Borsotti, 2009).

Perhaps due to their immature brains, young children are more likely than older children and adults to interject loosely related thoughts into conversations (Schacter, Kagan, & Leichtman, 1995). Children's stories are sometimes so preposterous that anyone would know they are "mental surfing,"[4] though some of their mind-wanderings sound credible. In one study, for example, interviewers ended each session by asking the following question while gesturing to a body diagram: "When you first came to play these games with me today, did I touch you in any of the places on this picture?" (Poole, Dickinson, Brubacher, Liberty, & Kaake, 2014, p. 104). Children who said "yes" or pointed were asked to tell what happened. Despite the fact that children and interviewers had met only minutes earlier and then sat on opposite sides of a table, some children reported that assistants had touched them. For instance, one boy said, "You touched me here so you could feel me am I burning up or not" (Poole, Dickinson, Brubacher, et al., 2014, p. 106), illustrating how general knowledge (in this case, memories of adults checking for fever) can infiltrate memory reports. Overall, children who responded less maturely on a battery of developmental tasks were most likely to confabulate.

The ability to distinguish specific event memories from self-produced information is a type of source monitoring called *reality monitoring*. Among adults, the prominence of a brain region in the prefrontal cortex predicts the ability to accurately report whether information was recently presented or self-generated in response to a cue (Buda, Fornito, Bergström, & Simons, 2011). In legal cases, accusations from young children that seem improbable (based on case features other than the quality of their reports) contain fewer of the perceptual, contextual, and other features that help witnesses distinguish event memories from self-generated information (Roberts & Lamb, 2010). Together, these findings suggest that reality monitoring can break down in laboratory settings and in real-world investigations, with some individuals being more prone to errors than others.

Because of children's desire to be cooperative during conversation, their incomplete language development, and their greater risk of retrieving inaccurate information in response to memory cues, adults' habit of asking a large number of focused questions is incompatible with the architecture of the developing brain (Poole, Dickinson, & Brubacher, 2014). Delivering more

---

[4] I borrowed this term from Stephen Ceci, who used it during conversations at a NATO Advanced Study Institute (*The Child Witness in Context*, May 1992, in Barga, Italy) to describe how some children go off on verbal tangents leading from one thought to the next.

open-ended prompts is a step in the right direction, but other skills are needed to converse skillfully with children. For example, even responses to open-ended invitations can contain ambiguities and errors, so interviewers need strategies that might clarify or confirm children's reports (Ceci, Kulkofsky, Klemfuss, Sweeney, & Bruck, 2007). Also, the social and cognitive processes that produce unreliable testimony are not the only challenges interviewers face: Sometimes, the challenge is a child who does not want to talk at all.

THE RESERVED CHILD: NOTHING HAPPENED AND I DON'T KNOW

A subset of children are chatterboxes around unfamiliar adults, but many are frustratingly restrained. To help professionals tackle this problem, interview guidelines include strategies for overcoming reticence stemming from the following issues.

Fear of Getting Into Trouble

A young boy found crouching in the backyard after a fire destroyed his bedroom will likely avoid talking, as will a teenage girl who has just been diagnosed with a sexually transmitted disease. The dynamics of these situations illustrate how fear of getting into trouble discourages children from talking.

Remarkably, juveniles account for about half of arson arrests in the United States, with bedrooms being the most frequent place of origin for house fires started by children. In these cases, the culprits are most often boys under 6 years of age (Evarts, 2011). Many backyard fires are unintentionally set by older children, and some arsonists are teenagers who intentionally caused damage. Regardless of whether fires were unintentionally or intentionally set, children will be motivated to conceal their actions. As one investigator remarked, "At the onset the children will most likely behave in a hostile fashion" (Bouquard, 2004, p. 107). Investigators' jobs are complicated by the fact that many juvenile fire-setters have had negative experiences with adults, thereby making it difficult to engage them in interviews (Gaynor, 2002).

There are numerous reasons why children may not want to disclose sexual abuse, including fear of getting loved ones into trouble, fear of being blamed for the abuse, and fear that illegal actions, such as drinking alcohol with perpetrators, will be discovered. Many factors predict the likelihood of disclosing (London, Bruck, Wright, & Ceci, 2008), including the structure of interviews (Lyon & Ahern, 2011). Jumping in and discussing sensitive matters without spending time to gain children's trust is always a barrier to conversation, but this overly abrupt style is especially counterproductive when children are afraid.

An Inhibited Temperament

A subset of children tend to freeze in the face of novel people and situations. Compared with their peers, these inhibited children have a lower threshold for activating the physiological pathways involved in responses to unfamiliarity and challenge (Kagan, Reznick, Clarke, Snidman, & Garcia-Coll, 1984). Individual differences in behavioral inhibition are partly due to genetic differences (Dilalla, Kagan, & Reznick, 1994), although supportive parenting helps some children outgrow their extreme reactions to novel situations (Fox et al., 2005).

In my laboratory, assistants watch for signs of hesitancy and provide more time and supportive social contact before trying to separate inhibited children from their parents. Reluctance to talk—whether from fear, temperament, or other reasons—can be spotted early in interviews as well (Lamb, Hershkowitz, Orbach, & Esplin, 2008, Chapter 8). But unlike laypeople, who sometimes respond to inhibited children by becoming more animated and intrusive (thereby scaring children into silence), forensic interviewers use the strategies described in Chapters 3 and 4 of this volume to build rapport with inhibited children.

Normal Memory Lapses

There are many reasons why memories can fail. When attention is directed to one part of an event, we may fail to create memories for other parts of the event. Memories that are not reinforced may fade, and we can have a strong memory yet still not bring it to mind when needed. Because of failures to create memories, store them over time, or retrieve them when needed, interview questions sometimes fail to prompt relevant memories even among cooperative witnesses. For example, when first confronted by a question, a sizable minority of adults do not retrieve memories of personally significant events, including car accidents in which someone was injured and hospitalizations that occurred within the last year (Loftus, Garry, & Feldman, 1994).

Children are especially prone to memory-retrieval failures. To understand why, it is helpful to explain that what we call *memory* is actually a collection of systems that develop at different rates. *Implicit memory* involves learning that occurs without conscious awareness, and this type of memory functions at birth. Implicit memory includes procedural skills, such as how to brush your teeth, and responses acquired through conditioning, such as flinching when an aggressor's hand comes near. *Explicit memory* retains information about the individual autobiographical events discussed during interviews. This type of memory comes online after the first year and takes longer than implicit memory to fully develop (Newcombe et al., 2007, 2012).

Because explicit memory functions early in development but continues to improve throughout early and middle childhood, memory experts describe children's eyewitness abilities as both stunning and deficient. For example, 2-year-olds usually have something to say about injuries that sent them to the emergency room 6 months earlier, but half recall little about these events (Peterson & Rideout, 1998). With increasing age, children become better at searching for specific event memories, and the completeness of their reports improves (Peterson, 2002, 2012).

There is an interesting consequence of the fact that memory probes sometimes fail to trigger recollection: It is not unusual for children to report an event and then, just minutes later, deny that event in response to a different question. For example, assistants working for Tom Lyon and his colleagues encouraged children not to disclose that toys had broken (Lyon et al., 2014). After initial questioning by another assistant, children were asked, "Did anything bad happen with any of the toys?" (Lyon et al., 2014, p. 1760). Remarkably, many children who had already reported a broken toy said "no." Similarly, children in another study often explained how a woman named Bonnie had showed them a dog apron but then said "no" when interviewers asked, "Did Bonnie show you anything in the room?" (Poole & Dickinson, 2014, p. 196). Focused questions such as these are notorious for producing inconsistent testimony, partly because children often respond "no" to questions containing the word *anything*, but also because some words suggest meanings to children that are different from what the questions intended.[5] Because familiar question forms may not be the forms that best prompt relevant memories, forensic interview guidelines include techniques for helping children search their memories more thoroughly. (See A. G. Walker, 2013, for a discussion of language issues that contribute to inconsistent testimony.)

Insufficient Effort

Getting children to acknowledge target events is a minor victory if they refuse to fill in needed details. Interviewers inadvertently discourage children from talking when they take control of conversation at the start by asking a long series of focused questions, such as "How old are you?" "How many brothers and sisters do you have?" and "What grade are you in?" After chit-chat like this, some children decide that interviewers are going to ask many

---

[5]I once experienced a remarkable memory retrieval failure when listing prior surgeries on a medical history form. I had recently had a bone graft and other procedures to replace damaged teeth with implants and had worn an awkward prosthetic for months. Despite the inconvenience of this treatment, I recalled these surgeries only after I had left the doctor's office. Apparently, the word *surgery* did not trigger memories for happenings above my neck.

questions and they should respond with short answers (D. A. Brown et al., 2013; Sternberg et al., 1997). This type of questioning lessens the chance that children will volunteer information about topics other than those in interviewers' questions, which can cause investigators to miss information about corroborating evidence, unrelated child protection concerns, or other important matters.

Conditions and Histories That Reduce Informativeness

Child witnesses are more likely than other children to have conditions and personal histories associated with lackluster performance during interviews (L. Jones et al., 2012). For example, risk factors for fire setting include impulsivity and problems establishing relationships (Gaynor, 2002), and sexual offenders often select victims who are vulnerable because of troubled family lives, depression, and other characteristics that reduce the risk of disclosure (Lyon & Ahern, 2011). As a result, forensic interviewers need a toolbox of strategies for conversing with children who have difficulty staying on topic and understanding questions, as well as with those who are simply uninterested in talking. Overcoming barriers to talking in ways that are forensically sound is an important goal of child interviewing research.

HOW PRACTICE GUIDELINES EVOLVE

From the discussion thus far, it is clear that adults' usual style of conversation is not conducive to maximizing the accuracy or completeness of children's testimony. When professionals train to be child interviewers, they learn a unique style of conversation, one that is "conceptually simple, but . . . structured to make social and linguistic sense to children" (Poole & Lamb, 1998, p. 153).

Where do the guidelines for this style of speaking come from? And why do professionals sometimes disagree about which strategies are best? As in any field, our knowledge contains information gleaned from a large set of high-quality research along with information resting on more fragile foundations. Understanding the strengths and limitations of different sources of authority can help interviewers appreciate the need to modify practice as new evidence irons out disagreements and interview guidelines evolve.

The Limits of Professional Intuition

It is natural to develop intuitions about how the world works from on-the-job experiences, but it is important to realize that these intuitions are both highly useful and notoriously subject to error. People acquire useful intuitions when they have (a) repeated experiences, (b) in environments that are sufficiently regular, and (c) that provide opportunities to learn through feedback (Kahneman, 2011). For example, seasoned firefighters and anesthesiologists have amazing abilities to spot cues of impending trouble, just as some of my assistants are especially good at sensing when children are not yet ready to separate from parents. In these cases, workers have had numerous opportunities to observe whether specific cues were present or not present and the circumstances following each of these situations. As a result, they learned which cues were typically followed by negative events and how their responses to those cues affected outcomes.

But the conditions that build useful intuitions are not always part of our jobs. For example, clinicians who regularly use one form of therapy have no information about what would have happened had they taken a different course of action. If many clients improve over time, these clinicians may erroneously conclude that the therapy works. However, the therapy would actually be harming clients if more clients improve without the therapy than with it. This was the case with critical incident stress debriefing, an intervention believed to ward off symptoms of posttraumatic stress disorder among people who had recently experienced horrific events. After studies found that clients who received this intervention had similar or worse symptoms than comparison groups, this form of therapy was added to a list of treatments that were probably harmful to some people (Lilienfeld, 2007). By the same logic, interviewers who always use a particular protocol have insufficient information about how children would have performed had they used another approach.

Even when interviewers try different approaches, frontline experience is not conducive to evaluating the risks and benefits of competing techniques. One problem is that interviewers may come to favor techniques that elicit responses from children, even though the accuracy of these responses is unknown. Also, children's behavior is highly variable, and the cognitive machinery that builds accurate intuitions performs poorly when information is not sufficiently regular (Kahneman, 2011).[6] As a result, many techniques that were once popular have not survived the scrutiny of systematic

---

[6]An interesting phenomenon called *illusory correlation* illustrates how difficult it is to draw accurate conclusions from personal observations. In one demonstration, Chapman and Chapman (1967) asked judges to look at pairs of information about hypothetical patients, with each pair consisting of a symptom the patient had and a drawing of a person that the patient had made. Later, judges overestimated the association between symptoms and seemingly related drawing features, such as suspiciousness and peculiar eyes. Seeing relationships where none exists is one of many human judgment errors that make scientists skeptical of claims proffered without solid evidence.

research.[7] Suggestions based on frontline experiences are highly valued not because these impressions are evidence of effective strategies but because practitioners' ideas can motivate the research that tests ideas.

Phases of Intervention Testing

The fields of medicine and child interviewing seem to have little in common, but their practice standards evolve in similar ways. For example, new drug treatments are born when findings from basic research or clinical observations suggest a novel drug. In early research phases, researchers administer the drug to small samples of normal volunteers, and then small patient samples, to explore whether the drug functions as expected. If the treatment looks promising, scientists progress to later phases of research involving larger numbers of patients in diverse treatment settings (U.S. National Institutes of Health, 2007). To understand how this process of intervention testing produces evidence-based interviewing guidelines, it is helpful to review the limitations of basic research findings, how scientists collect information in preliminary field and analog studies, and how policy makers craft guidelines when definitive evidence from large-scale field trials is not yet available.

Basic Research Findings Are Just a Start

The goal of basic research is to discover the fundamental principles that govern our physical and social words—without concern for whether those principles have practical applications (although they often do). Some scientifically based interviewing guidelines rest mainly on findings from basic research. For instance, the literature on language development contains a wealth of information about the words and question forms that confuse young children, and experts unanimously advise interviewers to avoid using these words and forms. Because it is unlikely that children will suddenly understand difficult language constructions during forensic interviews, these recommendations are sound, even if no studies have documented lack of comprehension in this context.

Tasks that challenge children in their natural environments will likely challenge them during interviews, but the reverse is not necessarily true: Children who are at or above the age of acquisition of a skill will not always

---

[7] Jim Wood, Kimberley McClure, and Rebecca Birch (1996) made the interesting observation that "interviewing procedures can become informal policy . . . even though their underlying purpose has been lost or forgotten over the years" (p. 224). For example, one agency routinely included a good touch/bad touch discussion, even though no child disclosed abuse during this portion of the interview in any of the tapes Wood and his colleagues reviewed.

demonstrate that skill during interviews. For example, most 2½-year-olds use the word *my* appropriately, yet older children sometimes misinterpret questions containing this word. There are several reasons why research to establish the age when children typically master a word, concept, or skill is not a sufficient foundation for choosing interview techniques:

- Many children master individual words, concepts, and skills after the age of acquisition. Child specialists define age of acquisition as the age when most children demonstrate proficiency most of the time, but that percentage could be 50%, 75%, or some other number (depending on the author). Clearly, a skill that 25% of children have not yet mastered has no place in a forensic interview.
- Children's performance varies across contexts. Children can demonstrate a skill during simple laboratory tasks yet fail during interviews, when cognitive demands are greater.
- The cognitive prerequisites for benefitting from an interviewing technique are often unknown. For example, it used to be widely assumed that children 5 years and older could accurately report touches by pointing to a doll or body diagram because these children usually understand the representational purpose of props. However, research reviewed in Chapter 6 has challenged the assumption that props are developmentally appropriate for all children who grasp the symbolic function of a prop. (See Chapter 6's Principles to Practice for another discussion of developmental norms.)

Because of the limitations of basic research findings, interviewing strategies that seem justified by basic research should be tested in studies that embed those strategies in eyewitness contexts. Preliminary field and analog research is usually the next phase of that testing process.

Preliminary Field and Analog Research

Field research observes children and interviewers in their natural environments. Coding interview transcripts and describing children's memories for naturally occurring events are examples of this research strategy.

Typically, children studied in the field have experienced a variety of events, event details are unknown, and interviewers did not strictly adhere to scripted procedures. Because of this lack of control, research teams usually mention one or more caveats when sharing the results of field research. For example, Lindsay Malloy, Elizabeth Shulman, and Elizabeth Cauffman (2014) reported fascinating data on the interrogation practices associated with self-reported true and false confessions in a sample of incarcerated youths. As expected, false confessions were associated with coercive interrogation practices, including lengthy interrogations and refusing requests for breaks. Yet despite clear criteria for selecting study cases, the research team was careful to point out that some respondents may have lied when they said their confessions were false, whereas some who truthfully reported a false confession may have exaggerated the coerciveness of their interrogations. The self-report nature of this study is not troubling to researchers, however, because there is converging evidence that coercive interrogations can lead people to confess mishaps they did not commit (Kassin & Gudjonsson, 2004). Scientists say there is converging evidence when findings from different methodologies—including basic research, case studies, field studies, and a type of study called *analog research*—point to the same conclusion.

In analog studies, researchers simulate real-world situations to exert more control over factors that might influence results. In a typical study, researchers stage target events and then interview children in various ways, sometimes manipulating the information children encounter before or after those events. Analog research is an important phase of intervention research because this methodology can provide information about the mechanisms underlying interesting phenomena (Poole & Bruck, 2012).

Later Phases of Intervention Testing

The final steps of interviewing research involve studies that systematically compare the effectiveness of new and existing approaches in actual investigations. For randomized controlled field trials, researchers randomly assign participants to one of two (or more) approaches to observe how people perform in the real-world environments where the new intervention will be used. Because this degree of control can be difficult to arrange with forensic interviews, some large-scale field trials use research designs that are not fully controlled. For example, investigators might analyze testimony elicited by two protocols implemented before and after an agency shift in practice. The research team that has contributed the most evidence from large-scale field trials is directed by Michael Lamb, and their studies have provided valuable information on the benefits of the National Institute of Child Health and Human Development interviewing protocol (named for the agency where Lamb worked when early versions of the protocol were crafted; Lamb et al., 2008). As with all protocols, this one continually evolves as new findings motivate improvements (see Chapter 7).

Intervention experts emphasize that the research phases preceding field trials should not be bypassed because the information obtained from small-scale field and analog studies reduces the risk of harming participants and provides information about why techniques function the way they do

(Rogers, 2009). The national movement for evidence-based practice in interviewing thereby rests on a foundation that includes basic research on memory, development, and other issues; early field and analog studies; and large-scale field trials. When a practice question has not been subjected to all phases of the testing process, ethicists recommend basing practice on the best available evidence, which will lie somewhere along the continuum of phases (APA Presidential Task Force on Evidence-Based Practice, 2006; Stuart & Lilienfeld, 2007). For the field of child interviewing, this book is a compendium of that evidence.

RECAP

Forensic interviewing of children is a collection of guidelines for mitigating the problems that can arise when professionals talk to young witnesses. Adults' usual style of conversing with children is inappropriate in forensic contexts because this directive style increases the risk that children will speculate, misinterpret questions, and answer falsely because of memory intrusions, source-monitoring errors, and confabulations. Also, this style fails to create a supportive environment for fearful children and those who are uninformative for other reasons. Guidelines for improving the accuracy and completeness of children's testimony continually evolve as new evidence accumulates from basic research on cognition and other topics, preliminary field and analog studies, and large-scale field trials.

2

THE FORENSIC PERSPECTIVE

Every day, adults around the world are trying to learn about children's lives through conversations such as this one:[1]

Father: So what did you do at the sleepover?

Son: Jake's mom took us bowling and I spilled a pop.

Father: You spilled a pop? Was Adam trying to wrestle with you again?

Son: No, I just spilled it. It took me a while to find Mrs. Linton, but she bought me another one.

Father: Did you have a good time?

Son: Yeah.

---

[1]Many parents share stories with me about times when a lack of skepticism led them to feel mortified. In a typical story, they confronted a teacher or neighbor about a situation involving their children only to learn that their assumptions about the event were wildly wrong. I penned this fictitious dialogue to illustrate how jumping to conclusions can lead to two types of errors: Adults can falsely accuse someone, but they can also miss real risks and harm.

http://dx.doi.org/10.1037/14941-003
Interviewing Children: The Science of Conversation in Forensic Contexts, by D. A. Poole

This style of inquiry is what I call a *story interview* (Poole & Dickinson, 2013): Adults prompt children to tell the story of an event, and often the inquisitors are mostly interested in particular subplots. This father had recently caught his son and an older boy roughhousing, which is why he asked about wrestling.

To appreciate why asking children to describe an event is not, by itself, a forensic interview, consider the fact that the son in this opening story was the wrestling instigator who had (once again) grabbed onto Adam just before the pop spilled. The father did not realize what triggered these events because he never generated alternative hypotheses about who started the wrestling. He also never encouraged his son to elaborate and did not ask whether anyone else saw the drink spill (which might have revealed witnesses). Most important, he was not at all curious about why Mrs. Linton was hard to find. Consequently, he never discovered that the boys were at risk because she spends most of these evenings with friends at the bar. Like many adults, this father is unlikely to discover unexpected truths because he has not adopted a forensic perspective. In the following discussion, I review this perspective by describing the characteristics that distinguish child forensic interviews from natural conversations, how the forensic perspective separates forensic and clinical roles ("play-your-position" recommendations), and how different procedures for briefing interviewers prior to forensic conversations serve different goals.

CHARACTERISTICS OF A CHILD FORENSIC INTERVIEW

Some professionals erroneously believe that interviews are competently conducted as long as interviewers avoid suggestive questions and progress through the series of phases dictated by a protocol. In fact, an adult can neutrally converse with children yet still conduct conversations that do not serve the needs of investigations. Interviewers shift from conducting story interviews to conducting forensic interviews when they build four characteristics into conversations: hypothesis testing, a child-centered approach, exploration that supports the broader investigation, and an eye on commander's intent.

Hypothesis Testing

The hallmark of the forensic perspective is *skepticism*, which is a questioning attitude in which professionals maintain doubt about evidence and witnesses' declarations. A critical skill in the skeptic's toolbox is the ability to generate and test alternative hypotheses. Forensic interviewers engage in *hypothesis testing* when they list plausible possibilities regarding the meaning of evidence and then look for information that will increase or decrease the likelihood of each possibility. Two types of hypothesis testing occur during child forensic interviews: (a) testing alternative hypotheses regarding the matters under investigation (primary-issues hypothesis testing) and (b) testing alternative interpretations of children's utterances during interviews (disambiguation).

The nature of *primary-issues hypothesis testing* is dictated by the type of case and individual case features. In arson investigations, for instance, primary-issues hypotheses are plausible accounts of how fires might have started. For sexual abuse investigations, alternative hypotheses for allegations might be that adults misinterpreted children's reports, that children were lying, and so forth. Knowledge of the dynamics of particular types of cases helps professionals generate alternative hypotheses. For example, one hypothesis about a distinctive pattern of bruising might be that parents used a popular folk remedy known to leave similar marks.

After generating alternative hypotheses about the matters under investigation, interviewers plan testing strategies. Some hypothesis-testing strategies are subtle. For example, asking what children were doing when something happened could reveal contextual information that changes the prevailing hypothesis. Similarly, asking children to describe what they saw or heard are hypothesis-testing questions if responses might lead to physical evidence that tests a hypothesis. Because it is often unrealistic to address every possible scenario, the goal of primary-issues hypothesis testing is to cover what can reasonably be covered given the age of the child and the case characteristics.[2] This type of hypothesis testing is a goal of child advocacy center interviews (e.g., Child Advocacy Center, 2014), an expectation of some forensic protocols (e.g., State of Michigan Governor's Task Force on Child Abuse and Neglect and Department of Human Services, 2011), and a recurring topic in resources on sexual abuse assessments (e.g., Ceci & Bruck, 1995; Faller, 2003; Kuehnle & Connell, 2009).

Three barriers hinder primary-issues hypothesis testing. First, some people believe that considering alternatives to a child's account is tantamount to disbelieving the child and, therefore, antiadvocacy. To respond, defenders of a skeptical approach point out that a powerful way to enhance a child's credibility is to rule out alternative explanations. Also, when children are misunderstood or manipulated by adults or peers, advocacy lies in uncovering the misunderstandings or manipulation.

---

[2]See State of Michigan Governor's Task Force on Child Abuse and Neglect and Department of Human Services (2011) for examples of allegations, possible alternative hypotheses, and test questions, along with a hypothesis-testing plan sheet.

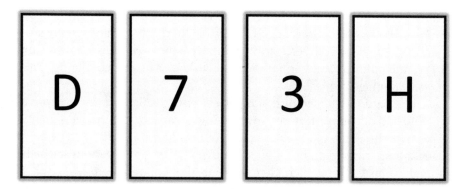

Figure 2.1. One version of the four-card task (Wason & Johnson-Laird, 1972). Assume there are only four cards. Each card has a number on one side and a letter on the other side. Which card or cards would you have to turn over to determine whether the following statement is true or false? Every card with a *D* on one side has a *3* on the other side.

The second barrier is more difficult to overcome: In most situations, hypothesis testing does not come naturally to adults. The classic demonstration of just how difficult hypothesis testing can be is a four-card task such as the one in Figure 2.1. To try this task for yourself, assume that there are four cards, each with a letter on one side and a number on the other. Now answer this question: Which card or cards in Figure 2.1 would you have to turn over to decide whether the statement (hypothesis) printed below the cards is true or false? ("Every card with a *D* on one side has a *3* on the other side.") The two answers people give most frequently, which are both wrong, appear in the footnote, along with the correct answer (which was achieved by only 4% of people in one set of studies; Wason & Shapiro, 1971, Table 1).[3]

The four-card task illustrates *confirmation bias* (also called the *myside bias*), which is the tendency people have to search for and interpret evidence in ways that confirm their beliefs while ignoring or downplaying evidence that would disconfirm those beliefs. Deciding what to turn over is analogous to deciding which questions to ask children, and neglect of the card with a 7 on one side illustrates that people often fail to search for critical evidence. Many studies have shown that professionals and laypeople alike find it difficult to maintain the open-minded perspective needed for forensic work. (For

---

[3]"*D* and 3" is the most popular answer, followed by "*D*." The correct answer is "*D* and 7": You should turn over the *D* to see whether there is a *3* on the other side, and you should turn over the *7* because a *D* on the other side of a *7* would prove the rule false. It does not matter what is on the other side of the *3*. For example, suppose there was an *F*: The rule "if *D* then *3*" says nothing about what has to be on the other side of any letter except *D*.

a review of reasoning biases, see Kahneman, 2011; for forensic implications of the confirmation bias, see Kassin, Dror, & Kukucka, 2013.)

The third barrier to primary-issues hypothesis testing is a "bottleneck" in the thinking process: the limited capacity of working memory. Working memory can be thought of as a temporary holding bin for the information we are thinking about while we talk, listen, and plan our next questions, and this bin can contain only a handful of items at any given time (Cowan, 2010). As a result, even when interviewers make plans to test alternative hypotheses, the cognitive demands of conversation can cause them to close interviews before they have explored critical issues. During forensic conversations, strategies for overcoming memory limitations include using interview breaks to receive feedback from coworkers (Chapter 5) and consulting checklists (Chapter 6).

In addition to testing alternative hypotheses about primary case issues, forensic interviewers have to continually envision possible interpretations of what children are saying and work to resolve ambiguities. This second type of hypothesis testing, *disambiguation*, occurs frequently during sexual abuse interviews because children use so many names for body parts and sexual acts. For example, when interviewers ask, "What do you use your bird for?" or "Is there another word for your bird? It's OK to say it," they are testing what a child means when he says *bird*. Likewise, after a child reports watching people "have sex," an interviewer might say, "What do people do when they have sex?" to explore whether the child equates sex with kissing. Meaning checks are also needed whenever children appear to no longer be talking about the topic of conversation. For example, a question such as "Was [something the child said] that time with John or another time?" is a type of disambiguation that prevents allegations from mushrooming when young children interject irrelevant people, places, and events into conversation. (See pp. 293–294 in Lamb, Hershkowitz, Orbach, & Esplin, 2008, for examples of how this type of hypothesis-testing is built into the National Institute of Child Health and Development protocol.)

An intriguing set of studies on the dynamics of adult–child conversation illustrates the need for skepticism and hypothesis testing throughout the life of a case. These studies were motivated by sexual abuse cases in which adults alleged that children disclosed, the children participated in one or more interviews, and interviewers took notes and summarized findings. The question researchers asked is how reliably information flows through this process. In one study, mothers had difficulty remembering whether they or their children had spoken specific utterances—even though conversations had occurred only 3 days earlier (Bruck, Ceci, & Francoeur, 1999). Experienced investigators also have difficulty recalling verbatim questions and answers (Warren & Woodall, 1999), and note taking does not fully resolve their memory limitations. For example, Lamb, Orbach, Sternberg, Hershkowitz, and Horowitz (2000) found that notes from trained forensic interviewers attributed fewer than half the details children reported to the correct eliciting utterance (even though interviewers were supposedly writing down literal questions and answers). But poor memory for what was said is not the only concern. Recordings have revealed that adults often mishear children and feed back information during interviews that is not what children said; in response, children sometimes go along with interviewers' distortions (e.g., Hunt & Borgida, 2001; Roberts & Lamb, 1999).

Because children's testimony can be misheard, misremembered, and transformed during conversations, it is disconcerting when professionals refer to unrecorded reports as *disclosures* (revealing a lack of skepticism) rather than *alleged disclosures*. Individuals with a hypothesis-testing mind-set would formulate several possibilities regarding reports of prior disclosures, including the possibility that the child said exactly what was reported, that the report is a distorted version of what the child said (with some accurate and some inaccurate information), and that a disclosure never occurred at all. The latter possibility does not assume that someone is lying, only that the type of cooperative behavior children show in the face of specific questions, as described in Chapter 1, might have combined with other factors to mislead adults. According to the forensic perspective, interviews are not simply opportunities for children to repeat something they might have discussed with others; instead, these conversations are opportunities to explore the origins of allegations.

As beneficial as hypothesis testing sounds in principle, there are good reasons for why the extent of hypothesis testing will vary across cases. For example, young preschoolers do not reliably answer questions about where or how they learned something, and many will have little to say about topics that might get at this information indirectly. Therefore, an interviewer's first priority when working with a young child is to elicit a sufficiently detailed narrative to allow the investigative team to evaluate the plausibility and coherence of information across reported disclosures. Hypothesis testing in such interviews might involve questions to assess whether children understand the forensically meaningful words they are using (which explores whether they are merely parroting words from television or some other source) and to determine that there have been no misunderstandings due to idiosyncratic uses or pronunciations of words.

A Child-Centered Approach

Another striking difference between adult–child conversations in everyday life (Chapter 1) and conversations in forensic contexts are the strategies forensic interviewers use to privilege children's participation. As one protocol explained (State of Maine Child and Family Services, 2010),

> Interviewers use open-ended questions to "transfer control" of conversations so children—not interviewers—are the information providers. Although interviewers direct the flow of conversation through a series of phases (steps), children determine the vocabulary and specific content of conversations as much as possible. Fact-finding interviewers are mindful to frame questions in ways that are developmentally and culturally sensitive. They choose techniques that empower children to be comfortable talking about potentially sensitive information. (p. 2)

A child-centered approach is often mentioned as the defining feature of professional child interviewing. As one training organization explained,

> The rationale for a child centered approach to forensic interviewing is anchored on the premise that a child's ability, willingness and competency to participate in the interview is greatly enhanced when the interview strategy is structured based on the child's emotional, cognitive, and developmental abilities. (National Association of Certified Child Forensic Interviewers, 2014, p. 1)

Unpacking these definitions reveals a daunting array of knowledge underlying skilled interviewing, including awareness of the emotional barriers that can inhibit children from talking, the cognitive strengths and limitations of different age groups, and how individual differences associated with victimization, disabilities, and cultural contexts affect interviewing choices. There are two approaches for taking these factors into account during interviews. In one, interviewers conduct developmental assessments to gauge children's language development, knowledge of concepts that will likely be part of the interview (e.g., numbers, the prepositions *in* vs. *on*), and ability to answer various types of questions. The goal of this approach is to use information about children's strengths and weaknesses to adjust interview plans (Morgan, 1995).

Today, developmental assessments make the most sense when professionals with specialized training in child assessment have multiple sessions to interact with children and their families, when concerns about children's developmental levels might affect case analyses, and when the content of assessments might inform these analyses. But these circumstances do not describe the majority of forensic interviews because the information obtained by assessments often is not useful. For example, children can recite numbers by rote and count small quantities yet still have trouble answering questions about the frequency of recurring events in their lives (Connolly, Hockley, & Pratt, 1996). For this reason, simple concept checks (e.g., "How many blocks do I have?" "Is this a weekday or the weekend?") only test foundational knowledge, not the ability to apply that knowledge in eyewitness situations.

As Michael Lamb and I pointed out, "At best, the presence of lengthy assessments only imparts specious authenticity to the interview process" (Poole & Lamb, 1998, p. 132).

An alternative to developmental assessments is to build child-centered strategies into the fabric of interviews. For instance, the conversational conventions of forensic interviewing help interviewers speak in ways that most children understand (Chapter 3), early interview phases encourage children to talk (thereby providing opportunities to observe their speech and narrative skills; Chapter 4), and case-specific decisions help ensure that children's individual needs are met (Chapter 6). A child-centered approach does not preclude delivering assessment questions when the information obtained might be useful, but it eliminates the need to do so for the majority of cases.

Exploration That Supports the Broader Investigation

In addition to testing hypotheses and taking a child-centered approach, forensic interviewers move beyond story interviews by delivering questions that might lead children to mention physical evidence, additional witnesses, and other information that could be explored outside the interview. In the words of one protocol, "Fact-finding interviews are part of broader assessments that sometimes involve retrieval of physical evidence, conversations with collateral contacts, and additional fact-finding efforts. Therefore, interviewers should explore topics that might lead to corroborative evidence" (State of Maine Child and Family Services, 2010, p. 2). After collecting such leads, interviewers should assist the investigative team by including this information in their interview summaries, even when interviews were recorded (Ministry of Justice, 2011).

The importance of supporting the broader investigation cannot be overstated. In child sexual abuse cases, for example, detailed narratives are important tools for eliciting confessions (Staller & Faller, 2010), and a confession or other corroborative evidence increases decisions to prosecute (e.g., Moore, 1998; Walsh, Jones, Cross, & Lippert, 2010). In five field studies, most evaluators judged allegations corroborated by evidence (e.g., medical findings, photographs or videos, other physical evidence, and suspects' confessions) "likely to be true" even when children did not disclose abuse, which reveals how much weight this evidence carries in the decision-making process (Herman, 2010). Corroborative evidence also reduces the stress felt by victimized children and directly benefits them by minimizing the duration of their involvement in the child protection and criminal justice systems (Goodman et al., 1992).

Because of the need to support broader investigative efforts, forensic interviewers do not give children full control over the pacing and direction of interviews. Instead, interviewers determine which topics should be covered, with topics determined by the age of the child, the type of case, and case-specific information. For example, if two teenagers made sexual abuse accusations against a teacher, interviewers would probably inquire about the history of each child's relationship with the alleged offender. Taking conversation in this direction probes for whether the children describe a consistent pattern of grooming behavior and whether there are details about specific places, persons, and physical objects that could be verified by other means.

There are challenges to moving interviews beyond the story model to one that fully supports investigations. Some interviewers have backgrounds that do not prepare them to immediately adopt a law enforcement perspective on evidence collection, and there is a persistent stereotype that corroborative evidence is rare in some types of investigations. In sexual abuse cases, the widespread belief that virtually all cases hinge solely on children's testimonies can discourage interviewers from looking for corroborative leads—even though some cases contain such evidence (Cross, Whitcomb, & De Vos, 1995; Herman, 2010). Thus, interviewers support investigative efforts when they repeatedly consider how converging evidence might corroborate children's testimonies, by delivering questions that explore possibilities, and by documenting findings in summary reports.

An Eye on Commander's Intent

The take-home message thus far is that forensic interviewing is problem solving embedded in a conversation. But problem-solving tasks are not all the same. Some, such as converting quantities in a recipe from U.S. units to metric, are well structured: These problems have clear initial states, defined end goals, and fixed strategies for getting from point A to point B. In contrast, most tasks in medicine, law, and child protection are ill structured, which means that "individual cases of knowledge application are typically multidimensional and there is considerable variability in the structure and content across cases of the same nominal type" (Spiro, Feltovich, & Coulson, 1996, p. 51). When problem-solving tasks are ill structured, initial states may not be completely spelled out, constraints on what problem-solvers can do are unclear, and end states are uncertain.

Because of the ill-structured nature of forensic work, interviewers are not always cognizant of the higher order goals of those who will use the information collected during interviews. This problem rears its head when interviewers ignore unexpected comments from children that do not relate to primary case issues, even though these comments strongly relate to the overarching goals of the interviewers' jobs. For example, I have listened to interviews in which child protection workers who were investigating physical abuse allegations ignored statements suggesting that a parent was leaving children unattended or failing to provide schooling. Listening to these interviews, I sensed that the mental resources needed to listen, plan questions, and keep precipitating issues in mind made it difficult for interviewers to think about and respond to unexpected comments. Ultimately, these interviewers ended conversations with sufficient information about the precipitating allegations but with serious questions about whether children were generally safe and receiving adequate care.

Whether children are safe and receiving adequate care is arguably the "commander's intent" of child protective services interviews. The concept of commander's intent was developed by the military to address the fact that plans for operations, even when enviably thorough, "often turn out to be useless" (Heath & Heath, 2007, p. 25). In their book *Made to Stick: Why Some Ideas Survive and Others Die*, Chip and Dan Heath (2007) shared how one colonel described this problem:

> "The trite expression we always use is *No plan survives contact with the enemy*," says Colonel Tom Kolditz, the head of the behavioral sciences division at West Point. "You may start off trying to fight your plan, but the enemy gets a vote. Unpredictable things happen—the weather changes, a key asset is destroyed, the enemy responds in a way you don't expect. Many armies fail because they put all their emphasis into creating a plan that becomes useless ten minutes into the battle." . . . Colonel Kolditz says, "Over time we've come to understand more and more about what makes people successful in complex operations." He believes that plans are useful, in the sense that they are proof that *planning* has taken place. The planning process forces people to think through the right issues. But as for the plans themselves, Kolditz says, "They just don't work on the battlefield." So, in the 1980s the Army adapted its planning process, inventing a concept called Commander's Intent (CI).
>
> CI is a crisp, plain-talk statement that appears at the top of every order, specifying the plan's goal, the desired end-state of an operation. At high levels of the Army, the CI may be relatively abstract: "Break the will of the enemy in the Southeast region." At the tactical level, for colonels and captains, it is much more concrete: "My intent is to have Third Battalion on Hill 4305, to have the hill cleared of enemy, with only ineffective remnants remaining, so we can protect the flank of Third Brigade as they pass through the lines."
>
> The CI never specifies so much detail that it risks being rendered obsolete by unpredictable events. "You can lose the ability to execute the original plan, but you never lose the responsibility of executing the intent," says Kolditz. (pp. 25–26)

The need for commander's intent statements strikes a chord with interviewing experts because children are masters at sabotaging interview plans.

When investigative teams agree on the commander's intent for an interview, they activate goals that help interviewers maintain the flexibility needed to establish new threads of conversation in response to unexpected information.

If the concept of commander's intent seems abstract, consider the goals of a sexual abuse interview conducted as part of a criminal investigation. A narrow goal would be to collect evidence pertinent to the hypothesis that Mr. Jones, the elderly neighbor of a 12-year-old boy, sexually abused the child. With this goal in mind, an interviewer could easily forget to ask whether the boy was victimized by other perpetrators or has knowledge of other children's abuse by the suspect. A broader goal would be to explore whether the boy has knowledge of sexual abuse against children (i.e., himself or others). An interviewer with this goal in mind would likely probe for knowledge about other possible victims but might not explore comments suggesting reckless endangerment or other criminal activity. Still another goal could be to determine the boy's knowledge of criminal activity against himself and others. This goal seems overly broad, however, because it encompasses such things as physical assaults and drug crimes over an unrestricted time period, thereby stretching conversation well beyond purposes of the investigation. A compromise might be to explore whether this boy has been the victim of sexual abuse and, following mention of any criminal activity, to fully explore those statements (including whether the boy has knowledge of other perpetrators and victims).

This list of possibilities illustrates why the goal of an interview is not always obvious. In practice, the type of case and local requirements will determine what the commander's intent is for a given interview. What does not change across contexts, however, is need to remain cognizant of the higher order goal. Collectively, hypothesis testing, a child-centered perspective, exploration that supports a broader investigation, and the specification of commander's intent distinguish story interviews (e.g., the conversation at the beginning of this chapter) from professional interviews in forensic contexts.

PLAY-YOUR-POSITION RECOMMENDATIONS

With relevant training and experience, mental health professionals can ethically work on cases involving known victims, alleged victims, and bystander witnesses in a number of capacities, including performing clinical evaluations to assess symptoms and to formulate treatment plans, providing therapy to children or parents, conducting forensic evaluations, consulting with attorneys, and serving as expert witnesses. There is a caveat, however: Because clinical and forensic roles have goals and practice standards that can conflict, there is consensus that professionals inappropriately engage in dual roles when they provide both therapeutic and forensic services within the context of a single case. As one protocol explained,

> Although information obtained from an investigative interview might be useful for making treatment decisions, the interview is not part of a treatment process. Forensic interviews should not be conducted by professionals who have an on-going or a planned therapeutic relationship with the child. (State of Michigan Governor's Task Force on Child Abuse and Neglect and Department of Human Services, 2011, p. 1)

No description of clinical goals and practices fits all situations, but clinical activities often have the following characteristics: the goal is to assess symptoms and/or provide treatment, the child or parent is the client, expressions of empathy and establishment of a therapeutic alliance are important, the client's perceptions of events may be given greater focus than factual accuracy, the clinician does not have authority to seek information from other sources without client consent, the information shared is private and subject to confidentiality restrictions, and clinicians have considerable leeway regarding their selection of therapeutic techniques. In a treatment relationship, the clinician's responsibility is to "promote the client's best interests," which is at odds with the objectivity required for a forensic analysis (Clark, 2009, p. 73).

In contrast, forensic interviews have a fact-finding purpose that supports a legal process: A representative of that process is the client, neutrality and an unbiased perspective are essential, the goal is to collect the most reliable evidence possible and support broader fact-finding efforts, there are limits to the confidentiality of findings, and the techniques used to elicit and document information should be scientifically justifiable and consistent with local (e.g., agency) practice. When clinicians provide forensic services, multiple relationships (assuming more than one role for a single case) are a threat to professional effectiveness. Other threats are personal histories or emotional issues that compromise objectivity, lack of appropriate training and skills, and the use of nonvalidated or unreliable methods (Clark, 2009; Koocher, 2009). Some threats, such as role conflicts and practicing outside one's scope of knowledge and experience, are discussed in the ethics codes of professional organizations for psychologists, psychiatrists, social workers, and counselors.

Clinicians providing treatment can inadvertently harm the credibility of children's allegations when they cross over into a forensic role by mining for disclosures or assuming an investigative role following disclosures. As Kathryn Kuehnle and Mary Connell (2010) explained,

> When therapists directly take on an investigative role, asking questions to "facilitate disclosure," they may interfere in the forensic investigation. Under such circumstances, the risk is that the child's memories and state-

ment become so tainted or inaccurate that a miscarriage of justice results. Abused children's statements may come to appear unreliable or the therapist may unwittingly shape and reinforce the erroneous statements of nonabused children. . . . Furthermore, children who are exposed to ongoing questioning and probing are effectively denied the needed therapeutic support that occurs within a relationship premised on neutrality regarding an unconfirmed allegation of sexual abuse. For example, when parents report to a therapist that their child made a specific comment about having been touched inappropriately, the therapist should follow mandated reporting laws and make an immediate report to CPS but should not conduct an interview of the child regarding the comment. However, if a child makes a spontaneous, suspicious but ambiguous statement during a therapy session (e.g., "Daddy touched my pee pee"), the therapist may need to respond with one or two open-ended questions (e.g., "Tell me about that") to determine if what is being described crosses the line from innocuous touch (e.g., wiping the child after toileting) and enters the range of reasonable suspicion (e.g., rubbing the child's genitals). (p. 557)

Activities during therapy that can compromise cases include repeated presentation of sexual abuse prevention books and detailed exploration following reports of abuse. Abuse prevention books can establish a strong atmosphere of concern about abuse while also imparting knowledge to the child that can lead to sexual acting out and verbal mimicry, thereby making it difficult to determine the source of the child's information. In turn, exploration of a potential disclosure that exceeds what is necessary to make a reporting decision (Kalichman, 1999) raises questions about the clinician's objectivity and influence on the report.

Forensic interviewers must also guard against the tendency to stray into another type of relationship. Emotional reactions to children's statements (e.g., "That's so horrible . . . I'm sorry that happened to you") and comments that label children's feelings (e.g., "You must have been scared") can become the focus of a defense team's strategy (especially when there is little else to attack). Therefore, interviewers protect cases by avoiding emotional comments that could be viewed as reinforcing children for one type of testimony over another. (See Chapter 3 for ways to express interest and support without making these errors.)

BRIEFING THE INTERVIEWER

Two models of interviewing, *blind* and *informed*, place different emphases on the need to remain unbiased versus the need to test alternative hypotheses. In blind interviews, interviewers know nothing about the situations triggering investigations. This approach prevents interviewers from acting in ways that might reinforce their own assumptions about the case while blocking future criticism about interviewer bias (Morgan, 1995). However, lack of knowledge makes it difficult to test alternative hypotheses. In practice, the approach interviewers use is usually dictated by local practices and requirements, with hybrid models incorporating features of both approaches.

Rationale for Blind Interviewing

In the 1980s and early 1990s, transcripts of interviews from highly publicized day care abuse cases revealed the danger of arming unskilled interviewers with details of allegations, as illustrated by this interview segment from the Kelly Michaels case (Ceci & Bruck, 1995):

Treacy:	I see and did the kids want Kelly to do that peanut butter stuff?
Child A:	I didn't even think that there was a peanut butter. . . .
Treacy:	Well, what about licking the peanut butter?
Child A:	There wasn't anything about peanut butter. . . .
Treacy:	Some of the kids told me that things happened with knives. Do you remember anything like that?
Child A:	No. [Although the child professes no knowledge of utensil abuse, at trial this child testified to numerous abuse allegations.]
Treacy:	. . . Well, what about that cat game?
Child A:	Cat game?
Treacy:	Where everybody went like this, "Meow, Meow."
Child A:	I don't think that I was there that day. [Although the child professes no knowledge of the cat game, at trial she described a cat game in which all the children were naked and licking each other.] (pp. 116–117)

In this biased style of interviewing, which is often called *confirmatory interviewing*, adults select questions and feed children information to confirm suspicions of abuse rather than exploring alternative explanations for those suspicions. Studies of adults who were not trained to follow current interview guidelines have found that preconceived notions alter the way people speak to children and how they report the content of interviews (Dent, 1982). For example, Gail Goodman and her colleagues showed adults a video containing misinformation about a target event and then asked this group and a group of uninformed adults to interview unfamiliar children (Goodman, Sharma, Thomas, & Considine, 1995). Compared with the adults who had not been misinformed, biased interviewers asked more questions about the misinformation, and their subsequent descriptions of what had happened to the children contained more errors.[4]

More recently, Heather Price and her colleagues conducted a study to connect the dots between interviewers' misconceptions, the types of questions they ask, and children's subsequent responses (H. L. Price, Ornstein, & Poole, 2015). In this study, one group of adults received only general information about the goal of the interview:

> Imagine that you are the director of [child care program name]. Recently, two parents expressed concern that their child may have participated in some activities that they did not give permission for with a male visitor who was doing some fitness activities with the kids. Your task is to find out if this child experienced something with this man and, if so, what took place.

A second group received longer instructions containing false information about the physical environment and what the man did with the children. In subsequent interviews of children ranging from 6 to 10 years of age, many prompts delivered by biased interviewers were suggestive, and some children acquiesced to this false information.

Yet despite the negative consequences of biasing information, the interviewing community rarely recommends keeping interviewers completely uninformed about the purpose of interviews. For example, Kevin Smith and Rebecca Milne (2011) advocated "minimal alleged offence information," an approach in which interviewers are informed about the following information but not the contextual details children should provide:

- The nature of the alleged offence;
- The time, frequency and location of the alleged offence;
- How the alleged offence came to the notice of the police;
- The nature of any threats or intimidation alleged to have been used by the suspect or their family or associates. (p. 92)

K. Smith and Milne said this approach is ideal but also acknowledged that in the jurisdictions where they consult (England and Wales), "minimal knowledge of the offence on the part of the interviewer is usually unachievable" due to interviewers' extensive involvement in investigations (p. 93).

Rationale for Informed Interviewing

There are drawbacks to keeping interviewers completely or minimally informed throughout the duration of interviews. One is that uninformed

---

[4]Misconceptions held by parents who converse with children can also lead children to report information consistent with those misconceptions and even prompt children to generate additional false information on their own (see Principe & Schindewolf, 2012, and White, Leichtman, & Ceci, 1997).

interviewers have few tools for introducing the target topic with general probes (e.g., "Tell me what you have come to talk to me about today"; Powell, 2003, p. 260). For this reason, Morgan (1995) suggested that blind interviews require highly trained interviewers and may not be maximally effective for young children.

Another concern is that uninformed interviewers lack the information needed for effective hypothesis testing. That is, uninformed interviewers cannot generate and plan tests of alternative hypotheses in advance of the interview and cannot detect discrepancies between information in prior reports and children's responses during interviews. As a result, it is unlikely that they will deliver the clarification questions needed to resolve contradictions across different sources of evidence. In a previous book, Michael Lamb and I used an example of an abuse report filed by day care workers who observed sexualized play and then conducted initial conversations with the children (Poole & Lamb, 1998). In this type of case, it is helpful to know what children's initial comments were when the play was discovered, which children are frequent playmates, and whether any surface features of the concerning play map onto recent events in the children's lives (in or out of school). Because it is difficult to figure out the source of a young child's behavior without such information, early recommendations from the National Center for Prosecution of Child Abuse (1993) asked interviewers to

> resist pressure for a "blind" interview. Interviewing a child without knowing any of the details revealed to others is analogous to performing a medical examination without knowing the patient's history or looking for an unfamiliar destination without a road map. (p. 59)

Later recommendations acknowledged that allegation-blind interviewing may have promise but that "measures other than allegation-blind interviews can be taken to assure reliable interview results" (National Center for Prosecution of Child Abuse, 2004, p. 39).

Why are there such discrepant opinions about how much information interviewers should have? One reason is that interviewers' skill levels influence the risks and benefits of prior knowledge, as a study by Martine Powell and her colleagues illustrated (Powell, Hughes-Scholes, & Sharman, 2012). In this research, police officers interviewed 5- to 8-year-olds about a staged event. Before the interviews, officers participated in mock interviews that assessed whether they were generally good (i.e., used many open-ended prompts) or poor interviewers and then were assigned to receive only general information about the target event or information containing numerous false details. Biasing information led poor interviewers to deliver a greater number of leading yes/no questions, but preinterview knowledge did not have a negative influence on skilled officers' techniques. This finding suggests that in situations where training and ongoing supervision are insufficient and staff turnover is high, blind interviewing might produce better results; with highly trained interviewers, however, the risks of prior knowledge may not override the benefits of having more information about children and allegation histories.

Hybrid Models

A compromise between blind and informed interviewing is a *hybrid model* in which interviewers (a) begin a conversation with only some background information about a child (e.g., the names of family members and the child's names for body parts), (b) take a break during the interview to review allegations and receive additional topics or questions from the investigative team, and (c) complete the interview. This approach reduces leading questioning early in interviews, thereby preserving the credibility of children's initial disclosures, while still providing opportunities to fully explore cases.

An evaluation of this model involved a child sexual abuse assessment center in Idaho, where a court decision prompted interviewing centers to switch from informed to initially blind interviewing (Cantlon, Payne, & Erbaugh, 1996). Results were optimistic, with a higher disclosure rate after the change to initially blind interviewing. The researchers suggested that lack of knowledge might have encouraged interviewers to take more time to develop rapport, although it is possible that changes over time in the strength of cases referred to the center contributed to the improved disclosure rate.

Also unknown is whether the encouraging results from this study generalize to other types of investigations. The success of initially blind interviewing at a sexual abuse assessment center could reflect the fact that the children interviewed at such centers typically know why they are being interviewed and interviews are scheduled shortly after referral, thereby making it less likely that giving interviewers additional case information would significantly increase disclosure rates. What this study does show is that an initially blind strategy does not leave interviewers completely unequipped to elicit abuse disclosures. (Turn to this chapter's Principles to Practice to read my answer to attorneys' questions about informed interviewing.)

RECAP

In everyday life, adults interview children to hear stories about their lives, including what happened and how children reacted to those events. Unlike these story interviews, forensic interviews are part of a problem-solving process that will decide which of several alternatives is most consistent with evidence. To collect sufficient evidence from children to assist this process, forensic interviews have four characteristics:

- A *hypothesis-testing approach*. Forensic interviewers maintain skepticism by testing competing hypotheses about the events in question (primary-issues hypothesis testing) and by clarifying the meaning of children's utterances during interviews (disambiguation).
- A *child-centered perspective*. Forensic interviewers use techniques that empower children to talk, always mindful that their techniques are compatible with witnesses' developmental levels and cultural norms.
- *Exploration that supports the broader investigation*. Forensic interviewers support broader investigative efforts by delivering questions that could lead to physical evidence, additional witnesses, and other important findings.
- An *eye on commander's intent*. Forensic interviewers keep the intended scope of interviews in mind. They adjust questioning plans to explore unexpected comments from children that are relevant to interview goals.

Because clinical and forensic roles have goals and standards of practice that can conflict, professionals should not provide both therapeutic and forensic services for an individual case or stray into the alternative role while providing those services. The nature of preinterview preparation will vary depending on the type of case and local practice.

PRINCIPLES TO PRACTICE: IS THIS BIASED INTERVIEWING?

Attorneys often contact eyewitness researchers to ask about the significance of a case feature. This is a composite of questions I have received about nonblind interviewing, along with my response.

Question From Defense Attorneys

I have a sexual abuse case involving a child who lives in ___ County, ___. The interviewer reviewed the police report before the interview, spoke with the officer, and had a conversation with the child's mother. Isn't this inappropriate? Doesn't that information seriously bias the interview?

My Response

In the United States, there is no national consensus that interviews have to be conducted blind, and this investigative team did not violate their county's protocol. That said, prior knowledge (bias) is an issue whenever (a) the interviewer mentioned case details before the child did and those details became an integral part of the child's testimony or (b) prior knowledge led the interviewer to omit needed hypothesis-testing questions.

The strongest interview analyses focus on what interviewers actually did and the possible impact of that behavior on children's reports. Experts question the reliability of children's testimonies when the case timeline, which is a document tracking the history of every alleged or recorded disclosure, contains concerning patterns. For example, it is troubling when most of the critical information in children's reports originated from adults and when details morphed over time in ways that exceed what is typical of children's eyewitness reports. When there is concern about interviewer influence, evidence of influence is more important than what knowledge an interviewer had going into an interview.

3

CONVERSATIONAL HABITS

There are probably many people you love to talk with and a few you would rather avoid. I tend to avoid people who dominate conversation, but I also steer clear of intent, quiet listeners. Because polite listening signaled lack of interest in my family's culture, insufficient feedback is a surefire way to get me to stop talking.

When scientists began studying eyewitness memory, they noticed something you likely noticed a long time ago: Some adults are simply better than others at getting people to talk. After observing what successful interviewers were doing, researchers trained volunteers to behave differently to document how conversational styles affected children's behavior. These studies mapped out a style of talking that helps interviewers elicit more information from children without lowering the accuracy of eyewitness reports.

For anyone interested in becoming a better interviewer, spending time mastering the conversational habits of forensic interviewing is time well spent. To understand why, the first section of this chapter explains why deeply

http://dx.doi.org/10.1037/14941-004
Interviewing Children: The Science of Conversation in Forensic Contexts, by D. A. Poole

engrained habits are crucial for expert performance. The remainder of the chapter unpacks a toolbox of interviewing essentials, including the interviewer behaviors that create socially supportive environments for children, the habit of cycling back to open-ended prompts throughout an interview, and the language choices that help children stay on topic and understand questions.

THE ROLE OF HABITS IN EXPERT PERFORMANCE

Expert interviewers maintain a unique set of conversational habits while they continually retrieve the background knowledge that directs their questions. These two components of skill—habits and knowledge—represent different types of learning. *Habits* are automatic reactions that occur when specific cues trigger responses. Deeply engrained habits are built by repetition and unfold without conscious awareness. When you learned to drive, for example, you developed habits for steering and using your feet, so today you are usually unaware of these tasks while you operate a car. Habits are part of the *implicit memory* system, which is a primitive system that helps even simple organisms return to food, avoid danger, and perform other repetitive but essential tasks.

Another memory system, *explicit memory*, houses the information you consciously manipulate. When you recall specific facts and prior experiences, you are relying on this more advanced system. At any given time, the information you are actively thinking about is held in working memory, which Chapter 2 described as the bottleneck of thinking because of the limited amount of information it juggles (perhaps as little as four units; Cowan, 2010). Because of working memory limitations, skill on many tasks improves when basic responses become so automatic that people can act without conscious effort, thereby freeing mental resources to deal with less routine matters.

Across a wide variety of tasks, *automaticity*—the ability to perform basic operations quickly and without mental effort—predicts performance.[1] Just as young drivers are accident prone because they still have to think about steering and changing speed, interviewers who have to think about how to phrase every question will not have the mental resources needed to detect ambiguities in children's utterances, flexibly shift the direction of interviews, and mentally review interview plans. By developing productive conversational habits,

---

[1]The ability to effortlessly retrieve information predicts many types of problem solving. For example, people who are good at mathematical problem solving tend to retrieve basic mathematical facts more quickly than those who are less mathematically inclined (G. R. Price, Mazzocco, & Ansari, 2013). Across domains, expert problem-solvers also notice patterns that novices miss, organize knowledge in ways that reflect deep understanding, consider a wider range of possibilities, and detect exceptions to the usual meaning of evidence (Donovan, Bransford, & Pellegrino, 2015; Feltovich, Spiro, & Coulson, 1997).

interviewers avert common errors and also make it easier to learn and execute the more challenging skills described in subsequent chapters of this book.

A SUPPORTIVE CONVERSATIONAL STYLE: FIRST IMPRESSIONS, DEMEANOR, AND THE RHYTHMS OF CONVERSATION

There is a simple way to upset a baby: Just interact normally for a few minutes and then freeze. When suddenly faced with a statue-like person, most babies become noticeably distressed and glance away, and they do not immediately shake their sadness when social life returns to normal. Negative reactions in this still-face paradigm are "one of the most replicated findings in developmental psychology"—an early indication that children are highly attuned to the rhythms of conversation (Goldman, 2010, para. 1; see Mesman, van IJzendoorn, & Bakermans-Kranenburg, 2009).

Children are not only social, in the sense that they are biologically built to collaborate with others, but they are also "ultrasocial" (Tomasello, 2014, p. 187). Even before they can talk, infants are obsessed with monitoring faces, have a keen sense of turn-taking in conversation, and look at others' reactions to gauge how they should react (through a process called *social referencing*; Kim, Walden, & Knieps, 2010). Children's social acumen is assisted by *mirror neurons*, collections of cells in the brain that become active when other people do something, promoting imitation, empathy, and as children mature, an increasing ability to read others' intentions (Bello et al., 2014). These skills help ensure survival because our young are built to accept care from a posse of people who pitch in to help raise them (Hrdy, 2009).

But our young do not allow themselves to be passed around willy-nilly. Instead, they carefully monitor situations and feel stressed when they are not in a trusted set of hands. Early in life, children use simple rules to judge whether someone is committed to their safety, including whether that person is similar to the usual parade of caregivers (with shopping mall Santas often losing the trust game). By early to middle childhood, our young have sophisticated abilities to size up unfamiliar adults. To do this, they evaluate other people's demeanors, their behavioral rhythms, and even the reactions these people elicit from others (Fusaro & Harris, 2008). If you want to quickly build rapport with children and then keep them talking, the key lies in first impressions, demeanor, and the rhythms of conversation.

Similarity and a Gentle Entry

Throughout life, we generally feel most comfortable with people who are familiar looking (Zajonc, 2001). In my laboratory, it is so common for children to fear distinctive-looking assistants that I ask new hires not to alter their appearance during data collection. This policy came in handy one fall when an assistant grew a beard for Halloween that frightened younger children. Happily, he took his job seriously and volunteered to shave it before I raised the issue. Our laboratory dress code also dictates modest clothing without words or logos (to avoid offending community members) and a casual appearance. Realistically, college students rarely show up to work in snappy professional clothes. When they do, however, the children worry about being in a medical office, which makes our jobs harder.

Though interviewers do not always have control over what they wear, protocols generally advise police officers against wearing uniforms or having guns visible (e.g., Oregon Department of Justice, 2012). Both of these items are strong authority cues that can reduce the accuracy of children's reports. For instance, children who witnessed a staged crime were more likely to erroneously select someone from a set of pictures that did not contain the perpetrator when interviewers wore police uniforms rather than street clothes (Lowenstein, Blank, & Sauer, 2010). To reduce authority cues and engender trust, it is also best not to wear clothing or jewelry that marks one as an outsider. Just as Mr. Rogers, the beloved children's television star, changed into sneakers and a cardigan at the beginning of every episode, many interviewers intentionally present themselves in ways that are nondistracting and familiar looking to children.

A familiar appearance is comforting, but behavior is crucial as well. Trying to engage children too soon and too fast is a recipe for rebuff, as observations of children's peer interactions have confirmed. From a young age, establishing social interactions is risky business, with children having a greater chance of being ignored than accepted. For example, even popular second- and third-grade children are rejected or ignored about a quarter of the time they make bids to join their peers' ongoing play (Putallaz & Gottman, 1981). Children are more likely to be rejected when they are highly involved early in social interactions, especially when these actions draw attention to themselves. Alternatively, successful children tend to hang back, get a sense of the social norms of a situation, and then gradually make contributions reflecting others' activities (Dodge, 1983; S. Walker, 2009). For interviewers, this means that children are accustomed to rejecting potential social partners, will do so quickly, and are more likely reject people who display an abrupt, pushy manner. A relaxed demeanor is important throughout an interview, but it is especially critical for trust building during the early minutes of conversation.

Positivity and Nonthreatening Attention

Among adults, nonverbal behaviors associated with *positivity*—the feeling that others are friendly and caring—create a sense of rapport with others

(Tickle-Degnen & Rosenthal, 1990). Nonverbal cues such as smiling, head nodding, leaning forward, having uncrossed legs, and frequently looking at others lead conversational partners to rate speakers as having more warmth, empathy, and understanding. These nonverbal cues are important to children as well. To illustrate, Ken Rotenberg and his colleagues (2003) trained interviewers to display high or low levels of smiling and high or low levels of looking (gaze). The interviewers then read a story to individual children while displaying a pattern of nonverbal behavior determined by random assignment of children to conditions. Afterward, the interviewers asked children personal questions to measure self-disclosure, and a teacher or another assistant asked questions to determine how likable and trustworthy children thought the interviewers were.

The results for smiling were clear: When interviewers displayed a higher frequency of smiling, children showed less nervous behavior and later disclosed more about themselves. This finding makes sense because emotional expressions are contagious: Adults and children often match the expression of social partners within a second of viewing them, and these rapid facial reactions influence their emotions (Beall, Moody, McIntosh, Hepburn, & Reed, 2008; Moody, McIntosh, Mann, & Weisser, 2007). Even school-age children rate adults who smile as friendly, helpful, and sincere, whereas nonsmiling, fidgeting adults are perceived as strict, bored, and stressed (Almerigogna, Ost, Akehurst, & Fluck, 2008).

In the Rotenberg study, results for gaze were more nuanced. Interviewers' frequency of gaze did not influence children's nervous behavior or disclosures. However, outgoing children rated interviewers in the high-gaze condition as more trustworthy, whereas shy children rated them as less trustworthy. Apparently, outgoing children enjoy attention and do not find a lot of eye contact off-putting, whereas shy children consider this behavior somewhat threatening or intrusive.

These findings explain why some people feel uncomfortable when others maintain constant eye contact: It feels too intense. But how much eye contact is too much? We get a sense of what children might be expecting from data on typical behavior during social conversation. With 3-year-olds, mothers spend less than a third of the time during play sessions actually looking at them, and the children look at mothers less than 15% of the time (Farran & Kasari, 1990). Patterns of eye contact vary across cultures, however, and are different for boys and girls. In general, mutual gaze is greatest in so-called contact cultures, such as Great Britain and Italy (which favor close interpersonal spaces and frequent eye contact), and lower in noncontact cultures, such as Japan and Hong Kong (Argyle, 1986; Matsumoto, 2006). Boys often show less eye contact than girls and prefer to seat themselves parallel to conversational partners, rather than directly facing them (Tannen, 1990). But regardless of the preferred amount of eye contact, comfortable contact is periodic and held only briefly. These patterns were evident when Thomas Schofield and his team observed European American and Mexican American children conversing with parents about a contested issue (Schofield, Parke, Castañeda, & Coltrane, 2008). The children engaged in mutual gaze about three to five times per minute as they repeatedly looked and then glanced away. Mutual gaze occurred less than half the time a parent was talking and was least frequent among Mexican American sons.

Because eye contact is a marker of status in some cultures, which leads many children to avert their eyes as a sign of respect or submissiveness, interviewers should not require children to look at them while talking. Adolescent boys in particular may be more willing to discuss difficult topics without the intensity of a forward-facing interaction (Tannen, 1990). As a general rule, it is best to avoid correcting behavior that is not interfering with the ability to hear children or their ability to participate in conversation.

In sum, positive facial expressions, a calm and nonintrusive manner, and periodic (but not excessive) eye contact create a comfortable conversational tone. Of course, interviewers have to behave differently during two major parts of interviews: in early phases, when they are building rapport but not talking about the matters under investigation, and after topic introduction, when they are exploring target issues. Incongruous or nervous smiling is inappropriate during evidence collection and could be viewed as reinforcing children for particular types of comments. Forensic interviewers therefore avoid nodding and smiling when talking about target issues while still maintaining a pleasant demeanor.

In-Sync Behavior

Social creatures are constantly judging whether unfamiliar others will be an asset to their group (i.e., people who bond with them and reciprocate) or a drain on resources (i.e., people who act selfishly). Two ways we signal a cooperative disposition are by syncing our behavior with others through brief, unconscious actions and by intentional imitation.

Mimicry involves fleeting behavior in which people reproduce each other's actions. Adults unconsciously lean in when someone else leans in, touch their faces after seeing a face touch, and fidget after spotting a fidgeting finger; they mimic accents, speech rate, and speech rhythm. Most of the time, we prefer people who mimic us to the out-of-sync types. The effects of mimicry are sweeping. We believe that people who mimic judiciously are more empathetic toward us, we behave more cooperatively with people who have mimicked us, and we are more easily persuaded by people who display in-sync behavior (Gueguen, Jacob, & Martin, 2009; but see Leander, Chartrand, & Bargh, 2012, for exceptions).

The discovery of mirror neurons initiated a surge of interest in how people fall in sync during social interactions. Philosopher Patricia Churchland (2008) suggested that mimicry "serves as a social signal because it indicates the presence of a crucial social capacity, namely the capacity to 'read minds'— know what others intend, believe, expect, and feel" (p. 411). Drawing from a large literature on neuroscience and social behavior, Churchland explained that mimicry increases in our social partners the production of hormones, such as oxytocin, that are the glue of social bonding:

> The idea is that adults respond positively to mimicry in social situations because imitative behavior is a powerful signal of social competence that inaugurates trust or assures the continuation of trust. If the newcomer is trustworthy, in this sense, he will probably behave in a way that is consistent with good citizenry. This means that mimicry, even if unconsciously produced and unconsciously detected, is a safety signal. The level of OT [oxytocin], and hence the level of trust, probably increase; defensive behavior and autonomic arousal decrease. Mimicry is not a fail-safe predictor of social competence and full acceptance will be gradual. As a first-pass filter, however, it may weed out the worst. (p. 411)

Children also mimic fleeting nonverbal behavior (though evidence is easier to find once they reach 5 years of age; van Schaik, van Baaren, Bekkering, & Hunnius, 2013). They also notice when others imitate them. For example, toddlers exposed to adults who imitated their actions were more likely than toddlers paired with nonimitating adults to invite these new friends to join play (Fawcett & Liszkowski, 2012), and 5- and 6-year-olds trusted the claims of adults who had previously expressed preferences matching their own (Over, Carpenter, Spears, & Gattis, 2013). These findings suggest that adults who are good at building rapport with children take time to enter children's worlds by temporarily withholding the barrage of questions and focusing on talk about what a child is wearing, holding, saying, or doing. Such child-directed and in-sync behavior sends a power signal that "I'm doing something *with* you today, not *to* you."[2]

Pacing and Still-Your-Turn Feedback

In Euro American cultures, extended silence during conversation makes everyone uncomfortable. The duration of pauses in daily conversation varies from extremely short to 3 to 4 seconds (and rarely as long as

---

[2]There is a large literature on the behaviors that foster cooperative behavior from children. For example, research on parent–child interaction therapy showed that parents can avert oppositional behavior by avoiding questions, imitating children's behavior, and delivering comments that describe what children are doing (Niec, Eyberg, & Chase, 2012).

7 seconds), but someone usually jumps in to say something after about a second (Jefferson, 1989). It is not surprising, then, that adults tend to quickly deliver new prompts whenever children stop talking. This fast-paced style is problematic, however, because immature brains work slower than adults' brains, so children need time to ponder (Nelson, 1976). Also, quick question delivery sends the message that children can end their talking turns simply by clamming up.

It is not entirely clear how long interviewers should wait before delivering the next prompt. In my laboratory, assistants are required to wait 10 seconds before speaking after a pause in children's free-recall responses, which distresses almost all new interviewers. I mention this example not to advocate for 10 seconds of silence but to illustrate how little time adults usually give children to speak.

There is anecdotal evidence that long pauses can be productive at critical times during interviews. One interviewer told me that after transitioning to the target topic, she simply remained silent for 5 minutes, after which the young child (who was playing with an activity in the room) turned around and reported abuse. The longest silence I have heard was about 7 minutes long, which felt like years but was followed by a disclosure from an adolescent. What is more typical than these long delays (which could be viewed as coercive) is that interviewers slow down the pace by tolerating silences longer than a second or two.

One strategy for making silence more comfortable is *selective note taking*. Some professionals find note taking distracting, and it can be. For example, school-age children often stop talking when interviewers write a lot, as if waiting for the adults to catch up. However, interviewers who jot down a few notes and then look up invite children to continue. Selective note taking keeps track of comments that should be explored later in the interview (Saywitz & Camparo, 2014; see also Chapter 4, this volume), prevents interviewers from using gestures suggesting desired responses (Broaders & Goldin-Meadow, 2010), and has the positive side effect of slowing interviewers down.

A better strategy to keep children talking is to interject conversation with *still-your-turn feedback* (*facilitators*, also called *minimal encouragers*; Powell & Snow, 2007). This feedback includes short utterances, such as "OK" or "uh-huh," that shift conversation back to the child (Hershkowitz, 2002). Interviewers also convey "go on" by nodding, remaining silent, or reflecting back part of a child's utterance (*paraphrasing*). Paraphrasing techniques include *simple paraphrasing* (e.g., Child: "And then I went home." *Interviewer*: "You went home"), *yes/no paraphrasing* (e.g., Child: "She has her boyfriend over all the time." *Interviewer*: "She has her boyfriend over?"), *expansion paraphrasing* (e.g., Child: "He told me to put it on for the pictures." *Interviewer*: "Tell me about him telling you to put it on for the pictures"), and *summary paraphrasing* (which combines information from several previous answers; Evans, Roberts, Price, & Stefek, 2010).

The limited research on paraphrasing suggests that yes/no paraphrasing prompts children to report fewer details than expansion paraphrasing does. Moreover, interviewers using yes/no paraphrasing more often distort what was said, and children often fail to correct these errors (Evans et al., 2010). Because yes/no paraphrasing is not effective and might be perceived as challenging children's statements, it makes sense to limit this type of feedback. However, both expansion paraphrasing and simply asking for more information effectively elicit new details (Evans & Roberts, 2009). The combined impact of giving children more time to respond, interjecting comments such as "uh-huh," and asking them to expand is a winning combination that helps even young children elaborate while maintaining their testimonial accuracy (Roberts & Duncanson, 2011).

Supportive Interviewing and Children's Testimony

Knowing that individual behaviors benefit testimony does not tell us the impact of packaging numerous techniques into a high dose of social support. One concern is that children may be more malleable to suggestion when interviewers clearly behave as pals rather than authority figures, as this anecdote from eyewitness researcher Bette Bottoms illustrates (Bottoms, Quas, & Davis, 2007):

> In a Chicago case several years ago, two very young suspects were wrongly suspected of killing a playmate. During their interviews with the child suspects, police officers used socially-supportive techniques such as giving the children food and talking with them in a friendly manner. The children made statements that placed them at the crime scene and were interpreted as confessions. When the real (adult) killer was identified, public outrage focused on the policemen's child-friendly interview techniques. In fact, [I] was contacted for expert consultation by a party exploring the feasibility of a lawsuit against the city based on the argument that the socially supportive interview techniques were inappropriate. (p. 137)

Bottoms declined the case because, as she explained to her caller, the "empirical evidence supports precisely the opposite conclusion" (p. 137).

Concern about interviewer-provided social support stems from the fact that interviewers in some high-profile abuse cases intertwined desirable conversational habits with suggestive techniques, making it impossible to tell which features of their behavior contributed to the wild tales children told (Wood, Nathan, Nezworski, & Uhl, 2009). Subsequent research proved the importance of distinguishing a supportive demeanor from suggestive behavior.

Interviewer-provided social support refers to such things as a relaxed body posture, a warm and friendly voice, and frequent gazes that do not reinforce the child for saying particular things.[3] In other words, interviewers who act in appropriately supportive ways are not withholding and delivering attention to shape the content of children's testimony.

The clearest way to test the impact of supportive interviewing on children's testimony is to expose children to a staged event and assign them to different interview conditions. For example, each child in one sample of 5- to 7-years-olds experienced either a supportive style with an interviewer who built rapport and displayed a number of warm behaviors or an intimidating style lacking these markers of trust (Carter, Bottoms, & Levine, 1996). Both groups were equally detailed and accurate when responding to open-ended prompts and abuse-relevant focused questions, but those interviewed by a supportive interviewer were more accurate in the face of less personally relevant questions.

As you would expect, the benefits of supportive interviewing are smaller when contrasting styles are more alike. For instance, style had no impact style on children's responses to focused questions when interviewers in the less supportive condition also smiled sometimes and complimented the children (Imhoff & Baker-Ward, 1999). The delay between events and interviews also matters because interviewer style makes a bigger difference when memories have faded (cf. Bottoms et al., 2007; Davis & Bottoms, 2002). In this situation, even school-age children make fewer errors in the face of suggestive questions when interviewers adopt a pleasant manner (e.g., Almerigogna et al., 2008; Almerigogna, Ost, Bull, & Akehurst, 2007). Interviewer support also reduces children's tendency to select perpetrators from target-absent lineups, proving they are less likely to respond thoughtlessly when interviewers help them relax (Rush et al., 2014). (For discussions of anxious and nonanxious children, see Quas, Bauer, & Boyce, 2004, and Quas & Lench, 2007.)

Field research with child witnesses confirms the benefits of a supportive interview style. One analysis recorded how many words interviewers spoke to alleged sexual abuse victims and how often interviewers delivered supportive (e.g., "Are you feeling comfortable here?") versus unsupportive comments (e.g., "We cannot help children who do not talk"; Teoh & Lamb, 2013, p. 151). Overall, children were more informative when interviewed by professionals who talked less and more frequently issued supportive remarks.

Because of such findings, experts have been tweaking protocols to emphasize interviewer demeanor. For example, the Revised National Institute of Child Health and Human Development Investigative Interview Protocol

---

[3]For evidence that suggestive techniques used in the McMartin preschool case can influence children's reports, see Garven, Wood, Malpass, and Shaw (1998).

recommended that interviewers express interest during initial rapport building (e.g., "I really want to know you better"), use children's names, and positively engage in other ways (e.g., by using partial repetitions, as in "You say you were [sad/angry/the feeling mentioned]"; Hershkowitz, Lamb, Katz, & Malloy, 2015, p. 9). In an evaluation, the revised procedure reduced children's reluctance (as evidenced by fewer unanswered questions) and increased the proportion of event details elicited with recall rather than recognition prompts. Quick Guide 3.1 summarizes some components of a supportive interview style.

QUICK GUIDE 3.1
Conversational Habits for Interviewing Children

A Supportive Conversational Style
- When possible, choose casual dress that is familiar to children.
- Be patient and do not try to engage children too quickly.
- Pay attention to children's demeanors. A child who is avoiding face-to-face interaction may feel more comfortable if you orient yourself at a slight angle to him or her, whereas one who is excitedly telling you about a favorite activity may enjoy a more engaged conversational style.
- Adopt nonverbal behaviors associated with positivity. During rapport building, for example, you can smile, nod your head, lean forward, keep your legs uncrossed, and look frequently—but not excessively—at the child.
- Avoid saying something immediately after the child has stopped speaking.
- Deliver still-your-turn feedback by using minimal encouragers (e.g., comments such as "OK" and elaborative paraphrasing—"You said [child's words]. Tell me more about that").

Privileging Open-Ended Prompts
- Begin exploring each topic by delivering a series of open-ended prompts.
- After a focused prompt, cycle back to an open-ended prompt as soon as possible.

Developmentally Appropriate Language Pronunciation[a]
- Speak to the child using proper pronunciation. Do not mimic the child's pronunciation or use baby talk (but do use children's terms for people, body parts, etc.).
- Do not guess what a child might have said. When you cannot understand, ask the child to repeat the comment.
- Remember that the child may mispronounce words. If there could be another interpretation of a comment (e.g., *body* or *potty*), clarify the meaning of the target word by asking a follow-up question (e.g., "I'm not sure I understand where he peed. Tell me more about where he peed").

Word Usage
- Avoid introducing new words, such as the names of people or body parts, until the child first uses those words.
- Avoid complicated legal terms and other adult jargon.
- Be aware that young children may have difficulty with words whose meaning depends on the speaker's context, location, and relationship (e.g., *come/go, here/there, a/the*, kinship terms).
- Words such as *she, he, that*, or *it* may be misinterpreted by the child. Avoid replacing names and action descriptions with these words.

(continues)

- Remember that a child's understanding of a word may be more restrictive than an adult's (e.g., bathing suits and pajamas may not be *clothes* to the child; only hands may be capable of *touching*), more inclusive (*in* might mean *in* or *between*), or idiosyncratic (i.e., having no counterpart in adult speech). Phrase questions to avoid late-acquired words.
- The ability to answer questions about the time of an event is limited before 8 to 10 years of age, and even the words *before* and *after* sometimes produce inconsistent answers from young children (e.g., "Did it happen before Christmas?"). Try to narrow down the time of an event by asking about activities or events that children understand, such as whether it was a school day or what the child was doing that day.
- When the child mentions a specific person, ask follow-up questions to make sure the person's identity is unambiguous (but do not interrupt the child's free-narrative account to clarify; if possible, wait until a natural stopping point).

Question Forms
- Use simple sentences with a subject–verb–object word order.
- Avoid embedding clauses. Place the primary question before qualifications. For example, say, "What did you do when he hit you?" rather than "When he hit you, what did you do?"
- Ask about one issue per question, and one question per turn.
- Avoid negatives, as in "Did you *not* see who it was?"
- Do not use tag questions, such as "It was his computer, *wasn't it?*"

Cultural Issues
- Different cultures and families have different ideas about how children should act around authority figures. Avoid correcting a child's behavior unless it is interfering with your ability to hear the child or impeding the interview in other ways.
- Language diversity includes diversity in how people structure narratives about past events. Avoid interrupting children, but when you need to redirect them then do so by repeating the topic (e.g., "I have a question *about that time you babysat your baby brother*").

Note. ªAdapted from *Investigative Interviews of Children: A Guide for Helping Professionals* (pp. 179–180), by D. A. Poole and M. E. Lamb, 1998, Washington, DC: American Psychological Association. Copyright 1998 by the American Psychological Association.

PRIVILEGING OPEN-ENDED PROMPTS

In Chapter 1, I introduced some frequently used terms for various types of interviewer remarks. To review, facilitators (also called *minimal encouragers*) include utterances such as "OK," and "Umm-hmm" that keep children talking. *Open-ended prompts* include initial invitations to talk about an event, such as "Tell me everything that happened" (*open-ended broad questions*); prompts that elicit more about the sequence of activities, such as "Then what happened?" (*open-ended breadth questions*); and cued invitations that spin off something children said, such as "Tell me more about the part where [action the child mentioned]" (*open-ended depth questions*; see Quick Guide 3.2 for

QUICK GUIDE 3.2
Introduction to Open-Ended Prompts and Still-Your-Turn Feedback
(Minimal Encouragers)

Local dialects and witnesses' cultures determine which prompts sound neutral and familiar to children. Using these examples as a starting point, professionals can create lists of open-ended prompts and still-your-turn feedback that are appropriate for the children they interview.

To Prompt an Initial Narrative (Open-Ended Broad Questions)
- Tell me what happened.
- Tell me everything that happened.
- What happened?

To Elicit More About a Sequence of Activities (Open-Ended Breadth Questions)
- Then what happened?
- What happened next?
- What else happened?

To Request Details About a Previously Reported Aspect of an Event (Open-Ended Depth Questions)
- Tell me more about [child's words; e.g., "what Sam showed you on the computer"].
- Tell me more about the part where [child's words; e.g., "he yelled at you"].
- What happened when [child's words]?
- You said [child's words]. Tell me everything about that.

To Take a Conversational Turn
- Uh-huh.
- Go on.
- OK.
- I'm still listening.
- [Last few words the child said.]
- [Silence, perhaps with a slight lean-in or nod to signal "go on."]

Note. The division of open-ended prompts into broad, breadth, and depth questions are from Martine Powell's research group (e.g., Powell & Guadagno, 2008; Powell & Snow, 2007). A variety of open-ended prompts appear throughout the literature on child forensic interviewing; for examples, see Lamb, Hershkowitz, Orbach, and Esplin (2008) and Poole and Lamb (1998).

other examples). *Open-ended questions* point children to an event or part of an event but do not specify which details they should discuss. *Focused questions*, which ask children to provide specific types of information, include *recall-detail questions* (i.e., specific recall questions, such as "Where did he touch you?"), *option-posing questions* (multiple-choice and yes/no questions), and *suggestive questions*. There is an increasing pull for particular answers as interviewers move from open to suggestive questions. Some training materials call this progression the hierarchy of questions (Poole & Lamb, 1998), whereas others refer to a continuum of question types (National Children's Advocacy Center, 2012).

Throughout conversation, skilled interviewers make careful decisions about the type of prompt to deliver. However, they reduce the need for play-by-play decisions by adopting a conversational habit, the *questioning cycle*, that increases their use of open-ended prompts while minimizing the problems associated with using only open or only focused prompts.

Benefits of Open-Ended Prompts

There are many reasons why forensic interviewers prefer prompts that are higher in the question hierarchy and, therefore, more open-ended (see Quick Guide 1.1). Children and adults alike report a larger number of details in response to open-ended prompts compared with focused prompts (at least by 5 years of age; Hershkowitz, Lamb, Orbach, Katz, & Horowitz, 2012; see also Lamb, Hershkowitz, Sternberg, Esplin, et al., 1996), and their accuracy is typically highest when responding to open-ended prompts (Lamb, Orbach, Hershkowitz, Horowitz, & Abbott, 2007; Poole & Lindsay, 2001, 2002). These findings make sense because open-ended prompts (a) do not narrowly restrict the scope of the information requested, so children have more to talk about; (b) allow children to follow their own trains of thought, which aids memory retrieval; and (c) are less likely than more focused questions to request details that are not remembered, which improves accuracy.

Transcripts of conversations with children who visited my laboratory illustrate two important guidelines involving open-ended questions. In each of the following examples, the interviewers took time to build rapport before asking the children a series of open-ended questions about some science activities. Here is how one 8-year-old girl responded:

Interviewer:	OK. I want to know what happened that day at Germ Detective. Start with the first thing that happened and tell me everything you can, even things you don't think are very important.
Child:	OK. He introduced me to the game. That's pretty much the first thing I remember.
Interviewer:	Mm-hmm.
Child:	Umm. We played the game. And then, do it, should, oh, shouldn't we, shouldn't we have played three of them? 'Cause I forget if we di-, if we played two.
Interviewer:	I don't know.
Child:	But the one that I, um, thought of, that he tau-taught me to wash my hands.
Interviewer:	Mm-hmm.
Child:	The right way, that's pretty much, then, um, I pretty much just went home.

Interviewer:	OK, so tell me a little bit more about what happened at Germ Detective.
Child:	OK. We had glitter, oh! There is a three, a third one, um, a sneeze, um, like, we should use the spray bottle to see the sneezes. Um. And I learned that sneezes can go 12, I mean a hundred miles per hour.
Interviewer:	Wow.
Child:	And 20 feet long. And we used glitter for the Germ Detective, and we, um, tried to find the hidden things that are, that were on, um, some things, with a magnifying glass.
Interviewer:	Mm-hmm.
Child:	That's pretty much it.
Interviewer:	OK. Sometimes we remember a lot about how things looked. So, tell me how everything looked at Germ Detective.
Child:	Um. Like the table looked glittery because we just did like a glitter thing.
Interviewer:	Mm-hmm.
Child:	And we put a, and um, the piece of paper that we were doing it with looked like, the spray thing with, um, it looked like a little bit of drops on it. And, uh, that's pretty much all I remember.

What is striking in my transcripts is how often children report only one or two events and then wait for the interviewer to speak. This child, for instance, mentioned only an introduction to the games in response to the first open-ended prompt and, after the interviewer delivered some minimal encouragers, a hand-washing activity. Subsequent prompts drew out information about a sneeze and glitter game. Because the event had recently occurred, she probably would have reported more had the interviewer continued to deliver open-ended prompts with still-your-turn feedback (e.g., "I'm still listening") followed by pauses. Clearly, it is a mistake when interviewers move to focused questions after only one or two open-ended prompts because they may not have exhausted children's ability to recall the events.

This next example, from an 11-year-old, illustrates a related point: Children often say they cannot remember more when, actually, they can:

Interviewer:	I want to know what happened that day in the science room. Start with the first thing that happened and tell me everything you can, even things you don't think are very important.

Child:	Well, he greeted me, he gave me a name tag, and I wrote my name on it and I put it on my shirt. And then we did some experiments like folding paper airplanes and doing things about pulley systems. And that's as far as I can remember.
Interviewer:	Tell me more about what happened in the science room.
Child:	Well, um, I really can't think of anything more.
Interviewer:	Sometimes we remember a lot about how things looked. Tell me how everything looked in the science room.
Child:	Well, it seemed darker than this room, and I don't remember there being a table, but there was a desk in the corner, only it was very cluttered. There was one or two chairs. And that's all I can remember.
Interviewer:	Sometimes we remember a lot about sounds or things that people said. Tell me all the things you heard in the science room.
Child:	Well, I heard the man's voice, I heard some people walking down the hall. I remember there was a beeping like, like some kind of computer or something. Like every once in a while just a sudden beep would come out. And that's it.

As both transcripts show, differently worded open-ended prompts do not sound unnatural or coercive, yet they elicit more information. Equally important, the information children offer in response to subsequent prompts is as accurate as their earlier responses were (Poole & Lindsay, 2001).

To illustrate the benefits of delivering a set of open-ended prompts, consider a fine-grained analysis of one data set (Poole & Lindsay, 2001). Children from 3 to 8 years of age interacted with someone called Mr. Science, participated in a short baseline interview, and then went home. Months later, parents received a book, *A Visit to Mr. Science*, with instructions to read the book to their children three times. Each book described two demonstrations the children had experienced, two nonexperienced (fictitious) demonstrations, and a description of nonexperienced touching. (Individual events were counterbalanced, meaning that an event that was experienced by one child was nonexperienced for another.) To measure how children responded after exposure to misinformation, interviewers questioned them a day after the last book-reading session. Following rapport-building chitchat, interviewers delivered the four open-ended prompts in the previous transcript excerpt, along with a fifth and final prompt: "Think about what you told me. Is there something you didn't tell me that you can tell me now?" Here are some findings:

- Children continued to report new information as interviewers delivered additional prompts. For example, almost half of the

3-year-olds and most of the 8-year-olds mentioned something new in response to the fourth open-ended prompt, and many children added information after interviewers delivered the fifth prompt.

- The amount of new information was meaningful. For example, 7- and 8-year-olds averaged nine pieces of new information in response to the fourth prompt.

- Accuracy did not decline across prompts. In fact, the percentage of information in children's reports that mirrored the fictitious narrative from the book was nearly identical for first and subsequent prompts.

- It is risky to omit topic markers. Notice that the final prompt did not clearly specify a topic. (It was "Is there something you didn't tell me that you can tell me now?" rather than "Is there something you didn't tell me about what happened in the science room that you can tell me now?"). Remarkably, although all prior questions had asked about the science experience, even older children did not always assume that this question did as well. Instead, they sometimes drifted off topic by mentioning unrelated events from their lives. For example, one 8-year-old boy told us, "We used to have a fish, but it died," and other children reported events that could be misconstrued as having occurred in the science room. To prevent misunderstandings due to topic drift, redundantly mentioning topics is a habit discussed in the language guidelines that wrap up this chapter.

Because it is unnatural for adults to deliver many open-ended prompts, it is helpful to memorize a selection of prompts from Quick Guide 3.2 and then practice using these prompts frequently in daily conversation.

Benefits of Focused Questions

Open invitations are important, but it is a mistake to think that good interviewing consists only of these prompts. Because children rarely describe events fully in response to open prompts, interviews without focused prompts are unlikely to elicit the event information and corroborative evidence needed to meet interview goals. As a result, thorough case exploration almost always requires focused questions (questions asking about specific aspects of events).

In addition to retrieving needed case information, focused questions are useful for double-checking responses to open-ended prompts. This is necessary because—counter to widespread belief—open-ended prompts are not a "magical elixir for truth" (Brubacher, Poole, & Dickinson, 2015, p. 17).

When experts say that information produced by open-ended invitations is largely accurate, they mean that accuracy is typically high among children who experienced suspected events. In fact, there are many reasons why inaccurate information can infiltrate freely recalled responses, including intentional lying, memory source-monitoring confusions (e.g., Principe, DiPuppo, & Gammel, 2013), and a type of error in which children provide descriptions matching familiar or expected circumstances that do not match the events under discussion (e.g., Erskine, Markham, & Howie, 2001). For example, a child in my laboratory elaborately described a type of dropped ceiling that is common in elementary schools even though this was not the type of ceiling in the location where the target event had occurred (see also Shapiro, 2009).

One goal of forensic interviewing is to deliver the least directive question that might retrieve needed information. For example, "Tell me about his truck" is less directive than the recall-detail question "What color was the car?" In turn, this question is less leading than a multiple-choice question, such as "Was the car red, blue, or something else?" or the yes/no question "Was the car red?" If a description of a car were needed, interviewers would start with an open-ended question, if possible (*Child*: "And then he drove me home." *Interviewer*: "What did he drive you home in?" *Child*: "His truck." *Interviewer*: "Tell me about his truck"). If this prompt did not return a color, the interviewer might say,

> I'm going to ask more about the truck now. Remember, if I ask a question and you don't know the answer, just say, "I don't know." But if you know the answer, I want you to tell me. What color was the truck?

("Do you remember what color the truck was?" would be understood by adolescents but might confuse younger children, as discussed later in this chapter.)

The accuracy of young children's responses to recall-detail and yes/no questions varies from study to study, but yes/no questions often return less accurate responses. For example, when Carole Peterson and Marleen Biggs (1997) interviewed 2- to 13-year-olds about traumatic injuries, the older children's responses to yes/no questions were only slightly less accurate than their responses to recall-detail questions. Among children 5 years old and younger, however, accuracy was lower for yes/no compared with recall-detail questions; among children 4 years and younger, accuracy was at chance when children said "no" (see also Peterson & Rideout, 1998). Because of findings such as these, one goal of training is to reduce interviewers' reliance on yes/no questions by providing *flexible question frames* (also called *question stems*), which are memorized phrases interviewers use to construct more open strategies for asking about various issues (see Quick Guide 5.2).

The Questioning Cycle: Balancing the Benefits of Open and Focused Prompts

Early descriptions of forensic interviewing sometimes depicted questioning as a two-step process: Interviewers were advised to start with open-ended prompts and then move on to focused questions once children's free-narrative accounts were exhausted. Today, the recommended conversational habit is a cycle, one in which interviewers continually return to the most open (and, therefore, least suggestive) prompt that might elicit needed information as they move conversation through various topics. By exploring new topics with a series of open prompts and trying to pair one or more focused questions with an open-ended prompt (Lamb, Orbach, Hershkowitz, Esplin, & Horowitz, 2007), interviewers encourage children to report information in ways that match the organization of their memories. Privileging open prompts does not prevent interviewers from asking targeted questions when necessary, but this conversational habit avoids lengthy series of recall-detail questions (which can train children to respond to each prompt with only a little information). In practice, it takes a lot of experience to cycle back to open prompts because this pattern is not adults' natural style of talking—nor is it the style of unskilled interviewers (who often deliver one or two invitations before initiating a lengthy series of focused questions; Powell, Hughes-Scholes, Smith, & Sharman, 2014).

DEVELOPMENTALLY APPROPRIATE LANGUAGE

In addition to encouraging children to do most of the talking, interviewers assume a child-centered perspective (see Chapter 2) by talking in simple ways that most witnesses understand. Developmentally appropriate language rounds out a set of conversational habits that also includes a supportive demeanor, a relaxed conversational rhythm, and a repeated cycle of returning to open-ended prompts after more targeted questions.

Children's linguistic needs are not always obvious. For example, word length is not a good clue to difficulty because many short words (e.g., the pronoun *in*) are conceptually confusing to young children. We also cannot assume that children have learned words they hear frequently. For instance, kinship terms (e.g., *aunt, uncle*) are challenging because of gender distinctions (e.g., one of my children called an aunt "Uncle Bonnie") and the fact that who you are (a mother or a daughter, a father or a son) depends on who is speaking (which is quite a brain teaser). To augment the discussion that follows, I recommend the *Handbook on Questioning Children: A Linguistic Perspective* (A. G. Walker, 2013).

Competent Babies and Confused Adolescents

Nature has a remarkable ability to equip children with the skills they need to survive without bogging development down by wiring up talents that can wait for a later time. Because of this biological triaging, from infancy through their early 20s our young are paradoxically precocious yet immature, which leads us both to underestimate and overestimate their abilities.

Whenever we spot remarkable achievements in a child, it is natural to expect competency in a related activity. For example, the capacity to make eye contact and take turns in conversation emerges so early that even 2-year-olds rarely interrupt their conversational partners or overlap speech (Kaye & Charney, 1981). Along with other linguistic achievements, this "you talk, then I talk" competency can trick us into thinking our young understand other conversational conventions, such as the need to say something relevant. But as I described earlier, even school-age children play fast and loose with conversational turns in the sense that they often say whatever comes to mind.

On the flip side, focusing on cognitive weaknesses can lead us to underestimate children's ability to recall meaningful events. For example, adults might be skeptical of a report containing inconsistent details even when those inconsistencies are easily explained by the way children answer certain types of questions (see this chapter's Principles to Practice). Before I describe some types of questions that child forensic interviewers should avoid, it is first helpful to summarize how language development typically unfolds:

- Receptive language (comprehension) usually outpaces expressive language (production). *Receptive language* is what children understand when people speak to them; *expressive language*, also called *productive language*, is what children can say. *Comprehension*— what children understand—usually outpaces production. In other words, children usually understand more language than they use themselves.
- Production does not imply comprehension. Just because children use particular words or respond to certain types of questions does not mean they understand those words and questions.
- Language learning is lifelong. It is tempting to set aside language guidelines when talking with older children and teenagers, but even these age groups lack a mature vocabulary and the ability to navigate difficult question forms. For example, some teenagers have only a vague understanding of basic legal terms (e.g., *jury*), most have little knowledge of more technical terms (e.g., *perjury*; Warren-Leubecker, Tate, Hinton, & Ozbek,

1989), and even college students find multiple questions a challenge (Perry et al., 1995).[4]

- Environmental factors, some medical conditions, and developmental disabilities affect language development. On average, maltreated children have poorer language skills than their peers (Lum, Powell, Timms, & Snow, 2015), as do children from low socioeconomic backgrounds. Also, many conditions, including early hearing loss, vision impairments, and developmental disabilities (e.g., autism spectrum disorder), affect language comprehension (Hoff, 2014). As a general rule, the vocabulary, sentence structures, and conversational practices that children master at a young age are easier for everyone to understand than later-emerging forms and conventions. Therefore, it makes sense to always use simple, concrete language in forensic conversations.

Guidelines for understanding children and phrasing questions during interviews address four language topics: (a) *phonology* (language sounds and the rules for combining sounds), (b) *semantics* (the acquisition of meaning or, to simplify, vocabulary), (c) *syntax* (the rules for combining words and their equivalents, commonly called grammar), and (d) *pragmatics* and conversational competence (the social functions of language). These terms are useful when searching databases for information about language issues, but here I use more familiar words to discuss how interviewers navigate children's unclear speech, avoid difficult words and question forms, and respect cultural differences.

Navigating Unclear Speech

Interview recordings often contain evidence of misunderstandings between children and adults, as in this excerpt from a sexual abuse interview:

Interviewer: Is it good or bad to tell a lie?

Child: G. A. touched me.

Interviewer: Jesus loves me? Is that what you said?

Child: Yeah. (Warren, Woodall, Hunt, & Perry, 1996, p. 235)

---

[4]Defense attorneys often ask children complex questions, yet in one study a confusing questioning style was associated with an increase in convictions (Evans, Lee, & Lyon, 2009). Because these data are correlational, there are several possible reasons for this finding: Attorneys who are less experienced with child cases could be more likely to question children inappropriately (and also lose cases), the strategy might turn jurors against the defense, or defense attorneys might evoke this strategy when prosecutors have a strong case. Regardless of the reason, it is interesting that violating language guidelines is risky for the defense and prosecution alike.

It is easy for communication to break down when interviewers guess what children said or take utterances literally because of a lack of familiarity with common pronunciation errors. I heard my favorite example during a workshop, when a child muttered, "He put some ting on my arm." Unfortunately, the interviewer heard this utterance as "He put some paint on my arm" and asked for information about the paint. Testimony quickly traveled down the wrong road, with the child giving a detailed report of events that never occurred. To the developmental psychologists in the audience, the child's initial statement ("He put something on my arm") was clear because he had merely deleted one of two consonants that should have occurred together (which is a frequent error).

To understand why some pronunciation errors occur more often than others, it is helpful to start with the smallest unit of language that signals a change in meaning: the phoneme. *Phonemes* are categories of sound that signal differences among words, and these categories vary from language to language. For example, /r/ and /l/ are two phonemes in English because we perceive *rice* and *lice* as two different words. Japanese speakers produce sounds similar to our /r/ and /l/, but substituting these sounds does not change the meaning of a word. In every language, children learn that some variations in sound mark changes in meaning whereas others do not (Poole & Lamb, 1998).

Although infants hear subtle differences between speech sounds, young children do not immediately know which differences are meaningful in their language—nor can they always articulate these sounds in words. At 4 years of age, children are still learning how to say many sounds of their native language, and some children do not master all sounds until about 8½ years of age (Reich, 1986).[5] During early language learning, a child's pronunciation is not always consistent from one utterance to the next, and the following errors are common (de Villiers & de Villiers, 1978; Reich, 1986):

- *Deletion of sounds* occurs when children drop consonants from consonant clusters (e.g., *tring* for *string*) or final consonants. Young children may also drop unstressed syllables in words (e.g., saying *way* for *away*).
- *Addition of sounds* occurs when children avoid a final consonant or consonant cluster by adding a vowel, as when they say *piga* for *pig* or *pulay* for *play*.
- *Sound substitution* occurs when children replace one sound with another. For example, a child in Sonja Brubacher's lab repeatedly said she was given *dope* (i.e., *soap*, the child's name for the hand

---

[5]Children may avoid saying words they cannot pronounce correctly. If a child seems to be avoiding a particular word, it is best to agree on another name for the object, action, or person.

sanitizer), illustrating how children sometimes substitute an easy-to-produce sound for one that is difficult (Poole, Dickinson, & Brubacher, 2014).

- *Reversal of sounds* is an uncommon error; for example, saying *puc* for *cup*.

The high frequency of such errors in children's speech dictates the following strategies during interviews:

- Do not mimic the child's mispronunciations. Because comprehension outpaces production, some children become agitated when adults speak in baby talk or reproduce their pronunciation errors. Instead, interviewers should pronounce words correctly (while using children's terms for people, body parts, etc.).
- Ask the child to repeat words and phrases that were not understood. If the child mumbles the name of a person, for example, the interviewer might say, "I didn't hear that . . . what did you say?" Interviewers should avoid guessing what children said by saying, "Did you say [possible word or phrase]?"
- Follow communication slip-ups with questions that might clarify what words or phrases mean. For example, if the child repeats a name but is still unclear, the interviewer might ask, "Who is that?" If the child used a verb, as in "He [inaudible] me," follow-up questions could be "Tell me how he did that" or "I don't know that word. Tell me what that is" (Poole & Lamb, 1998).

Avoiding Difficult Words and Question Forms

There are many reasons why a child might not understand a question: A word in the question could be difficult because it is not used often (or at all) in the child's environment, because it refers to a concept that is cognitively challenging, or because it has a linguistic function in the question that is difficult to master. But even when the individual words an interviewer uses are understood, these words can still be assembled into confusing questions by putting too many ideas into a question or by ordering ideas in ways that are cognitively challenging. Here are examples of potentially confusing words:

- *any*: Children sometimes say "no" to questions involving the word *any* (e.g., "Did anything happen?") and then contradict this answer later in their testimonies. There is not a simple reason for these inconsistencies, which occur among adults as well (e.g., "Did you have anything for breakfast?" "No, just a piece of toast"). The best approach for avoiding these questions is to try to get needed information with open-ended prompts (e.g., "You said John picked you up at school. What happened next?"). When the use of *some* would not be overly leading, questions with this word are less likely to produce thoughtless "no" responses (e.g., "Did you hear something?" followed by "Tell me what you heard").

- *before/after*: Children say these words before they understand their appropriate meanings in all contexts (usually around age 7, according to Reich, 1986), although mastery can be as late as 14 or 15 years among children speaking English as a second language (according to A. G. Walker, 2013). Comprehension is better when the order of events in a question matches the past order of events. For example, it is easier to comprehend "Did you tell someone before you told your teacher?" than "Before you told your teacher, did you tell someone else?"

- words describing touch and penetration (i.e., *in*, *inside*): Sexual abuse interviews often discuss touching and penetration, but children's meanings for common words about these issues can be more restrictive or broader than that of adults. To young children, the word *touch* might mean only a specific type of contact administered by the hand, which can lead them to deny falsely that touching occurred (e.g., *Interviewer*: "Did he touch you?" *Child*: "No." *Interviewer*: "Tell me what happened." *Child*: "He kissed my pee-pee"). Once touching has been established, interviewers have a challenge because the prepositions *in* and *inside* can be confusing to young children (especially when these words are embedded in questions about unfamiliar anatomy). For example, young children might describe a penis between the legs as *inside* their bodies yet deny that penetration breeching the labia majora was *in*.

- *know, think, remember, guess*: Words about mental states are challenging to preschoolers, who are just beginning to think about thinking. For example, some children believe that to remember something, they must have forgotten it first. Therefore, a child might say "no" to the question "Do you remember when __?" yet mention that event a few moments later.

- time words: The words *yesterday* and *tomorrow* are confusing because these words refer to a time relative to the present rather than a particular day. To preschoolers, yesterday could be any day in the past whereas tomorrow is any day that has not yet arrived. (Most children understand *today*.) Relatedly, asking young children which day of the week or which month something happened is risky because they may not yet grasp these words and tend not to organize memories around these concepts. Generally, accuracy is better for recent, isolated events than for repeated events and those that occurred a long time ago. (For information about children's ability to identify the time of past events, consult articles by William Friedman; e.g., Friedman, 1991; Friedman, Reese, & Dai, 2011.)

- kinship terms: As mentioned earlier, young children sometimes confuse male and female kinship terms (e.g., *aunt* and *uncle*) and fail to shift perspectives to grasp that, for example, their mother is their grandmother's daughter. Therefore, "Does Nanna have another name?" might identify a grandmother more accurately than "Is that your momma's mom or your daddy's mom?"

- pointing words: In conversation, adults often mention a specific person or action (e.g., "John came by yesterday and brought the divorce papers") and then use words that refer back to what was discussed earlier (e.g., "I got mad when *he* did *that*"). Words whose meanings depend on what was said earlier go by a variety of names, including pointing words, deictic words, and indexical words. In interviews, many pointing words are pronouns (e.g., *him*), although words such as *there* also derive meaning from the context. Children have difficulty identifying the meaning of pointing words, especially when a lot of conversation intervenes between statements mentioning a person, place, or action and subsequent pointing words referring back to these referents. Therefore, it is best to restate the names of people, actions, and so forth, rather than replacing unambiguous words with pointing words.[6]

In addition to avoiding problematic words, developmentally appropriate language avoids the following question forms:

- left-branching questions: English speakers are most accustomed to *right-branching sentences*, which are sentences that put the main subject (e.g., "You") before actions and objects (e.g., "drove Mark's car on Friday before the party"). In contrast, *left-branching sentences* start with modifying information, which the

---

[6]A study by Debby Hulse (1994) illustrated how challenging interviews can be for children. She counted the number of conversational turns that transpired (interviewer and child utterances) between the time interviewers mentioned something by name and the time they used a pronoun referring back to the referent. When interviewers questioned children 2 to 6 years of age, that distance was 7; for older children (7–13 years), it was 32.

listener has to keep in mind while waiting for the main point to arrive (e.g., "On Friday, before the game, you drove Mark's car"). Generally, it is best to keep the main subject and verb at the beginning of a question and near each other (e.g., "Did you drive Mark's car on Friday?" rather than, "Did you, on Friday, drive Mark's car?").

- passives: In *passive* sentences, the subject is the receiver of the action rather than the individual who acted. For example, "Mom hit Sam" is active voice, whereas "Sam was hit by mom" is passive voice. It is best to always use active voice because children do not gain mastery of passives until late in development. For example, an interviewer would ask, "Did he pick you up from school on Monday?" rather than "Were you picked up from school by him on Monday?"

- multiple questions: Children often respond to one of several questions delivered in a single utterance even though it is unclear which question they are answering. However, they are tolerant when interviewers catch the error and say something like, "I'm sorry, let me start again."

- do-you-remember-X questions: A frequent question form in courtroom transcripts is "Do you remember" followed by mention of an event ("... the last time he babysat?") or other topic ("... what the pictures looked like?"). Answering these questions requires sophisticated linguistic knowledge and the ability to remember multiple parts of the question. Children sometimes respond to these questions without actually understanding them, as in the following example from A. G. Walker (2013; transcript question and answer from A. G. Walker, 1993):

  Q. Do you remember telling T. J. that Harv pulled Doug's shirt up and dug at his eyes with a spoon?

  A. No
  A logical adult interpretation of that response would be that the "No" meant that the child had no recollection of saying such a thing. And that is a possibility. But it could also have a number of alternative interpretations from the child's point of view: 1) that Harv did not pull up Doug's shirt; 2) that Harv did not dig at Doug's eyes with a spoon; 3) that it was not Harv but someone else who did one or both of those things; 4) that the child did not tell T. J. that, but told someone else. In fact, as further questioning revealed, her responses meant none of these things. It simply meant, in her words, "I don't remember what you said." (pp. 56–57)

(See Chapter 5, Phrasing Detail Questions, for a discussion of research on children's responses to do-you-remember questions.)

- questions with negatives in them: Children's answers to questions with negatives (e.g., "Did you not see the computer?") are unreliable, but they do well with more straightforward wording (e.g., "Did you see the computer?"; Perry et al., 1995).

These examples are just some of the many words and question forms that can cause miscommunications during interviews. Children respond in a variety of ways to utterances they do not understand, including saying nothing, offering answers, and—as in the following example—by repeating something the interviewer said or saying something irrelevant (Saywitz, 1988):

Attorney: When you were at your grandma's house with your daddy, whose mamma is your grandma?

Jenny: Grandma Ann. (gives grandma's name)

Attorney: Is she your daddy's mamma?

Jenny: Huh? (doesn't understand the question)

Attorney: Is she your daddy's mamma? (leading question requiring only a nod)

Jenny: Daddy's mamma. (repeats the end of the sentence; common response when communicating with children fails)

Attorney: Is grandma daddy's mother? (requires only a nod to force the adult to stop this line of questioning)

Jenny: She has a boyfriend, two boyfriends. (irrelevant response) (pp. 38–39)

Because children who are confused by questions sometimes repeat interviewers' comments or move on to unrelated topics, it is important to not assume that witnesses who produce a few silly answers are simply fabricating information.

Respecting Cultural Differences

While children are learning to pronounce sounds, building their vocabularies, and mastering various sentence forms, they are also learning about the social uses of language. This layer of language learning includes skills such as changing the way we speak in different situations, knowing how to tell a "good" story, and showing appropriate nonverbal behavior during conversation. In some cultures, children tend to position themselves close to adults, maintain eye contact, and get directly to the point of questions they have been asked; in others, children avoid invading adults' personal space and looking them in the eyes, and their narratives about past events often start with a lot of background information. This latter style can appear uncooperative to interviewers from a more direct, get-to-the-point culture.

As mentioned earlier, interviewers should avoid correcting children's behavior unless this behavior is interfering with the ability to hear responses or is impeding interviews in other ways. It is also best to not interrupt children, even if they are not quickly addressing the point of a question. Once it becomes clear that a child is truly off topic, the interviewer should repeat the topic in a redirecting prompt (e.g., "I have another question about the time you babysat your baby brother").

In sum, forensic interviewers minimize miscommunications by following the language recommendations in Quick Guide 3.1, which round out the conversational habits for talking with children. As with all recommendations, interviewers are free to adjust their behavior depending on the needs of individual cases and children. For example, it is not a mistake to adopt a more formal demeanor with an unusually playful child or to insist that a highly distractible one sit in a chair. Forensic interviewers deviate from the general guidelines in this chapter when doing so will help them elicit testimony that is distorted as little as possible by reluctance, thoughtless compliance, or other factors.

RECAP

Professionals master the conversational habits of forensic interviewing to avert common interviewing errors and to the free cognitive resources they need to problem solve during interviews. They accomplish these goals through three sets of techniques:

- A *supportive conversational style*. Forensic interviewers put children at ease by avoiding clothing that draws attention to their authority, having a relaxed and patient demeanor, adopting nonverbal behaviors associated with positivity during early interview phases (e.g., smiling, leaning forward, nodding), showing interest without a threatening amount of eye contact, observing children's reactions and adjusting their own behavior accordingly, giving children adequate time to talk, and delivering still-your-turn feedback (comments such as "uh-huh" and "You said [child's words]; tell me more about that"). Child interviewers maintain a neutral yet warm demeanor throughout conversations.

- *Privileging open-ended prompts.* To elicit testimony representing children's ideas, forensic interviewers explore each topic with a series of open-ended prompts and cycle back to such prompts after one or more focused questions.
- *Developmentally appropriate language.* Forensic interviewers use the adult pronunciation of words (rather than mimicking children's) and strive to deliver one question at a time, phrase questions in the clearest way possible (e.g., subject–verb–object), repeat names and actions (rather than replacing these words with pronouns), avoid conceptually difficult words, monitor for possible miscommunications, and ignore behavior that is not interfering with the process of delivering prompts and hearing answers.

In the field, children's ages and individual characteristics, along with the goals of interviews and local standards, determine how interviewers translate these conversational conventions into practice.

PRINCIPLES TO PRACTICE: IS THIS CHILD AN UNRELIABLE WITNESS?

Professionals often wonder about the significance of discrepancies across related questions in an interview. Though every case is unique, my transcript analyses usually include a step explained here.

Question From a Forensic Psychologist

I have a sexual abuse case involving a 5-year-old girl who was interviewed at a child advocacy center. She reversed her answers to several questions, and some answers seemed evasive. Should I assume she did not actually experience the events she describes?

My Response

Occasional inconsistencies and peculiar answers are not uncommon when young children talk about events they have experienced. To analyze a transcript, it is helpful to first strike out question–answer pairs containing inconsistencies that are easily explained by the type of questions the interviewer asked. For example, children often say "no" to questions containing the word *any*, so it is unremarkable when young children describe touching but also say "no" to a question such as "Did he touch you anywhere?" I also (a) strike out question–answer pairs when the questions contained words or sentence structures the child may not have understood, (b) note discrepancies to differently worded questions when related questions could have been interpreted differently by the child, and (c) watch for times when the child might have been off topic (due to fatigue or to take a conversational turn after a difficult question). After eliminating issues that are easily explained by routine developmental and memory issues, I evaluate the rest of the child's report (always considering the broader case context). This step eliminates minor inconsistencies and lapses of attention without explaining away every concerning response.

4

CONVENTIONAL CONTENT: EARLY INTERVIEW PHASES

Trained interviewers maintain the conversational habits of child interviewing (see Chapter 3, this volume) while they direct discussion through the set of interview phases (sections) suggested by their preferred or required protocol. Individual protocols use different names to describe these phases, recommend different sets and orders of phases, and suggest different ways of wording prompts within each phase. Nevertheless, in every protocol phases are designed to solve challenges that arise when adults talk to children about sensitive issues.

This chapter describes how early interview phases prepare interviewers and children to discuss the matters under investigation, the research supporting each phase, and some ways interviewers assemble and deliver these phases in current practice. Early phases include planning the interview, preparing the interview space, introducing the interviewer and beginning the rapport-building process, discussing interview ground rules, conducting a practice

http://dx.doi.org/10.1037/14941-005
Interviewing Children: The Science of Conversation in Forensic Contexts, by D. A. Poole

narrative, and discussing useful background information. Collectively, the phases described here and in Chapter 5 represent the conventional content of child forensic interviews.

The tradition of breaking conversations into phases is a long-standing yet often misunderstood feature of child interviewing. Some interviewers believe they have mastered forensic interviewing once they have learned to deliver a set of phases, even though their conversational habits are inexpert, they fail to explore unexpected information that emerges during interviews, and they sometimes close interviews without collecting needed information. Defense attorneys make a related mistake when they attack interviewers for not following a protocol simply because an interview phase was reordered or delivered differently from protocol examples. In both of these cases, professionals erroneously equated good interviewing with a rigid walk through a list of phrases. Experts, however, view interviewing as a set of decisions professionals make about how to solve conversational challenges to achieve case goals. From this perspective, the phases in this chapter are simply modules that appear in many interviews because many interviews face similar challenges. (To read more about flexibility in practice, turn to this chapter's Principles to Practice.)

PLANNING THE INTERVIEW

Professionals interview children for many purposes, in different environments, and with varying amounts of time to plan conversations. Because of this variability across cases, guidelines for individual jurisdictions and specific purposes direct the extent and nature of preinterview preparation. (See Chapter 2 for an explanation of fully informed interviewing, blind interviewing, and hybrid models.) A unifying theme is the understanding that "planning investigative interviews is an essential aspect of the interview process" (K. Smith & Milne, 2011, p. 87). This process often involves four activities: (a) compiling background information about the child and the matters under investigation, (b) articulating the purpose (commander's intent) of the interview, (c) constructing alternative hypotheses and planning strategies for testing these hypotheses, and (d) deciding how the interview will be conducted.

Compiling Background Information

When preinterview preparation is desired and possible, the following information can help an interviewer (a) schedule conversation for a time when the child is unlikely to be tired or in need of a break for medical reasons (e.g., to take medication), (b) assess the need for an interpreter or bilingual interviewer, (c) recognize the names of people the child may discuss, and (d) choose scripts for early interview phases that are appropriate for the child's age and level of cognitive ability.

Child information includes the following:

- child's name, preferred name, age, and gender identity;
- developmental considerations, such as developmental delay, hearing or speech impairment, and mental health diagnoses;
- medical treatments and conditions, along with the implications of medication and/or treatment for scheduling the interview;
- cultural considerations, including which language is spoken in the home;
- family composition and custody arrangements;
- caregiving environments and schedules (including day care and babysitting arrangements);
- family names for body parts (for abuse investigations); and
- relevant family routines and recent events (e.g., for sexual abuse investigations, family practices regarding nudity and recent sexual education).

Circumstances and local practice dictate how much information interviewers will have about the matters under investigation, which can include some of all of the following *alleged offense information*:

- general nature (e.g., physical abuse, sexual abuse, neglect) and circumstances of the allegation (e.g., time, location, frequency);
- how the allegation came to the attention of the authorities;
- possible motivations to conceal or distort information (e.g., alleged threats, family or neighborhood hostilities predating the allegations); and
- for fully informed interviewing, the allegations and circumstances surrounding these allegations (e.g., allegations of touching by the babysitter during baths).

Information about the child and the matters under investigation helps an interviewer or investigative team articulate the purpose of the interview, construct alternative hypotheses and testing strategies, and plan a child-centered and developmentally appropriate conversation that will support broader investigative efforts. (See Chapter 2 for an introduction to these characteristics of the forensic perspective.)

Articulating the Purpose of the Interview (Commander's Intent)

Interviewers or investigative teams articulate *commander's intent* when they define the scope of topics to explore. For example, a child protection worker who conducts an interview triggered by a sexual abuse allegation may be charged to also explore for other forms of child maltreatment. The scope of this interview is likely broader than that of a sexual abuse interview conducted for a criminal case, which in turn will be more comprehensive than a minimal facts interview (i.e., a short interview conducted by a responding investigator used to determine whether a more extensive interview is warranted; e.g., San Diego Child Protection Team, 2013). Regardless of whether an interview's scope is broad or narrow, interviewers should have a clear sense of what their obligation is to explore (a) issues beyond those that triggered the interview and (b) unexpected comments that might have criminal or child protection implications.

Constructing Alternative Hypotheses and Testing Strategies

After gathering available information about the case and defining the scope of an interview, it is time to plan strategies for testing alternative hypotheses. A simple form for listing alternative hypotheses and planning ways to test those hypotheses can organize thoughts before an interview (see State of Michigan Governor's Task Force on Child Abuse and Neglect and Department of Human Services, 2011, for an example).

When abuse or neglect is under investigation, alternative explanations could include the possibility that alleged statements by a child were misunderstood, that an injury was accidental, that a child's statements were unintentionally or intentionally influenced by another person, and that the child is lying to achieve some goal. As discussed in Chapter 2, some alternative hypotheses are tested directly, as when an interviewer says, "Does Grandpa have another name?" (which can clarify the identity of an alleged offender). Other times, simply asking for contextual information ("What were you and Mom doing when [child's words]?") tests an alternative hypothesis. The dynamics of specific types of cases (e.g., physical abuse, sexual abuse, arson) and children's ages dictate what the most plausible alternative hypotheses are and common ways of testing those hypotheses.

Deciding How the Interview Will Be Conducted

This planning articulates where the interview will occur; what recording equipment (if any) will document the interview; who will be present, their roles, and where they will be positioned during the interview; and what the structure and content of the interview will be. Content planning decides how the delivery of interview phases will be adjusted to accommodate the child's age and level of cognitive ability, how the topic of concern will be introduced, whether drawing materials or other props will be on hand, and which topics should be raised to support broader investigative efforts.

Overview of a Successful Interview Plan

Interview planning ranges from a mental run-through while driving to a local school to team-based meetings in which several professionals discuss the purpose and structure of an upcoming interview. Successful planning means that within the constraints of the situation and local practice, the interviewer (a) understands the goals and scope of the interview, (b) has considered the implications of available case information for hypothesis testing, and (c) has translated general interviewing guidelines into a developmentally appropriate plan for conducting an interview that will support the broader investigation.

PREPARING THE INTERVIEW SPACE

Ideas about the structure of a child-friendly interview space have changed considerably since the days when play therapy rooms were a popular location (D. P. H. Jones & McQuiston, 1988). Today we know that toys and other distractions can capture children's attention, making it more difficult to keep them on topic. Also, playroom environments create opportunities for critics to say that children were engrossed in fantasy (rather than recalling from experience) or that objects mentioned in testimony were merely suggested by the setting. For example, a child could be reminded of pornographic images because the schoolroom used for an interview had a computer, but a defense attorney might argue that the child was merely looking about the room and weaving suggestions into the report. By taking time to prepare the setting, interviewers improve children's engagement in interviews and avert this type of criticism.

Characteristics of the Interview Space

Many guidelines list the following characteristics of a supportive interview space (for more information, see National Children's Advocacy Center, 2012; Saywitz & Camparo, 2014):

- *Quiet and with minimal distractions.* Noise from people, traffic, and electronic equipment can startle young witnesses and reduce their ability to search through memory. As much as possible, interviewing spaces should be free from distractions, including personal items (e.g., guns) that might capture attention. Because some children become distressed when adults try to separate them from interesting activities, it best to stock waiting areas with objects that are not highly novel or engaging.

- *Private*. It is preferable to interview children without others in the room. If a support person is required, it is best if that person sits behind the child and leaves after the early interview phases. (See Chapter 7 for a discussion of support persons.)
- *Informal and somewhat familiar*. Young children will be less nervous in settings that look more like home or school than a medical office.
- *Neutral and age-appropriate*. The best furniture and decorations are thematically neutral and inviting for children.
- *Safe*. It is best to interview children in a location where they will not fear the presence of alleged perpetrators.
- *Functional*. The rooms in interviewing centers are designed to seat children and interviewers for conversation, permit video recording equipment to capture whatever happens, and store supplies (e.g., paper and markers) out of sight until needed. Waiting areas and a bathroom (which children should be invited to visit before interviews begin) are nearby. Interviewers working outside a specialized center should select the location that best mirrors these features, avoiding large spaces that invite children to roam.
- *Culturally inclusive*. Many images, objects, and commercial logos have negative connotations to some families and cultural groups. For example, Halloween images, fairies, and wizards are offensive to some religious groups, and the ways Native Americans are depicted in some Thanksgiving decorations are disrespectful. Professionals should (a) research the appropriateness of images and objects in waiting areas and interview rooms and (b) take care that interview aids depict boys and girls with a range of physical appearances.

Overview of a Child-Friendly Interview Space

The best interview spaces are neutrally decorated, quiet, furnished to encourage conversation between adults and children, and pleasant without being overly distracting. Professionals who interview in the field should consider which of the available locations will work best, take a minute to remove distracting objects from the room, and remove personal items that could capture children's attention.

INTRODUCING THE INTERVIEWER AND BEGINNING THE RAPPORT-BUILDING PROCESS

Starting the Interview

Some children are unusually social, but many tend to freeze in unfamiliar situations (Bishop, Spence, & McDonald, 2003). The goals of initial introductions and chitchat are to acclimate the child to the interview environment, address any misunderstandings the child may have about the interviewer's job, begin the rapport-building process (which continues throughout the interview), and convey that the child should do most of the talking. This phase is also an opportunity to elicit speech, which provides information about the child's developmental level, willingness to talk, and pronunciation patterns.

Although some protocols script opening introductions, many interviewers write their own. Because of developmental differences, it makes sense to use a short version for young children and a more maturely worded version for older children and adolescents. During the opening introduction, most interviewers (a) tell children their names, (b) say something about their jobs, and (c) orient children to the room and any recording equipment. In interviewing centers, local requirements dictate whether children will be introduced to an observation room and/or told about observers, and interviewers may be required to vocalize labeling information for a recording. The general principle is that introductions should be "simple and to the point, as well as tailored to the child's culture and developmental stage" (National Children's Advocacy Center, 2014, p. 2). Consider this example (State of Michigan Governor's Task Force on Child Abuse and Neglect and Department of Human Services, 2011):

> Hello, my name is [interviewer's name]. My job is to listen to kids. Today is my day to listen to you.
>
> As you can see, I have a video camera/recorder here. It will record what we say. Sometimes I forget things and the recording helps me remember what you said. (pp. 9–10)

Here the interviewer used the word *kids* because this is the term community members use in daily conversation, but interviewers should adjust their language to accommodate regional differences and children's ages. Another striking feature of this example is the lack of mention of a specific job category. The law enforcement professional who suggested this example conducted sexual abuse interviews in plain clothes and did not want children to fear that they or a family member might be in trouble. This second example, though worded differently, is also short and straightforward (Lamb, Hershkowitz, Orbach, & Esplin, 2008).

> Hello, my name is ___ and I am a police officer. [Introduce anyone else in the room; ideally, nobody else will be present.] Today is ___ and it is now ___ o'clock. I am interviewing ___ at ___.
>
> As you can see, we have a video-camera and microphones here. They will record our conversation so I can remember everything you tell me. Sometimes I forget things and the recorder allows me to listen to you without having to write everything down.
>
> Part of my job is to talk to children [teenagers] about things that have happened to them. (p. 283)

Because some children have fears about social workers and police officers, it is appropriate to take a moment to address possible misunderstandings (e.g., by explaining that not all police officers do the things children see on television) but without misleading the child or making promises that might not be kept.

Initial Rapport-Building Conversation

After a brief introduction, interviewers begin a back-and-forth dialogue that helps children relax and improves their cooperativeness (Vallano & Schreiber Compo, 2015). A valuable habit is to always use a transition comment before shifting to a new topic or phase. These comments, which I call *topic shifters*, give children time to mentally process changes in the direction of the conversation.

The wording of a topic shifter depends on which protocol the interviewer is following. Some interviewers proceed directly from the opening introduction to other early interview phases, such as the ground rules and narrative practices phases, without any chitchat about the child's age, family members, or other such issues. In this style of interviewing, these other phases help interviewers develop rapport and encourage children to talk, thereby reducing the need for more rapport-building conversation (Lamb et al., 2008).

In other interviewing styles, early rapport building involves general questions about the child's life and interests. When interviewers adopt this approach, the topic shifter can be something such as "I'd like to get to know you a little better now," followed by the first prompt. A common error during this phase is peppering a child with many questions that can be answered by a word or short phrase (e.g., "How old are you?" "What grade are you in?" "What is your teacher's name?"), which quickly trains the child that the interviewer will be in control of the conversation and that the child's job is to respond to each query with minimal information (H. L. Price, Roberts, &

Collins, 2013). It is also an error to prolong initial chitchat beyond what is necessary to put the child at ease.

Because it has proven difficult to stop interviewers from making these mistakes, some protocols provide a script to move conversation into open-ended questions more quickly. For example, the interviewer might elicit the child's names for people who might be discussed later in the interview by starting with "Tell me all the people who live with you." Less structured protocols suggest using open-ended questions to show interest in the child while demonstrating a warm and patient demeanor: "Now I want to get to know you. Tell me some things about yourself. What kinds of things do you like to do for fun?" (National Children's Advocacy Center, 2014, p. 3).

In the National Children's Advocacy Center's (2014) interview, discussion of who lives in the child's household occurs as a separate phase, just before the interviewer transitions into talk about abuse allegations. I included "Discussing Useful Background Information" as a separate phase later in this chapter to highlight that interviewers are free to elicit information about family structures or other useful background information before raising target issues.

Interviewers balance two goals when they deliver early interview phases: This part of the conversation should not be overly long and fatiguing, but jumping too quickly into sensitive issues can solidify a pattern of uncooperativeness. There is evidence that children who say little about the matters under investigation are less informative even before interviewers raise target topics, which suggests that interviewers who detect reluctance may want to prolong conversation about neutral topics, thereby providing more opportunities to deliver socially supportive comments (Katz et al., 2012). For example, interviewers can use children's names ("Thank you, Emily, for telling me about your family. I know a lot more about you now"), deliver the types of reinforcing comments that are permissible before target issues are under discussion ("I know a lot more about playing soccer now that you explained that"), and make use of pauses and facilitators (comments such as "OK" and repetition of a few words children just said) to encourage children to talk.

Introductory Comments and Early Rapport Building for Repeated Interviews

Although most resources about child interviewing describe guidelines for conducting a single interview, the phases of a forensic interview, in modified forms, describe repeated conversations as well. For example, you usually greet people at the start of any conversation, and you sometimes avoid awkward situations by reminding casual acquaintances about how you know them. These social rules should not be disregarded simply because the other person is a child. Introductions to a familiar child will not be worded the same as initial introductions were, but it is still necessary to deliver comments that orient children to what is happening and warm them up to the current conversation.

As for one-time interviews, interviewers meeting a child they have spoken with before would use the early minutes of conversation to (a) model the supportive demeanor that recruits children's cooperation and (b) deliver open-ended prompts that get children talking without jumping immediately into questions about target issues. Interviewers should plan these comments to achieve the rapport-building goals of an introduction in ways that are appropriate for the type of conversation, the child's age, and the interview environment.

To demonstrate the flexibility of the introductory phase, consider how a worker might begin conversation during the first of many monthly meetings with a child in nonparental care (State of Maine Child and Family Services, 2010):

> Start the interview (monthly face-to-face contact): Hi ___. My name is ___. I'm here today to check in about how things are going with [your family, your placement, etc.].
>
> Explain your job (assessment or monthly face-to-face contact): I'm a social worker and part of my job is to talk with children and to help them. I talk with a lot of children in [name of town or specify living arrangements].
>
> Orient the child (monthly face-to-face contact): I talk about how things are going for children. We are going to talk for a while and then I'll [e.g., tell your mom to come back in, talk with your caregiver, talk with your siblings, etc.]. (p. 11)

Following orienting comments such as these, the worker would begin the rapport-building process by delivering a few open-ended prompts (e.g., "I see you were building something interesting when I came in. What kinds of things do you like to build?"). In the next visit, the worker would greet the child and briefly remind him or her of the earlier visit and the general purpose of the visits. In a similar way, an investigative interviewer meeting a child for the second time would deliver a reminder introduction and some early, open-ended chitchat.

Overview of a Successful Introduction Phase

Productive introductions give children time to transition from their earlier thoughts and feelings, help them orient to the interview setting, begin the rapport-building process, convey that children should do most of the talking, and provide interviewers with information about children's behavior patterns and ways of speaking. A skilled interviewer maintains a calm, patient demeanor and moves quickly to open-ended prompts that encourage the child to talk. Common mistakes include talking rapidly during initial introductions, providing little time for the child to look around the environment, and peppering the child with specific questions that create an overly long introduction in which the interviewer does most of the talking.

DISCUSSING INTERVIEW GROUND RULES

In Chapter 1, I described how a child in my laboratory, Paige, answered question after question even though the questions were "impossible" (designed so children would not know the answers). It makes sense that children would do this because adults typically expect children to try to answer. But there is another reason why children can be compliant during interviews: More so than adults, they simply react to environmental cues without thought. Put a stuffed dog and a brush in front of some children and they brush the dog—ask a question and they answer it; punch the blow-up doll and they punch the doll—use a word in a sentence and they use the word (Hunt & Borgida, 2001).

The purpose of a ground rules phase is to improve children's testimonies by explaining that interviewers are naïve to the events in question and want children to (a) share only accurate information stemming from their own experiences, (b) say "I don't know" when they have no knowledge of what is being asked, (c) tell interviewers when they do not understand a word or question, and (d) correct any mistakes interviewers make. This phase is sometimes called *interview instructions* to capture the educational purpose of this early interview phase.

Research on ground rules instruction and practice questions converges on six broad conclusions:

- It takes little time to deliver a ground rules phase. For example, the average length of the ground rules phase was about two minutes in one study, and ground rules rarely took longer than 4 minutes to deliver (Dickinson, Brubacher, & Poole, 2015).
- Children perform well during ground rules instruction. "Don't-guess" instructions and questions about truth and lies are the easiest for children to navigate. Young children find it more difficult to express lack of understanding and to correct the interviewer, but the majority of younger children successfully demonstrate these skills with adequate instruction (Dickinson et al., 2015).

- When children err on practice questions, additional instruction improves their performance. For example, it is common for children to mention a dog's name in response to "What's my dog's name?" even after interviewers have told them to say "I don't know" when necessary. After interviewers correct this behavior, however, most children say "I don't know" to the next practice question (Dickinson et al., 2015).
- Ground rules instruction is more effective when children have opportunities to practice the rules. There is little benefit from simply telling children rules, but providing opportunities to practice increases appropriate responses later in interviews (Brubacher, Poole, & Dickinson, 2015; but see Danby, Brubacher, Sharman, & Powell, 2015).
- Scripted instructions help interviewers deliver ground rules instruction. In my studies with Jason Dickinson, interviewers were more likely to continue instruction for children who failed the first practice question after we added scripted dialog (Dickinson et al., 2015).
- Some question wordings confuse children. Another reason it is best to script ground rules instruction is that some of the questions adults generate confuse children. For example, some older children in my laboratory did not correct interviewers who asked, "How do you like being 4 years old?" perhaps because these children interpreted the question as "How *did* you like being 4 years old?"

The ground rules phase begins with a topic shifter that flags the transition to a new topic. The specific comment used will depend on the interviewer's style, where ground rules appear in the protocol, and the first rule chosen for discussion. A topic shifter can be as simple as the following: "Now that I know more about you, I need to talk about some rules that we have in this room. One rule is that [we don't guess, it is important to tell the truth, etc.]."

Some interviewers prefer a more developed transition for school-age children, as in this example:

> Now that I know more about you, I want to talk about some rules that we have in this room. You probably have rules you follow at home and at school. What is one rule you have at school? [Wait for child's response.] Oh, so you can't [child's words]. Well, we have some rules for talking to each other here today. One rule is that [first rule].

Next, the interviewer delivers instruction for a predetermined set of rules, modifying instructions, as needed, to accommodate children's linguistic and social cultures. The sample instructions in this chapter illustrate how, for each rule, an interviewer might (a) introduce the rule, (b) give the child an opportunity to practice the rule, and (c) ask whether the child will agree to follow the rule.

"Don't Guess"

"Don't-guess" instructions are among the easiest for children to understand, with 98% of the 4-year-olds in two samples eventually mastering this instruction. Nonetheless, even children 8 years and older sometimes speculated in the face of the first practice question, confirming the need for this instruction (Dickinson et al., 2015).

A concern about don't-guess instruction is that children might avoid difficult questions later in the interview by saying "I don't know." However, reinforcing children for describing what they do remember reduces unwanted "don't know" responses (Saywitz & Moan-Hardie, 1994), and interviewers can ask questions to clarify the meaning of unexpected "don't know" responses (Scoboria & Fisico, 2013; also see Chapter 5).

For the following example, I modified protocol language (State of Michigan Governor's Task Force on Child Abuse and Neglect and Department of Human Services, 2011, p. 11) by adding instructions following a wrong answer, an agreement to say "I don't know," and reinforcement for sharing known information:

> One rule is that we don't guess. If I ask a question and you don't know the answer, just say, "I don't know." For example, what is my dog's name?
>
> > Right answer: That's right; you don't know my dog's name, so "I don't know" is the right answer.
> >
> > Wrong answer: Do you really know my dog's name? If you don't know the answer, just say, "I don't know." Let's try again. What is my sister's name?
>
> Will you say "I don't know" when you don't know the answer today? [Wait for response.] Good. But if I ask about something you know, I want you to tell me. For example, what is your last name? [Wait for response.] Thank you for telling me.

"Tell Me When You Don't Understand"

There is little evidence on the efficacy of "tell-me-when-you-don't-understand" instructions. One research team delivered extensive training, first requiring children to signal lack of comprehension to mumbled speech and then to difficult questions (Saywitz, Snyder, & Nathanson, 1999). Although this training helped children signal lack of comprehension, Meaghan Danby and her colleagues (2015) found that a less time-consuming instruction was ineffective, at least among 5- to 9-year-olds. Perhaps because trained interviewers rarely ask difficult questions, some protocols simply ask children to tell when they do not understand and leave it at that (e.g., "If I ask a question that you don't understand, just say, 'I don't understand.' OK?"; Lamb et al., 2008, p. 284).

When my colleagues and I used a word children did not understand for a ground rules practice question ("Is my shirt gridelin?"), over a quarter of the 9-year-olds attempted to answer (rather than saying, "I don't understand"). However, only the 4- and 5-year-olds continued to perform poorly after another practice opportunity (Dickinson et al., 2015). Unfortunately, we do not know whether children's initial performance was poor because the task was challenging or because they found the practice question confusing. Until more data are available on alternative practice questions, I illustrate delivering this rule using a rule statement from Karen Saywitz and Lorinda Camparo (2014, p. 75–76), followed by practice questions containing low-frequency color words.

> If I ask a question you do not understand, tell me. You can say, "I don't get it," or "I don't understand," and I will ask it again with different words. For example, is my shirt gridelin?

> Right answer: Thank you for telling me you didn't understand. I'll ask a different way. What color is my shirt? [Wait for response.] Good.

> Wrong answer: "Do you know what gridelin is? Actually, it is a color. If I say something you don't understand, just tell me you don't understand. Let's try another one. Is my shirt burnet?" [Wait for response.]

> Thank you for telling me you didn't understand. I'll ask a different way. What color is my shirt? [Wait for response.] Good. While we are talking today, will you tell me when you don't understand?

"Tell Me if I Say Something Wrong"

Few studies have trained children to resist interviewers' false statements, and some that tried asked practice questions referring to events on training videotapes (Brubacher, Poole, & Dickinson, 2015). Consequently, there is not a collection of proven questions that do not require an interview aid. As I mentioned earlier, asking "How do you like being [wrong age] years old?" confuses children: Some children who are older than the stated age begin talking about their lives at that age, whereas some younger children begin talking about what they are looking forward to in the future (Dickinson et al., 2015).

It is curiously difficult to come up with a fact that all children would know and reject. For instance, many young children do not know the town they live in, and even a child's gender identity may not be known to the interviewer (which precludes using "What if I said, 'How do you like being a boy?'"). During the fall and winter months, my team asked a follow-up question that worked well for children 6 years and older ("What did you do at the water park today?"), but even then a few children discussed visiting a water park. These errors teach us that children sometimes focus on key words in questions and answer different questions than the ones interviewers asked.

To avoid the concept of time, it is best to talk about the here and now, as in this example.

> Sometimes I say something wrong by mistake. I want you to tell me if I say something wrong. For example, what color is this pair of scissors? [Show a pen.]
>
> > Right answer: That's right—this isn't a pair of scissors, so I'm glad you told me.
> >
> > Wrong answer: But this isn't a pair of scissors, right? I made a mistake when I said scissors [slap head]. It's OK to tell me if I say something wrong. Let's try another one. What animal is on my shirt? [Wait for response.] That's right, I didn't wear my animal shirt today, so I'm glad you told me.
>
> While we are talking today, will you tell me when I say something wrong? [Wait for response.] Thank you.

"Tell the Truth"

There are many reasons why child witnesses might deny knowledge of a crime or report what another person has asked them to report. For example, sexual perpetrators sometimes instruct children not to talk about their abuse, and mothers may ask children to say that intentional injuries were accidental. To encourage honesty, some protocols instruct interviewers to discuss the need to tell the truth.

Children's understanding of the word *truth* is not a reliable predictor of their testimonial accuracy (Goodman, Aman, & Hirschman, 1987; Pipe & Wilson, 1994), but promising to tell the truth nonetheless improves honesty even among children who cannot demonstrate understanding (Lyon, Malloy, Quas, & Talwar, 2008). Because comprehension tasks can underestimate children's knowledge, some protocols simply ask children to tell the truth without formally assessing their understanding of the concept: "It's really important that you tell the truth. Do you promise that you will tell me the truth? Will you tell me any lies?" (Lyon, 2005, p. 1).

Protocols that assess understanding do so to document that children knew what they were promising to do and to provide prosecutors with information about how young witnesses might perform when asked such questions in court.

Although the legal and psychological justifications for assessing children's understanding of the truth are weaker than many people realize (Lyon, 2011), widespread inclusion of comprehension questions in protocols has nonetheless prompted interest in the best ways to deliver these questions. To work around the fact that young witnesses have difficulty describing what "the truth" means, forensic interviewers prefer concrete ways to help children demonstrate knowledge. One approach asks children to label simple statements, as in this example:

> It is also very important to tell the truth today. First I need to make sure you know what the truth is. "I'm sitting down right now." Is that true or not true? [Wait for response.] That's right; I am sitting down, so sitting down is the truth. "You are running right now." Is that true or a lie? [Wait for response.] That's right, you are not running, so running is a lie.

In one study, over half of the 4-year-olds correctly answered "true" in response to this first question, and 75% either said "the truth" or "yes" (Dickinson et al., 2015). Some interviewers provided additional explanation when necessary, in which case over 90% of 4-year-olds answered correctly. By 6 years, over 90% of children answered correctly the first time interviewers delivered the question, and nearly all did so with additional instruction.[1] Thus, most children 4 years and older can demonstrate understanding without an elaborate training process.

Another way to make questions concrete is to ask about a picture. For example, Tom Lyon and his team developed pictures showing a child looking at a target object, such as a cat, while talking about another object, such as a dog (Lyon, Carrick, & Quas, 2010). Their assistants asked, "What is this?" (while pointing to the cat) and then, "This boy/girl [pointing to the child in the picture] looks at the cat and says, 'That's a dog.' Did the boy/girl tell the truth?" (For a young child, interviewers can ask, "Is that a dog?" which could demonstrate that the child understands the difference between a correct and incorrect statement.) This approach does not require the child to discuss lying or to accuse someone of lying yet shows that the child appreciates the difference between true and false statements while setting up the interviewer to ask the child to tell the truth (or to say only things that are "right"; Lyon, Quas, & Carrick, 2013). (For a picture task that asks children which of two people "told the truth" or "told a lie," see Lyon & Saywitz, 1999.)

As with all ground rules questions, wording is important. In one study, assistants asked children to label statements as true or a lie and then said the following: "I see you understand what the truth is. It is important to tell me the truth—what really happened. Will you tell me the truth today?"

---

[1] In Dickinson et al. (2015), children's performance was similar for questions about the truth and questions about a lie, but see Lyon, Carrick, and Quas (2010) for evidence that the concept of lying can be more difficult.

(Dickinson et al., 2015, p. 89). This question confused many children, who interpreted the prompt as a request to start talking about things that were true. The following interchanges illustrate this problem:

Interviewer 1: Will you tell me the truth today?

4-year-old boy: I didn't do anything wrong.

Interviewer 1: Right, you didn't do anything wrong, so you'll tell me the truth right?

4-year-old boy: Mm.

Interviewer 2: Will you tell me the truth today?

4-year-old boy: Um, Aaron took Mom, Aaron was at school, from me. It's the truth.

Interviewer 2: OK. So will you tell me the truth today then?

4-year-old boy: Um, th-that's what he did.

These responses suggest that interviewers did not say enough for children to understand that the question referred to future answers. A less ambiguous question would (a) include the words *promise* and *will* (Lyon & Evans 2014) while (b) placing the question in context (e.g., "Today I am going to ask you some questions. Do you promise that you will tell the truth when I ask you a question?")

In sum, whether interviewers discuss the truth or not is determined by local tradition, requirements, and prosecutors' preferences. When interviewers preface the oath with questions that assess understanding of the *truth* and a *lie*, it is best to ask children to label statements spoken by the interviewer or those made by a story character (rather than asking children to define these terms). Finally, it may be acceptable to substitute language that young children understand. For example, interviewers can ask whether a statement is right or wrong and explain that the purpose of the interview is to talk about "things that really happened and that are the truth" (National Children's Advocacy Center, 2014, p. 3).

"I Don't Know What Happened" (Interviewer Naïveté)

To encourage children to describe events completely, some interview guidelines include a statement explaining that the interviewer does not know what has happened to the child. One sample of 6-year-olds benefitted from this statement, but 8-year-olds—who are beyond the age when children think adults know everything they know—did not (Waterman & Blades, 2011). "Ignorant interviewer" instructions can be simple, as in this example: "I don't know what's happened to you. I won't be able to tell you the answers to my questions" (Lyon, 2005, p. 1).

Selection and Placement of Ground Rules

There are two schools of thought on selecting which ground rules to include in an interview. Because even young children perform quite well during a well-delivered ground rules phase, some experts recommend using a fixed set of rules for all typically developing children age 4 years and older (T. Lyon, personal communication, October 10, 2014). Another approach is to deliver fewer rules to young and developmentally delayed children by omitting some challenging rules. For example, the National Children's Advocacy Center (2014) recommended delivering four rules to children 5 years or older: (a) "It's OK to say 'I don't know,'" (b) "Tell me if you don't understand," (c) "Correct me if I say something wrong," and (d) "It is important to tell the truth." These guidelines mentioned that children 10 years and younger benefit the most from opportunities to practice these rules but that adolescents, who might be offended by such questions, need to hear the basic instructions even if not required to demonstrate them.

There are different views on when to deliver interview instructions. Some interviewers prefer to do this immediately after initial introductions, which gives them opportunities to reinforce rules during the subsequent narrative practice phase (La Rooy, Brown, & Lamb, 2012). Others prefer to place ground rules just before they transition to the matters under investigation, which increases the chance that children will still have the rules in mind during later interview phases. Conducting the practice interview before ground rules instruction may also help interviewers build rapport with reluctant children, especially when interviewers take time to use children's names, show interest in their experiences and feelings, and thank them for sharing (Hershkowitz, Lamb, & Katz, 2014). Regardless of where interview instruction appears, it is a good idea to take advantage of opportunities to reinforce rules throughout the interview, as this research assistant did (Dickinson et al., 2015):

> *Interviewer:* I see you understand what the truth is. It is important to tell me the truth—what really happened. Will you tell me the truth today?
>
> *Child:* I don't understand that. Like, tell you what happened today?
>
> *Interviewer:* Yeah, so when I ask you a question in the interview will you say, will you tell the truth when you answer them?
>
> *Child:* Yes.
>
> *Interviewer:* Okay, good. And thank you for telling me you didn't understand. (p. 95)

Ground Rules During Repeated Interviews

Professionals can modify effective interviewing techniques to accommodate the goals of different types of conversations. For example, child protective services workers who conduct monthly supervision visits would not preface every conversation with a comprehensive ground rules phase. But even in this situation, it is important for children to know they should be honest and can correct misunderstandings workers have, ask when there is something they do not understand, and say "I don't know" when appropriate. Also, even older children may believe that workers already know what has been happening in the home through conversations with adults. In this situation, workers might use a modified ground rules discussion when they first get to know a child, remind the child of one or more rules during the next few visits, and then revisit rules as needed during subsequent visits (e.g., interviewer naïveté: "I haven't talked with your Grandma in a while, so I'm really interested in hearing you talk about everything that has happened since my last visit").

Overview of a Successful Ground Rules Phase

An effective ground rules phase takes only minutes to deliver and covers five basic rules for typically developing children 4 or 5 years of age and older: "It's OK to say 'I don't know.' 'Tell me if you don't understand.' 'Correct me if I say something wrong.' 'It is important to tell the truth.' and 'I don't know what happened.'" In a comprehensive ground rules phase, the interviewer explains each rule in turn, giving the child an opportunity to practice the rule using a concrete example and asking whether the child will follow the rule. Individual interviews can be customized by deleting one or more rules, adding rules, or eliminating practice questions for adolescents (while still instructing them about the rules and eliciting a promise to tell the truth).

CONDUCTING A PRACTICE NARRATIVE

The opening introduction, initial rapport-building chitchat, and ground rules discussion typically take only minutes to deliver. After these phases, few children have the level of comfort that promotes an uncensored account of events, and even relaxed children likely expect that interviewers will direct subsequent conversation by delivering a long list of focused questions. A *practice narrative* (also called a *practice interview* and *episodic recall training*) aims to improve the amount and accuracy of testimony by accomplishing the following goals (Roberts, Brubacher, Powell, & Price, 2011):

- *Strengthening rapport.* A narrative practice provides more time for the child to acclimate to the interviewer and the setting, thereby continuing the rapport-building process.
- *Encouraging children to talk.* The interviewer's behavior during this phase transfers control of conversation to the child by conveying that the child—not the interviewer—should do most of the talking.
- *Providing narrative training.* It takes mental effort to search memory, recall event details, and organize a narrative that makes sense. By training children to provide complete descriptions in response to open-ended questions, the interviewer establishes a pattern of behavior that can improve the coherence of children's testimony (D. A. Brown et al., 2013; H. L. Price et al., 2013; Roberts et al., 2011; Roberts, Lamb, & Sternberg, 2004).
- *Establishing good interviewer behavior.* The behaviors the interviewer displays during a well-conducted practice interview may persist into later interview phases, increasing the amount of information elicited by open-ended prompts and facilitators.

A practice interview also helps interviewers learn how children pronounce words, which can reduce misunderstandings, and gives them a sense of how individual children typically respond to questions about past events.

Techniques That Train Children to Describe an Event

During a practice narrative, interviewers use facilitators (e.g., "Oh"), motivational phrases (e.g., "I'm really interested in __"), and open-ended prompts (e.g., "Tell me more about __") to train children to provide detailed information in response to open-ended prompts. By asking children to describe an event from the first thing that happened to some end point and by using prompts such as "And then what happened?" interviewers help children organize temporally structured narratives that are rich in contextual detail.

A transcript from my laboratory, in which an assistant asked a child to describe a "script" (what usually happens during an activity), illustrates this process of training children to describe an event:

Interviewer: So what grade are you in?

Child: Kindergarten.

Interviewer: I'm interested in what children do in kindergarten now. Tell me about a day at your school, from the time you get to school until the time you come home. Tell me everything you can about a day at school.

Child: What?

Interviewer: So, um, tell me everything that you can about a day at school, from the time you get there until the time you come home.

Child: Well, when I get home I usually watch TV.

Interviewer: Mmm.

Child: And when I first get to school I usually play at the playground, playground, but if it's rainy day I have to go in the gym.

Interviewer: OK, so what happens after you play in the playground?

Child: You go inside and you, you can, actually you line up and then you, then you, then you wait for the teacher to let your line go. And then you can, when you get in you put your coats away. And then you go, come into the classroom.

Interviewer: Mm-hmm.

Child: Actually, you put your, actually, and go and then you go into the classroom, and then you, when you're in the classroom you can play at your station, and at each station has a different toy.

Interviewer: Cool. What happens next?

Child: And then you, then you, then you do morning meeting, and then, and we, and we usually do the calendar. Actually, we do a song.

Interviewer: Uh-hm. What happens after that?

Child: Then we do, then we hear what's on our calendar, to see what, what we, what we do today at school.

[Eighteen interchanges occurred here. Each time, the interviewer turned conversation back to the child with a facilitator or by saying "Then what happens?" or "What happens next?"]

Interviewer: OK, so then once you're sitting at your bus tables, what happens? What's after that?

Child: We, well, if, if your bus teacher comes in you get to line up at the door, and you get to go to your bus.

Interviewer: Mm-hmm.

Child:	And then if your family teacher, if your mom or your dad like comes in, comes in outside and the teacher sees them, you can, they, you can go, and they tell you, you can go, you can go and see them. But you have to get your backpacks 'cause if you grab your backpacks and you put 'em at your spot so you can take 'em with your mom, your mom or your dad or both.
Interviewer:	OK so then, where do the buses or your parents take you?
Child:	Uh, they take you to your house, but the bus takes you to different houses that people go.
Interviewer:	OK. Cool.

In this example, an initially hesitant child eventually provided longer, more informative responses without the interviewer resorting to yes/no or leading questions.

The topic of conversation in the previous example (a typical school day) is not the optimal practice topic because asking children what usually happens does not encourage them to describe specific episodes, that is, events that happened at particular places and times. Whether interviewers discuss a scripted event (i.e., what usually happens during a repeated activity) or a particular incident (e.g., the child's recent birthday party) is important because speaking styles early in conversations can shift the way children describe events. When interviewers discuss what usually happens, children often use generic language themselves (e.g., "She hits . . ."), rather than language describing specific episodes (e.g., "She hit . . .," "And then on Monday . . ."), and they are less likely to spontaneously mention multiple incidents of an experience (Brubacher, Roberts, & Powell, 2011).

To encourage children to talk about specific episodes, the best practice topics are events that happened at particular places and times. Questions that elicit scripts memories are usually reserved for children who refuse to talk about other topics and for times when there is no obvious or suitable special event. In these cases, an interviewer who gets a child talking by asking about a typical experience can still ask about a specific episode. For example,

> Is there a favorite place you like to go to eat with your family? [Wait for child's response.] Tell me everything that happens when you go to ___. [Wait for child's response.] Was there a time you went to __ when something different or surprising happened? [Wait for child's response.] Tell me everything about that day, from the time you got to ___ to when you got home.

When the matter under investigation involves repeated events, choosing a repeated event for the practice narrative, such as swimming lessons or sleepovers with a best friend, provides an opportunity to ask about individual incidents ("What happened the last time you_____?") and may help children describe multiple incidents later in the interview (Brubacher et al., 2011).

Structure of a Practice Narrative Phase

There are several ways to select a practice event. When interviewers know children's cultural backgrounds, a recent school, national, or religious holiday (e.g., Christmas day) is an opportunity to ask children what they did on those days. Sometimes interviewers ask parents to identify a recent significant event, such as a family trip or a party. Early rapport-building talk about a child's hobbies, after-school activities, and favorite versus least favorite school "specials" (e.g., activities such as gym and art that occur only once or twice a week) can also lead into a practice narrative about the most recent time children participated in a particular activity (Roberts et al., 2011).[2]

As with all interview phases, the practice narrative begins with (a) a topic shifter, after which the interviewer (b) attempts to raise the practice topic and (c) provides motivation to recall the event from the beginning to the end. There are numerous ways to accomplish these goals, as in the following examples:

1. Transition: I want to know more about you and the things you do.

   Raising the topic: A few [days, weeks] ago was [special event]. Tell me everything that happened on [special event].

   Encouragement to report completely: Think hard about [event] and tell me what happened on that day from the time you got up that morning until [the end of the day or a portion of the event mentioned by the child]. (Adapted from Lamb et al., 2008, p. 286)

2. Transition: I'm interested in getting to know more about you.

   Raising the topic: Was there something fun or special that happened in your life recently?

   Encouragement to report completely: Well, you know I'd really like to know about that. Tell me everything you can remember about [special event], from the very beginning to the very end. (Adapted from Roberts et al., 2011, p. 130.)

---

[2]As long as the matter under investigation did not occur in the last few days, school-age children could be asked to describe everything they did yesterday, but this will not be as memorable or interesting as a special event would be. Because preschoolers sometimes interpret *yesterday* to mean *not today*, a question about yesterday may not trigger young children to remember a specific day.

3. To encourage school-age children to report particular instances of a repeated event.

Transition: As I said earlier, I talk to a lot of children in [name of town]. I like to learn more about the things children do when they are not in school.

Raising the topic: Your mom told me you take [activity] lessons, is that right?

Encouragement to report an individual event completely: Tell me everything you can about the last time you went to [activity], from the very beginning to the very end. [Explore this event with a series of open-ended prompts and encouragements.]

Encouragement to report another instance of the event: That's really interesting—I never went to [activity] when I was in school. What day at [activity] do you remember the best? [Wait for response.] Tell me everything about that time at [activity].

Training-to-describe begins after these opening remarks as interviewers repeatedly turn conversation back to the child with a series of facilitators (e.g., "Mm-hmm"), encouragements (e.g., "Good for you"), and open-ended prompts such as these:

- And then what happened?
- What happened next?
- Tell me everything that happened after [something the child mentioned].
- Tell me more about [something the child mentioned].
- You said [something the child said]. Tell me everything about [what the child mentioned].

Throughout this phase, the interviewer displays the conversational habits of a child forensic interview (see Chapter 3) by avoiding threatening attention and rapid-fire questioning. The duration of this phase can be extended if the child needs extra time to warm up (perhaps by choosing a second topic or event), but an effective practice narrative phase should not be long and tiring. Practice narratives in my laboratory take less than 7 minutes to complete, and one of the studies that found benefits from practice narratives limited interviewers to 5 to 7 minutes of practice (Brubacher et al., 2011).

Professionals will be interested to hear that adding a practice narrative did not increase the length of interviews in one experiment, largely because children "described their experience more efficiently when prepared well beforehand" (D. A. Brown et al., 2013, p. 379). An analysis of front-line abuse interviews found that interviewers who used practice narratives did produce longer interviewers than their peers, but the length difference had little practical significance (32 minutes for interviews with a practice interview vs. 22 minutes for those without; H. L. Price et al., 2013).

Overview of a Successful Practice Narrative Phase

A well-delivered practice narrative continues the rapport-building process by encouraging children to talk about a specific but nonthreatening event. Throughout this phase, the interviewer models the conversational habits of forensic interviewing by maintaining a calm demeanor, showing interest with appropriate (but not excessive) eye contact, and waiting patiently after the child stops speaking before making another remark. After a topic is raised, the interviewer repeatedly turns conversation back to the child by using minimal encouragers and open-ended prompts (e.g., "What happened next?") that prompt the child to search memory, relate more than just a few words, and report a temporally organized narrative. This phase usually takes less than 7 minutes to deliver, but an interviewer can prolong this phase if a reluctant child might benefit from having more time to warm up to the interview.

DISCUSSING USEFUL BACKGROUND INFORMATION

Interviewers can add an early interview phase to collect any background information that might be useful during the interview. For example, abuse interviews sometimes include a discussion about the people who live with the child and the names of other family members, caregivers, and close friends. Eliciting children's names for people in their lives can prevent misunderstandings and help interviewers gauge whether children are willing to discuss these individuals (National Children's Advocacy Center, 2014). Because children who are hesitant to talk during early interview phases are also less likely to disclose suspected events later in the interview, adding a background information phase also gives interviewers the opportunity to prolong rapport building when talking with reticent children (Hershkowitz, Orbach, Lamb, Sternberg, & Horowitz, 2006; Orbach, Shiloach, & Lamb, 2007).

Some interviewers ask about family members at the beginning of interviews, but delaying this phase can create a smoother transition into the matters under investigation. Moreover, placing this phase after the ground rules and practice narrative phases ensures that the flow of the interview will be less disrupted should the child spontaneously begin talking about target issues. Instructions such as the following can be modified to meet the needs of individual cases:

- I'd like to know more about where you live and who lives with you. [Child's name], do you live in an apartment, a house, or something else?
- Tell me all of the people who live there with you.
- Does someone else live with you? [Repeat until the child says "no."]
- Is there another place where you stay when you are not [at home with your mom, in school, etc., and repeat until the child says "no"]?
- Tell me about the people at [child's name for caregiving environment].
- Does someone else ever take care of you when [your mom, your dad, etc.] is gone?
- Is there someone else who also takes care of you? [Repeat until the child says "no."]

In this phase, the specific questions and level of detail requested will vary depending on which alternative hypotheses require exploration later in the interview. For example, when influence from peers is a concern or peers might also be victims, questions about the child's friends, both inside and outside of school, are useful.

There are two styles for discussing family members and friends during a background information phase. In one, interviewers record children's responses by drawing with a marker on a flip board or piece of paper, quickly producing and labeling a face for each individual mentioned. When a name does not match what interviewers expected based on case material, it is easy to ask, "Does [name child mentioned] have another name?" or "What does your [mom, dad] call [name child mentioned]?" Most often, interviewers ask questions without using markers and paper, but this decision is a matter of individual style (Poole & Dickinson, 2011).

RECAP

Early interview phases prepare children to discuss the matters under investigation. Six phases occur most often in protocols:

1. *Planning the interview.* After assembling initial facts about the child and the case, the interviewer or investigative team plans

an interview strategy to achieve the goals of the conversation in a developmentally appropriate manner. In this phase, professionals think about ways to explore alternative hypotheses for allegations and strategies for eliciting information that might assist the broader investigation.

2. *Preparing the interview space.* Within the constraints imposed by case circumstances, the interviewer considers which of the available locations is the most emotionally safe and quiet, taking care to remove distracting objects and personal items that might capture children's attention.

3. *Introducing the interviewer and beginning the rapport-building process.* The interviewer starts conversation with a short introduction (e.g., the interviewer's name and the nature of his or her job) and quickly transitions into a back-and-forth conversation with the child. When the protocol encourages initial chit-chat about the child's life or interests, the interviewer delivers mostly open-ended questions that encourage the child to do most of the talking.

4. *Discussing interview ground rules.* After delivering a topic shifter (a transition comment, such as "Now that I know more about you . . ."), the interviewer explains a set of rules for the interview, giving preadolescent children an opportunity to practice each rule and asking all children to declare that they will follow the rule.

5. *Conducting a practice narrative.* The interviewer signals a topic change (e.g., "I'd like to know more about the things you do") and continues the rapport-building process by encouraging the child to talk about a specific but neutral event (e.g., a recent birthday party). The interviewer delivers open-ended prompts and encourages the child to describe the event completely.

6. *Discussing useful background information.* The interviewer elicits information that might be helpful when discussing the matters under investigation, such as information about the child's family, caregiving arrangements, and friends. The topic shifter for this phase can follow any of the early interview phases (e.g., "I'd like to know more about where you live and who lives with you").

The set of phases selected and the way each phase is delivered will vary depending on the protocol in use and other considerations, including the purpose of conversation and the child's level of cognitive development.

PRINCIPLES TO PRACTICE: WHICH INTERVIEW PHASE SHOULD I START WITH AFTER AN UNEXPECTED DISCLOSURE?

Most discussions of child interviewing focus on abuse investigations, but child protective services workers also monitor children in nonparental care. When children make new allegations during these visits, local policies dictate how extensively workers will fact-find during the current conversation. The following question, from a worker trained to conduct forensic interviews, asks how to progress through interview phases after a spontaneous report of maltreatment.

Child Protective Services Worker's Question

If you were in a noninvestigative conversation with a child, and that child began disclosing abuse or neglect, how would you handle it? There are two ways I can think of. The first is allowing the child to disclose. Once the child is done, I could test for forensic competency, ask whether the child told the truth, and ask whether the child needed to correct any of the story. The second way would be to stop the child from disclosing, test for forensic competency, complete a practice interview, and then attempt to reengage in the disclosure.

I have tried both methods, and I am never satisfied with either. In the first, I question the validity of the disclosure. The second stops any momentum the conversation had, and it is hard to get the child back to the disclosure. What are your thoughts?

My Response

Remember that each interview phase is designed to solve a set of problems that arise when talking with children, but the flow of conversation should be customized for each situation. For example, you introduce yourself to a child you do not know, but you do not have to introduce yourself to a child you know well.

There are a number of reasons for the ground rules phase: This process provides time for unfamiliar children to become comfortable with you, the rules empower children to say "I don't know," and children are more likely to disclose wrongdoing after this step (Lyon et al., 2008). A ground rules phase is not, however, a test of forensic competency.

If you know the child and the child spontaneously discloses during a noninvestigative conversation, just let her or him talk. Use facilitators, such as "Um-hmm," to turn conversation back to the child, and deliver numerous prompts such as "Then what happened?" If you are in a jurisdiction where workers explore more in the current conversation, then before transitioning to some focused questions (if necessary), you can decide whether to deliver ground rules (depending on the types of questions you will be asking). If the child makes a minimal or ambiguous disclosure but then does not talk, you can always say, "I'm interested in hearing more about [child's words] today. But first I just want to spend a few minutes [catching up on what's been happening at school since our last visit, or another neutral topic], is that OK?" Encouraging a reluctant child to talk about a neutral topic first might help them provide more information about the unexpected disclosure.

To sum up, when a child you know spontaneously discloses, you can transition to the case-issues phases of a forensic interview and behave as you usually would during these phases, with the extent of exploration determined by standards of practice in your agency for disclosures that occur during non-investigative conversations. As in any interview, you can always return to an earlier interview phase if needed. Your intuition to keep it simple and to start by following the child's train of thought is sound.

5

CONVENTIONAL CONTENT: CASE ISSUES PHASES

After delivering the early interview phases, interviewers transition into the matters under investigation and direct conversation through the case issues phases. These latter phases are squarely focused on eliciting testimony, but the entire interview is a forensic conversation because key facts can emerge in any phase. For example, a practice narrative could reveal that a preschooler mispronounces sounds in ways that might have created misunderstandings, or a child could discuss activities that account for injuries. Even so, early phases typically function to prepare children for the work of interviews, with case issues phases focusing on eliciting testimony.

Guidelines for discussing the matters under investigation help interviewers (a) prompt detailed accounts of events, (b) clarify multiple interpretations of those accounts, (c) explore alternative hypotheses for allegations or physical evidence, and (d) direct conversation in ways that support broader fact-finding efforts. As with early interview phases, interviewers take different

http://dx.doi.org/10.1037/14941-006
Interviewing Children: The Science of Conversation in Forensic Contexts, by D. A. Poole

journeys through case issues phases depending on the goals of conversations, the protocols in use, and children's behavior. For example, minimal facts have narrow purposes that preclude extensive exploration of children's accounts (DuPre & Sites, 2015), and child protection interviews often explore a broader range of topics than interviews conducted for criminal investigations. Yet despite these differences, most forensic conversations follow the general pattern of raising the topic, eliciting a free narrative, questioning and clarifying, and closing the interview.

RAISING THE TOPIC

Conversations about target issues begin when interviewers signal a change of topic and deliver one or more prompts to raise the first issue. Most guidelines recommend strategies that encourage children to mention key information, including the names of suspects and the nature of events, before interviewers do. Following a brief discussion of the rationale for a nonsuggestive approach, I explain some popular ways of establishing the interview topic.

Benefits of Nonsuggestive Topic Prompts

As mentioned in Chapter 1, some children impulsively say "yes" to yes/no questions and then spin narratives around words in those questions when interviewers say something such as "Tell me about that." An earlier example was a boy who said "yes" when an unfamiliar research assistant asked whether she had touched him. This boy went on to describe how the assistant had checked for fever by feeling his stomach, thereby showing confabulating behavior in which he retrieved memories that were irrelevant to the current situation. Children who respond in this way do not have a mental filter that reliably separates relevant from irrelevant thoughts.

Only a subset of young children are prone to confabulate, but many generate false narratives after exposure to misinformation. When this occurs, children make source-monitoring errors (see Chapter 1) by reporting what they heard others say or imply rather than what they actually experienced. Misinformation can infiltrate responses to open-ended prompts, but yes/no questions are more likely than open forms to trigger reports from sources other than participation in target events. Expert interviewers avoid yes/no questions early in interviews because, unfortunately, these errors are not completely eliminated by telling children to talk only about things that really happened (Poole & Lindsay, 2001, 2002).

What motivated the use of yes/no questions as a topic opener in some early protocols was the conviction that children cannot convincingly describe experiences they have not had—especially when those experiences involve sensitive issues, such as sexual abuse. Indeed, some interviewers have told me they are unconcerned about the risks of yes/no questions because they can identify erroneous "yes" responses based on the quality of the narrative descriptions following these answers. However, the idea that true and false narratives are easy to distinguish has not been supported by studies that questioned children after exposure to misleading conversations: In these situations, children's false narratives sometimes had as much (or more) detail as their true narratives did (Ceci, Kulkofsky, Klemfuss, Sweeney, & Bruck, 2007).

Because interviewers rarely know about individual children's tendency to confabulate or the nature of previous conversations, guidelines advise them to start with the least specific prompt that might raise the topic and then progress, when necessary, through prompts that gradually become more specific but without mentioning a complete allegation (i.e., a suspect plus the alleged event). This cautious approach has widespread acceptance from the interviewing community because many children disclose in response to open-ended prompts when interviewers prepare them by delivering the early interview phases described in Chapter 4 (Lamb & Malloy, 2013). Most protocols, however, give interviewers the discretion to progress to direct questions about allegations if they can justify that choice, such as when case features reduce the risk of false reports, there is physical evidence, or there is a need to explore a previous report. When the protocol in use allows interviewers to directly mention allegations, the decision about how directly to probe to raise target topics is best made during preinterview preparation.

Structure of a Topic-Raising Phase

The interviewer transitions to the matters under investigation with a topic shifter, as in the following examples:

> Practice narrative precedes topic raising: Thank you for telling me about [practice narrative topic]. I am going to ask about something different now.

> Ground rules precede topic raising: Now it's time to talk about something else.

How the interviewer proceeds depends on the case. Sometimes the event under investigation is not in doubt, such as when children are interviewed about a family altercation that summoned law enforcement. In these cases, the interviewer avoids mentioning a specific hypothesis (e.g., he or she would not say, "Did your dad hurt your mom?"), but there is no need to dance around the reason for the interview. After the topic shifter, the interviewer could initiate the free narrative phase with an open-ended prompt that invites the child to start talking ("Tell me everything that happened at your house last night").

In other types of cases, such as most sexual abuse investigations, it is unknown whether children actually experienced the alleged event or not. For these situations, most protocols recommend an indirect approach to topic raising. The idea is to deliver one or more prompts that might start a child talking about the matters at hand, starting with a general prompt that does not mention any specifics about the allegation. Because children often know why they are being interviewed, many protocols begin with a "How come you're here today?" question (National Children's Advocacy Center, 2014, p. 1):

- Now that I know you a little better, I want to talk about why [you are here] today. (Lamb, Hershkowitz, Orbach, & Esplin, 2008, p. 288)
- Tell me why I came to talk to you. Or, Tell me why you came to talk to me. (Lyon, 2005, p. 2)
- Tell me what you have come to talk to me about today. (Powell, 2003, p. 260; this prompt accomplishes the purpose without asking *why* the child came, which implies that the child initiated the visit.)

If the child says "I don't know" or ignores this prompt, the interviewer progresses through a series of prompts, usually starting with prompts that do not mention a suspect, action, or location of an allegation. One way of accomplishing this is to ask the child about a detail that led to the concern. If the child confirms the detail, the interviewer can then ask what happened, as in these examples:

- Your mum said you told her something in Coles [a store] and she got upset and took you outside to talk about it. Did you tell your mum something that upset her in Coles? (Powell, 2003, p. 261)
- Is your mom worried that something may have happened to you? (Lyon, 2005, p. 2)

If the child acknowledges an earlier disclosure or concern, the interviewer can proceed with an open-ended prompt, such as "Tell me what happened to you" or "Tell me what she is worried about." Some protocols omit an initial yes/no question, as in these examples:

- I heard something might have happened to you—tell me what happened. (American Professional Society on the Abuse of Children, 2012, p. 19)
- I understand some things have been happening in your family. I'll listen while you tell me about that.

- I heard that someone might have bothered you. Tell me everything about that. (Lyon, 2005, p. 2)

If the child participated in a prior documented conversation, a prompt such as the following might be sufficient to elicit the topic (taking care not to disclose a protected source):

- I heard you saw a policeman last week. Tell me what you talked about. (Lyon, 2005, p. 2)
- I heard you talked to [your teacher, a doctor, some other professional] [yesterday, last week, or some other time]. What did you talk about?

More directive prompts could mention such things as physical evidence or a location but without articulating details of the allegation or concern:

- I see you have a bruise on your face. Tell me how that happened.
- I heard something happened at camp. Did something happen at camp? [Wait for child to confirm.] Tell me everything about that.

When the child does not respond to open prompts and there is a decision to prompt more specifically, the next set of topic openers might ask about specific people but without mentioning an action. ("I heard that you know a man called Big John. Do you know a man called Big John?" ["Yes."] "Have you ever met Big John yourself, or have you just heard about him?" ["I met Big John at his house last week."] "I've never been to Big John's House. So I don't know what happened there. Tell me what happened when you went to Big John's house last week. Start at the beginning"; Powell & Snow, 2007, p. 79). Sometimes, physical evidence provides a way to raise the topic without mentioning allegation specifics (e.g., "Did you leave your pajamas at Grandpa's house?" ["Yes."] "Tell me what happened"). A more suggestive, and therefore less desirable, approach mentions an action without mentioning a suspect (e.g., "Did somebody [give you beer to drink, etc.]?").

How interviewers plan topic openers depends on the reason for concern. For example, when sexual play triggered the interview, starting with a general question about that play can lead into subsequent questions. ("Your teacher said you were playing a game with James, and she asked you to stop. Did your teacher ask you to stop a game?" ["Yes."] "Tell me how you play that game." [Wait for a response.] "Tell me about the first time you played [child's words] with someone"). Two general principles direct how interviewers design prompts for individual cases. First, they avoid mentioning details of the allegation (e.g., the suspicion that a father's behavior precipitated sexual play) to protect children's credibility, but also because hearing children's words helps interviewers detect any earlier misunderstandings on the part of adults who reported concerns. Second, interviewers avoid language that asks children to speculate or imagine what might have happened.

Even children who have recently disclosed to a parent, teacher, or friend sometimes need time to realize the purpose of the current conversation or to begin talking. During topic raising, it is appropriate to give children time to pull their thoughts together but without creating verbal pressure for a disclosure. One way to provide this time is to create a pause in the conversation. For example, the interviewer could say, "I'm going to look over the things we've talked about for a minute. You can think about whether there is something I should know about [your family, things that have happened at school]." Another strategy is to return to neutral conversation for a few minutes before revisiting the purpose of the interview. (I discuss interview breaks later in this chapter.)

Overview of a Successful Topic-Raising Phase

The basic principle for topic raising is to avoid mentioning case hypotheses and unknown details. After a topic shifter (e.g., "I am going to ask about something else now"), the interviewer starts with a broad and open-ended topic opener, such as "Tell me what happened here today" (when responding to violence in the child's home) or "Tell me what you have come to talk to me about today" (for a sexual abuse interview). If the initial prompt does not start conversation, the interviewer progresses through a list of prompts, with the degree of specificity decided before the interview or during a short break (when the interviewer or investigative team considers alternatives). A first choice could invite the child to confirm a detail that led to the concern (but without mentioning specific actions or suspects) or mention neutral information about a particular day (with an invitation to discuss what happened that day). Approaches that include more allegation details include mentioning a suspect (but not the alleged action) or an action (but without mentioning a suspect). Asking whether someone did something wrong, which does not label a specific transgression or suspect, is preferable to asking a question containing more details.

It is appropriate to return to neutral conversation for a few minutes if the child needs more time to acclimate to the interview. A topic-raising phase is successfully conducted whenever the interviewer follows a process that gives the child opportunities to mention case details before the interviewer does. As one protocol reminded, "Closing the interview without a report of abuse is an acceptable outcome" (State of Michigan Governor's Task Force on Child Abuse and Neglect and Department of Human Services, 2011, p. 15).

ELICITING A FREE NARRATIVE

Once children acknowledge the topic of conversation, interviewers encourage them to describe events by delivering a series of open-ended prompts that allow them to follow their unique trains of thought. Compared with responses to focused questions, responses to open-ended prompts are longer and more informative, contain a higher proportion of accurate details, and provide more leeway for children to mention unexpected information (Lamb, Hershkowitz, Sternberg, Esplin, et al., 1996; Sternberg et al., 1996, 1997).

Structure of a Free Narrative Phase

The interviewer delivers an initial free-narrative prompt after a successful topic opener:

> Topic shifter and topic opener: Now that I know you a little better, it's time to talk about the reason you are here today. Tell me why you came to talk to me today.

> Initial free narrative prompt: Tell me everything you can about [topic the child mentioned].

Teenagers may benefit from a longer invitation modeled after instructions from the cognitive interview that emphasize the need to report details (Fisher & Geiselman, 1992; see also Chapter 7, this volume): "I want to understand everything about [what child mentioned]. Start with the first thing that happened and tell me everything you can, even things you don't think are very important."

While the child is speaking, the interviewer maintains a relaxed demeanor, avoids staring, and gives the child adequate time to think. Instead of jumping in as soon as the child stops speaking, the interviewer uses minimal encouragers (comments such as "OK" and partial repetition of the child's words) to encourage the child to continue (e.g., *Child*: "And then I went across the street to Mrs. Manning's house." *Interviewer*: "You went across the street"). The interviewer repairs breaks in conversation by delivering open-ended prompts that encourage the child to construct a narrative that has breadth and depth, as in these examples (adapted from Powell & Snow, 2007):

> Open-ended breadth questions: What happened next/after that? What else happened that time [child's words for the broad event]?

> Open-ended depth questions: Tell me more about the part where [child's words]. What happened when [child's words for something that happened]?

To encourage an older child to situate events in a broader context, the interviewer can use this invitation from the National Institute of Child Health and Human Development protocol (Lamb et al., 2008): "Think back to that [day/night] and tell me everything that happened from [some preceding event mentioned by the child] until [alleged abusive incident as described by the child]" (p. 291). A young child may benefit from a conceptually simpler question, "Tell me about the part where [earlier event mentioned by the child]," followed by a series of "Then what happened?" prompts (M. Powell, personal communication, July 27, 2015).

In some jurisdictions, interviewers focus on what happened (actions) and do not try to elicit other types of information. This philosophy aims to prevent children from being discredited because of misreported or changed details resulting from expected memory lapses. In other jurisdictions, interviewers are encouraged to elicit contextual details in age-appropriate ways. According to this philosophy, photographs of the location of the event or retrieval of physical evidence can demonstrate the reliability of children's reports. When interviewers are authorized to seek contextual information, asking children to report more about what they saw and heard elicits new details. Perhaps because these prompts allow children to select what they remember best, in analog studies the information obtained from these questions is as accurate as the information in earlier narrative responses (adapted from Poole & Lindsay, 2001, p. 30):

> Sometimes we remember a lot about how things looked. Tell me how everything *looked* in/at/when [child's words for the location or event].

> Sometimes we remember a lot about sounds or things that people said. Tell me all the things you *heard* in/at/when [child's words for the location or event].

In this phase, the interviewer continues to deliver open-ended prompts that encourage the child to describe each event component mentioned (e.g., "You said [child's words]. Tell me about that"). When necessary, the interviewer asks the child to repeat something that was difficult to hear (e.g., "I couldn't hear that name. What did you say?"), gives neutral permission to discuss difficult topics (e.g., *Child*: "And then he touched my . . ." *Interviewer*: "It's OK to say it"), and encourages the child to continue ("I'm still listening." "I'm going to give you a minute to think about that time [child's words], in case there is something else you can tell me"). A common interviewing error is shifting into focused questions prematurely, without attempting to keep the child in the free narrative phase (Davies, Wilson, Mitchell, & Milsom, 1995; Lamb, Hershkowitz, Sternberg, Esplin, et al., 1996). Although the interviewer will want to know more about actions and objects mentioned, interrupting a free narrative to ask about the type of car a child rode in or other details would interrupt the child's train of thought. Only when it is clear that the child is not going to volunteer additional information should the interviewer shift into the questioning and clarifying phase.[1]

Requesting a Double Check

Children are tolerant of requests to repeat information when adults provide reasons for double checks. Asking children to review information a second time can be helpful when their first descriptions contained confusing details, events that seemed out of sequence, or diversions that could have been irrelevant stories. And because of a phenomenon called *reminiscence*, children and adults alike often recall new information with each retelling (La Rooy, Katz, Malloy, & Lamb, 2010). Thus, when conversation stalls, an interviewer can elect to ask for another review, as in these examples:

- You've told me a lot, and that's really helpful, but I'm a little confused. To be sure I understand, please start at the beginning and tell me [how it all started/exactly what happened/how it all ended/etc.] (Lamb et al., 2008, p. 292).
- I want to make sure I heard everything right. It helps me check my notes when I hear things one more time. Tell me one more time what happened [last Sunday, etc.].

Discussing Repeated Events

Many interviews discuss events children have experienced multiple times (Trocmé et al., 2010). To meet charging needs, it is often necessary to identify one or more individual events by restricting the time, place, and nature of those events (with requirements for particularization differing across jurisdictions). This can be challenging because it can be hard for witnesses to remember single incidents of repeated events. Over time, children and adults develop *scripts*, which are memories of what usually happens that preserve the typical features of repeated events (general event representations, such as "When I get ready in the morning, first I . . ."). Script recall is evident when children talk in the present tense using language that describes typical activities, as in this example from Sonja Brubacher, Martine Powell, and Kim Roberts (2014):

Whenever mum goes out, like sometimes she works in the evenings, he–, she works on Wednesday, Thursday, and Friday nights, whenever she

---

[1]Other common interviewing errors are trying to elicit a free narrative when the child's statement of the topic was vague or ambiguous, repeatedly using only a few open-ended prompts, and phrasing prompts in ways that encourage short responses (e.g., "Can you tell me a little bit about . . .") or are difficult for children to understand. For a discussion of these and other errors, see Powell and Guadagno (2008).

goes he just comes in, like while I'll be watching TV or something, and does the thing. So, if I have to say about one time, it's probably like a Friday night and I'm watching my movies, usually I'm wearing my pajamas by then—so yeah, had my pajamas on—and he sits down on the couch. (p. 326)

Yet even after memories become organized as scripts, children can often remember a number of specific incidents. Therefore, a primary objective of research on repeated events is to discover strategies that help children discuss a number of discrete episodes.

Perhaps because scripts are sturdier and easier to recall than memories of specific instances, children who have had repeated experiences report more event information when, before exploring individual events, interviewers first ask them to report what usually happens. Compared with children who first recall a specific episode, those who start by describing what usually happens describe more of the unique features of individual occurrences later in the interview—without decreasing their accuracy or responsiveness to questions about individual events (Brubacher, Roberts, & Powell, 2012; Connolly & Gordon, 2014). Experts therefore recommend paying attention to the language a child uses: When a child's initial statements contain generic language, such as "Grandpa keeps touching me," the first prompts should also be generic (e.g., "Tell me what Grandpa does").

Following a child's generic description, the interviewer prompts for specific instances. Techniques for drawing out individual occurrences include asking about the time the child remembers the most (T. Lyon, personal communication, December 22, 2015), the last time it happened, the first time it happened, and so forth. Because atypical events are especially memorable, it can be productive to ask children whether there was a time when something "different" happened. A spontaneous comment from the child in the previous example illustrates the salience of this type of information (Brubacher, Powell, & Roberts, 2014):

> Oh, but this one time I remember he just started, like, he had the zip down on his jeans, and it was nearly my bedtime—just about 9, and the neighbor came to the door. He jumped up like, just like "I wasn't doing anything" and quickly went to—cause, we were right in the lounge room that's right by the window at the front door, so he zipped up quickly and answered the door. (pp. 329–330)

Whenever a child discloses an individual incident, the interviewer should label that incident to reduce confusion and make it easier to ask follow-up questions. The child's words make the best labels because these words are more likely than labels chosen by the interviewer to reference a unique occurrence and to trigger the desired event memory (e.g., *Interviewer*: "Let's call that the time Jason [child's words]"). In an analysis of police interviews, children were less responsive to interviewer conversational shifts when interviewers ignored children's labels or replaced their words with other identifiers (Brubacher, Malloy, Lamb, & Roberts, 2013).

Children are highly attuned to adults' language and will shift from generic ("First he closes the drapes") to episodic language ("First he closed the drapes . . ."), and vice versa, depending on the way interviewers phrase prompts (Brubacher & La Rooy, 2014; Brubacher et al., 2013; Schneider, Price, Roberts, & Hedrick, 2011). Consequently, interviewers should monitor their language choices to effectively direct children's narratives, using generic language to elicit scripts ("Tell me *what happens* when Dad gets angry") and language referring to specific episodes to elicit individual instances ("Tell me everything that happened *this morning*"). (See Quick Guide 5.1 for examples of generic and episodic language.) In this example, based on the sexual abuse interview described earlier, Brubacher, Powell, & Roberts (2014) annotated the interview to illustrate how the interviewer assigned and clarified labels:

Child: . . . When the neighbor went, he just did the things he normally does but a bit less—yeah, because it was, he had less time before mum got home.

1. *Use the child's episodic leads to create labels and make labels explicit:*

Interviewer: OK, thank you for telling me about that. I'd like to talk about that time you just mentioned, let's call that the time the neighbor came at the door. Tell me everything that happened that time when the neighbor came at the door.

QUICK GUIDE 5.1
Generic and Episodic Prompts

Generic prompts	Episodic prompts
Tell me what happens.	Tell me what happened that time.
Then what happens?	Then what happened?
What happens next?	What happened next?
What else happens when [child's words for the repeated action or other information that identifies the topic, e.g., "The other children leave"]?	What else happened when [child's words for the event or other information that identifies the topic, e.g., "The other children left"]?
You said [child's words; e.g., "She starts yelling"]. Then what happens?	You said [child's words; e.g., "She started yelling"]. Then what happened?
You said sometimes [child's words; e.g., "She uses a belt"]. Tell me what happens when [child words; e.g., "She uses a belt"].	You said once [child's words; e.g., "She used a belt"]. Tell me about that time.

Note. Generic prompts elicit information about what usually happens during repeated similar events, whereas episodic prompts elicit details about individual incidents.

Child:	Well, it just started out as normal, so as I've said he–, I was watching my, uh, ok, that time I was watching a TV show, it was Glee, and he came in the room and sat beside me on the couch. He said, "What are you watching?" and I just said it was my program like—, sort of trying to ignore him, like . . .
Interviewer:	OK.
Child:	So, uh, so he started playing with the, um, with the button and zipper on his jeans. He–, sometimes he would get the blanket so that when, so nobody would see if they come to the door. So, he puts that over him, and over me, just–, over our legs. And then he just does it.

2. *When unsure, ask if labels are unique:*

Interviewer:	Ok, were there any other times when the neighbor came at the door, when he did it?
Child:	Yeah, um, the neighbor comes sometimes when mum's at work, just to say hi and you know. I think the neighbor came a few times so he started putting the blanket over, but this time it was already so late–, like, it was almost 9 so my mum gets home at 9, so–, I don't think he thought anyone would be there.

3. *Adjusting labels for clarity:*

Interviewer:	OK, so let's talk more about this time when the neighbor came and it was almost 9 . . . [interview truncated]

4. *Prompting for another occurrence after recall for the previous is exhausted:*

Interviewer:	Can you tell me about another time? (p. 331)

Notice that throughout this example, the interviewer only asked questions to clarify which event was under discussion but otherwise continued the free narrative phase with open-ended prompts, such as "Tell me everything that happened." Only when the child had exhausted her ability to recall discrete events did the interviewer shift into the questioning and clarifying phase by delivering questions to elicit detailed information about each incident.

During the incident-labeling process, and sometimes later in the interview, it is common for children to make new disclosures (e.g., "Oh, but this one time . . ."). Whenever this occurs, the interviewer should clarify whether this is a new incident or an elaboration of a previously mentioned one and then use free narrative prompts to elicit descriptions of new incidents. In this way, the interviewer will cycle several times from eliciting free narratives to questioning/clarifying and back, always trying to draw out as much information as possible using open-ended prompts.

It is common for children to mix up details from related events and to focus on different details each time they remember an event (La Rooy et al., 2010; H. L. Price, Connolly, & Gordon, 2015). As a result, they often insert details from one episode into narratives about other episodes (i.e., internal intrusion errors) and report different sets of details across multiple accounts of an event (e.g., mentioning a conversation in one interview but not in another). Adults seem to realize that memories are not described exactly the same from one retelling to the next (Connolly, Price, & Gordon, 2009, 2010), and interviewers should expect some variation in reports of repeated events across interview phases (Connolly, Price, Lavoie, & Gordon, 2008).

Overview of a Successful Free Narrative Phase

During the free narrative phase, the interviewer delivers a long series of varied open-ended prompts that encourage the child to provide an elaborated report of events. When a child's initial disclosure is generically phrased (e.g., "He touches me"), the interviewer starts with generic language to elicit script recall ("Tell me about the touching"); when the initial disclosure refers to a specific episode ("He touched me in his car"), the interviewer uses episodic language to elicit information about specific incidents ("Tell me everything about the touching in his car"). Initial prompts are typically broad (e.g., "Tell me what happened.") and followed by encouragement to continue (e.g., "Tell me more"), with facilitators ("Uh-huh" and pauses) conveying that the child should continue talking. Subsequent prompts can ask the child to elaborate on something mentioned ("You said he [child's words]. Tell me about that").

At any time during a free narrative phase, the interviewer can ask the child to repeat a comment or can request a double check by asking the child to review an event one more time. If the case involves repeated similar events, the interviewer repeats this process to draw out information about multiple incidents (e.g., "Tell me about the first time this happened"), using the child's description to label each event (or, if necessary, assigning labels themselves: "Let's call that the first time in the yard").

Because children are tolerant of pauses in conversation, it is better to stop and think about ways to continue the free narrative phase rather than entering the next interview phase (questioning and clarifying) too soon ("Give me a second; I'm thinking"). Once the child has stopped providing new information, the interviewer transitions into questioning and clarifying, always cycling back to free narrative prompts when the child mentions new incidents.

QUESTIONING AND CLARIFYING

After children have provided a free-narrative account, interviewers deliver a wider variety of questions to test primary-issues alternative hypotheses and to clarify ambiguous information (e.g., the identity of people mentioned; see Chapter 2). During this phase, interviewers also try to elicit the information needed to meet charging needs and details that could support the broader investigation (e.g., mention of other witnesses and physical evidence that might be retrievable). The following discussion reviews general guidelines for delivering the questioning and clarifying phase, with Chapter 6 ("Case-Specific Decisions and Exploration") suggesting strategies for customizing interviews.

Topic Shifters, Topic Markers, and Topic Drift Checks

Children do not always mentally shift gears when interviewers raise new topics, do not always understand questions requiring them to match words such as *he, she,* and *that* to referents (people, places, events, and objects), and do not always assume that the current question is asking about the same people and events that earlier questions addressed. Compared with older children, young children are more likely to interweave relevant and irrelevant narratives, but their habit of basing narratives on the name of a recently mentioned object, person, or activity makes it difficult to tell when they are talking about the matters under investigation. In this example from my laboratory, a 5-year-old boy who could not remember a visit with Mr. Science that had occurred 3 months ago simply began talking about rooms in his home:

> *Interviewer:* Can you tell me more about what happened in the science room?
>
> *Child:* For everything like, just like, I can't like go down in the basement or up in the attic. I can only go upstairs and be downstairs and like, that's all. There are like boxes up there and there's some stuff down there.

Off-topic talk can lead cases to spin out of control if investigators erroneously come to suspect a multitude of events involving numerous people. Therefore, it is important for interviewers to clearly alert children whenever a new question deals with a different topic from the previous question, to embed topic markers into questions (e.g., "Tell me what happened *at your birthday party*"), and to verify what children are discussing when conversation might have drifted off topic. To avoid confusion, it is best to follow a child's train of thought by first exploring information mentioned during the free narrative phase and then to cluster questions regarding additional topics together (rather than jumping from a question about one issue to a question about a different issue).

Because the questioning and clarifying phase continues conversation about events the child has just described, there is no need to verbally flag the beginning of a new interview phase. Instead, throughout this phase the interviewer clearly signals changes in the topic of questions and marks questions in ways that help the child stay on topic. For instance, after questioning about the most recent of several incidents, the interviewer might shift to another incident by saying, "Let's talk about the time the neighbor came over and it was almost 9 o'clock." Following this topic shifter, the interviewer would periodically embed topic markers into questions to clarify which event is under discussion. For example, by saying, "You said that he rented a movie *the night the neighbor came over*. What movie did you see *that night?*" the interviewer could help the investigative team identify the date of the event (from rental records). Also, this question could begin a discussion to explore whether the child was exposed to adult movies. Throughout this phase, the interviewer asks which event is under discussion (i.e., delivers a topic drift check) whenever there is suspicion the child might be talking about an unrelated event (e.g., "Are you talking about the time [current topic] or something else?").

Because of the need to keep children on topic and reduce the potential for confusion, the conversational style of forensic questioning is subtly different from the way adults typically speak. In daily life, we often establish a topic and then assume that our conversational partner knows what we are discussing. As a result, dialogue such as the following sounds natural to us:

Mother: So can you tell me what happened at school today?

Child: Umm.

Mother: What was the first thing you did?

Child: Umm. Wait that was easiest! [Child playing with a toy]

Mother: Did she have morning work for you?

Child: Stations.

Mother: What did you go to first?

Child: Table 1.

Mother: What did you do there?

Child: Magnet words.

With this style, a distracted child can answer by attending only to key words in the mother's comments without staying on topic (in this example, what happened *today*). As transcripts from interview studies show, children can appear to be talking about a target event when they have actually shifted into talk about other days and happenings. In my laboratory, this is one of the reasons some children tell us they made a volcano with Mr. Science or did other activities associated with the word *science* that are not part of our target events.

I created the previous dialogue by removing the topic markers an astute mother in my laboratory actually included to keep her son on task. The actual transcript reads like this:

Mother: So can you tell me what happened at school today?

Child: Umm.

Mother: What was the first thing you did *at school today, when you got there?*

Child: Umm. Wait that was easiest!

Mother: Did she have morning work for you, *when you got there this morning?*

Child: Stations.

Mother: What *station* did you go to first?

Child: Table 1.

Mother: Can you tell me what you did *at Table 1?*

Child: Magnet words.

Of course, there are other ways to make these questions less ambiguous. For example, the mother could have said, "Did *your teacher* have work for you when you got there this morning?" (instead of "Did *she*") and "What station did you go to first *today?*" (to keep conversation clearly about this morning's activities). As a general rule, forensic interviewers prefer to use names or other identifying information (e.g., "your teacher") instead of *he, she,* or *they;* prefer to mention actions instead of saying *that* (e.g., "Where did that happen?" would be rephrased as "Where were you when [child's words for the event]?"); and try to frequently mark the topic under discussion (e.g., "Was someone else with you *that day at the beach?*"). The following hypothetical example illustrates the use of topic shifters, topic markers, and a topic drift check. Here the interviewer is asking follow-up questions about a day when the child's brother was bitten by a dog:

Child: And then we drove home from the hospital.

Interviewer: Let's talk about what was happening when Pepper bit Sam [topic shifter]. Where were you *when Pepper bit Sam* [topic marker]?

Child: On the deck.

Interviewer: Where was Sam?

Child: Sam threw the ball over the deck and went to get it.

Interviewer: Where was Pepper?

Child: I don't know, but Uncle Matt came home and let him into the yard.

Interviewer: Then what happened?

[Child described the event in response to a series of open-ended prompts.]

Child: And, then . . . he bit Uncle Matt on the finger. Auntie Lou hit him and put him in the kennel.

Interviewer: Is that the time Pepper bit Sam or another time [topic check]?

Child: That's another time. My mom told me.

Because it can feel wordy to completely avoid words such as *he, she,* and *that,* interviewers take children's ages and cognitive abilities into account when phrasing questions. As a general rule, typically developing children who are 10 years and older are more skilled than younger children at keeping referents in mind, so interviewers speak more naturally when talking to older children and adolescents. Nonetheless, it is always best to be mindful of how many interchanges have occurred since a person, action, or object was explicitly mentioned and to repeat these unambiguous words (i.e., referents) periodically.

The Questioning Cycle Revisited

As discussed in Chapter 3, forensic questioning is best described as a cycle in which interviewers continually return to the most open prompt that might produce a response as they move conversation through various topics. During the questioning and clarifying phase, interviewers initiate this cycle numerous times as they mentally (or physically) check off topics that have to be covered. Often, they ask a recall-detail question to raise a topic and then return to an open-ended prompt that encourages children to report information in ways that match the organization of their memories.

In this hypothetical example of a sexual abuse investigation involving an 11-year-old boy, the interviewer is interested in eliciting information to demonstrate a consistent pattern of behavior across multiple alleged victims:

- Detail question to explore delayed disclosure.

Interviewer: How do you think he got away with this so long?

Child: He told me I'd get in a lot of trouble because we drink beer.

- Child answered generically, so interviewer asks an open-ended question to elicit a generic description.

  Interviewer: Tell me about the beer drinking.

  [Child answers.]

- Interviewer asks an open-ended question to elicit a specific incident when a threat was made.

  Interviewer: Tell me about a time he said you'd get in a lot of trouble.

  [Discussion of that time, with the interviewer delivering a series of open-ended prompts.]

- Interviewer clarifies which incident the child is discussing.

  Interviewer: Was that the sleepover time, last Friday's, or some other time?

Some questions do not require a subsequent open-ended prompt (e.g., *Interviewer*: "Do you have one Uncle Bill or more than one Uncle Bill?" *Child*: "One"). Nevertheless, the idea of a questioning cycle underscores that the transition into questioning and clarifying is not a transition from open-ended questions into a long list of focused questions. Instead, the interviewer continually moves conversation back to open-ended prompts, when appropriate, to encourage elaborated reports in the child's own words.

Phrasing Recall-Detail Questions

Many questions that ask for contextual detail or clarification are *Wh*-questions: questions starting with *when, where, who, what,* or *how* that ask children to recall details of an event. When delivering these questions, skilled interviewers maintain the conversational habits of forensic interviewing (see Chapter 3) by adopting a relaxed tone, giving children adequate time to add new information, and using simple language. They also follow the recommendations in Quick Guide 3.2 for navigating pronunciation issues, choosing words children will understand, and selecting the most direct question forms. For example, interviewers ask about one concept per question, avoid negatives (e.g., "Did you *not* see who it was?"), and do not use tag questions (e.g., "You must have been afraid, *weren't you?*"). Because interviewers prefer questions that require more than a "yes" or "no" answer, they ask, "What did the car look like?" rather than "Was it a red car?" and "Where was your mom when Ben . . .?" rather than "Was your mom in the room when Ben . . .?" (See A. G. Walker, 2013, for a review of developmentally appropriate language.)

One question form that often befuddles children is a type of indirect question called a *do-you-know* (DYK) question. For example, adults sometimes ask a question such as "Do you know (or do you remember) what the car looked like?" instead of the direct question, which is "What did the car look like?" Although DYK questions seem less suggestive than direct questions (because they do not assume that children know the desired information), the two layers of meaning in these questions are difficult for young children to navigate. As Angela Evans and her colleagues explained, "Indirect speech acts directly to ask *if* respondents know, while indirectly asking *what* respondent know" (Evans, Stolzenberg, Lee, & Lyon, 2014, p. 776).

In a set of courtroom transcripts, 4- to 9-year-old children responded only by saying "yes" to DYK questions almost half the time, showing that these questions do not always prompt children to search memory for the desired information (Evans & Lyon, 2012, as cited in Evans et al., 2014). Although DYK questions can reduce confabulation when children have no knowledge of the detail in question (Poole & White, 1991), there is no reason to routinely preface requests for details with "Do you know?" (Evans et al., 2014).

Experts also suggest caution when asking about why something happened. One reason is that questions such as "Why did you wait to tell your mom?" sound accusatory: Children could believe these questions are asking them to defend their behavior rather than asking them to explain the circumstances surrounding an event. The second reason for caution is that *why* questions require advanced cognitive and linguistic maneuvers, including self-reflection, reasoning about causes, and the ability to accurately articulate that information. As Anne Graffam Walker (2013) explained,

> Children are rarely prepared to meet this kind of challenge before they are at least 7 to 10 years old (Perry & Teply, 1985). The ability to respond reliably to questions that ask for inferences about the internal processes or behavior of others is not well established until children are 10 to 13 years old. (pp. 71–72)

For children less than 8 years of age, Karen Saywitz and Lorinda Camparo (2014) recommended rephrasing *why* questions in alternative ways that reflect common language usage in the children's cultures. For example, interviewers can request children's reasoning by saying, "What makes you think so?" and use forms such as "How come?" and "What made that happen?" (p. 117). Questions such as "How do you think he got away with this so long?" or "How did you feel when . . .?" can start a productive line of questioning about threats or fears.

Although some jurisdictions avoid questions about feelings (M. Powell, personal communication, July 27, 2015), "How did you feel?" can be a powerful prompt for eliciting children's reactions to events, which can bolster their credibility. Children rarely provide information about feelings and reactions in response to questions that do not contain evaluative words, but they often do so when interviewers ask about feelings. Furthermore, "How did you feel?" is more likely to elicit information than questions phrased more specifically, such as "How did your [body part] feel?" (Lyon, Scurich, Choi, Handmaker, & Blank, 2012). The questions "How did you feel when [abuse occurred]?" and "How did you feel after [abuse occurred]?" frequently elicit reports of feelings and reactions, and these questions also return new information about abuse, such as threats and subsequent events. For example, one 10-year-old responded to a feeling question by saying, "Scared 'cause he told me not to tell anybody and I didn't know what was gonna happen if I told somebody" (Lyon et al., 2012, p. 7). Another 10-year-old gave a compelling description of her abuse experiences:

> *Question:* How did you feel when he touched you?
>
> *Answer:* Kind of angry at him cause he shouldn't be doing that and sometimes I thought that he was doing that 'cause I wasn't his daughter (oh, o.k.) I felt kind of mad, disappointed. 'Cause in front of my mom he always say that he love me really. And on my mind I say that if he loves me why was he doing that to me.
>
> *Question:* Okay. How did you feel after he touched you?
>
> *Answer:* I felt like nasty. Like dirty.
>
> *Question:* Really. Tell me about that, dirty and nasty.
>
> *Answer:* 'Cause he touch, if he touches me, he touch me, right. Then he just leaves and like if like if I didn't work anymore just leave me like that (uh-huh). And I felt like mad and at the same time felt kind of dirty because he shouldn't be doing that because I'm just a little girl. (Lyon et al., 2012, p. 7)

In sum, interviewers minimize the need for numerous focused questions by delivering supportive early interview phases (Chapter 4) and not exiting the free narrative phase too soon. During questioning and clarifying, they enhance children's productivity and accuracy by delivering simply worded questions and questions that have been proven effective in eyewitness studies. The art of asking good questions requires a toolkit of knowledge and skills that includes information about the next topics in this chapter.

Memorizing Question Frames (Stems)

Throughout conversation, interviewers have to keep case features in mind, remember what they have already asked and what children have said, and mentally revisit interview plans. When the strain on working memory is high, interviewers sometimes ask long series of focused questions that appear to have no clear purpose or direction. Skilled interviewers are less prone to this behavior because they have memorized strategies for dealing with frequently occurring situations, thereby freeing mental resources they use to monitor higher order goals.

It is especially helpful to memorize flexible *question frames* (also called *question stems*), such as the examples in Quick Guide 5.2. Professionals who

---

QUICK GUIDE 5.2
Exploring Issues With Open-Ended Prompts
and Question Frames

Familiarity with a list of frequently used comments and prompts helps interviewers ask questions that children understand. *Question frames* (also called *question stems*) are memorized phrases used to construct individualized prompts about issues under discussion.

Managing Topics

Raising the Topic
Topic opener: Tell me what you have come to talk to me about today.

Keeping the Child on Topic
Topic marker: Tell me everything about [child's words; e.g., *those pictures*].

Conducting a Topic-Drift Check
Topic-drift check: Are you talking about the time [current topic] or something else? Are you talking about [person under discussion] or someone else? Are you talking about [object under discussion] or something else?

Shifting the Topic
Topic shifter: I am going to ask about something else now.

Eliciting Information

Asking for a Free Narrative
Open-ended broad question (also called a free narrative prompt): Tell me everything that happened.

Asking for Elaboration
Open-ended breadth question: What happened next/after that? (or "Then what happened?") What else happened that time [child's words]?
Open-ended depth question: Tell me more about the part where [child's words]. What happened when [child's words]?

Asking About Feelings and Reactions
How did you feel when [child's words]?
What did [name of person] do that made you [child's words: scared, nervous, etc.]?
Is there something that would make you feel less [scared, nervous, etc.]?

Asking About Reasons
What made [name of person] [action child described]? (For example, "What made your mom get mad?")
How did [description of the situation]? (For example, "How did your pajamas come off?" "How did the lighter get on the table?")

(continues)

Asking for Sensory Details

Sometimes we remember a lot about how things looked. Tell me how everything *looked* in/at/when [child's words for the location or event].

Sometimes we remember a lot about sounds or things that people said. Tell me all the things you *heard* in/at/when [child's words for the location or event].

Exploring for Other Incidents

Did that happen one time or more than one time?

(If child says, "lots of times"):

Tell me about the last time something happened.

Tell me about another time you remember.

Tell me about the time you remember best/most.

Was there ever a time when something different happened? Tell me about that time.

Clarifying Reports

Clarifying Ambiguities

Person: You said [grandpa, teacher, Uncle Bill, etc.]. Do you have one _____ or more than one _____?

Which _____?

Does your _____ have another name? (or "What does your _____ [mom, dad, etc.] call _____ ?")

Object or action: You said [child's words]. Tell me what that is.

Object: You said [child's word]. What does the [child's word] look like?

Location: I don't know anything about the [child's words]. Tell me about the [child's words]/What is the [child's words]?

Clarifying "I Don't Know" Responses

You don't know, or you don't want to talk about this right now?

Clarifying Inaudible Comments

I couldn't hear that. What did you say?

Resolving Inconsistent Information

You said [child's first words on the issue], but then you said [child's second words on the issue]. I'm confused about that. Tell me again how that happened.

You said [child's first words on the issue], but then you said [child's second words on the issue]. Was that the same time or different times?

Encouraging Responses

Overcoming Embarrassed Pauses

It's OK to say it.

It's OK to talk about this.

Is there something that would make it easier for you to talk about this? (Children sometimes continue when interviewers give them a choice, such as "Would you like to sit here instead?" or "Would you like to make a picture while we talk?" The choices offered should permit continuous recording and should not involve unauthorized interview props.)

Repairing Conversational Breaks

Tell me more about that.

And then what happened?

I'm still listening.

Note. Data from Lyon, Scurich, Choi, Handmaker, and Blank (2012); Poole and Lamb (1998); Powell (2003); and Powell and Snow (2007).

learn to conduct interviews for specific purposes add content-specific frames to this basic list. For example, practice guides for abuse-focused interviews discuss ways to clarify sexualized acts and explore for nudity, force, pornography, and other relevant topics (see Saywitz & Camparo, 2014).

Revisiting Ground Rules and Clarifying "I Don't Know" Responses

An excessive number of recall-detail, option-posing, and yes/no questions can derail cases if clearly erroneous or inconsistent answers become the focus of efforts to discredit children. One way to reduce impulsive responding is to remind children before asking for information they might not remember (while also reminding them to answer if they do know) that it is acceptable to say "I don't know."

In truth, "I don't know" is an ambiguous response that can mean "I don't have a memory of that detail" (i.e., "I don't know whether the detail referenced in the question existed/happened or not"), "I never saw/heard that" (i.e., the detail did not exist/happen), or "That detail existed/happened, but I cannot describe it" (Scoboria, Mazzoni, & Kirsch, 2008). Thus, witnesses sometimes have more information than "I don't know" conveys. For this reason, adults who answer a mix of answerable and unanswerable questions provide higher quality testimony when they are allowed to say "I don't know" but interviewers clarify the meaning of those responses (Scoboria & Fisico, 2013).

Sometimes, children say "I don't know" because they have lost track of the topic, are confused by an ambiguous question, or just do not want to talk about the issue under discussion (e.g., *Parent*: "What happened at school today?" *Child*: "I don't know"). Therefore, it can be useful to provide another opportunity to respond without pressuring children to answer in a particular way. For example, a question such as "What did he say?" might elicit "I don't know" if the person under discussion did not say anything while performing the last action the child described—even though this person did talk. In this situation, the interviewer could say, "I didn't ask that very well. I meant 'Did [person's name] say something while [child's words for the broader event] or was he quiet the whole time?'"

When a child seems reluctant to discuss a sensitive issue that was already described briefly, a question such as "You don't remember or you don't want to talk about that right now?" gives the child an opportunity to admit knowledge while deferring discussion for a later time. If the child says, "I don't want to talk about it," the interviewer can shift to a more neutral topic for a few minutes, offer reassurance ("Oh, I talk about this kind of thing all the time with children . . . it's my job. It's OK to tell me [what it looked like, etc.]"), or explore the child's feelings about the best way to continue (e.g., "Is there something that would make it easier for you talk about this?" "Could you draw what [item under discussion] looked like?").

Asking About Age, Size, and an Individual's Appearance

Children are not very skilled at describing where something falls on a dimension relative to other similar things. When asked which of two people is older, for example, children less than 8 years old may say that whoever is taller is older (Kuczaj & Lederberg, 1977), and their answers to "How big was [some person or thing]" are often exaggerated or do not reflect adults' sense of size. In general, children's and youth's reports of age, height, weight, and interior facial features (e.g., the shape of someone's eyes and nose) are not very accurate (Pozzulo, 2007, 2013). When it is necessary to ask such questions, or when interviewers regret a poorly worded question, A. G. Walker (2013) recommended following up with another question that might clarify answers. For example, an interviewer might ask, "What made you think she was old?" (p. 62).

Asking About Number and Time

Young children sometimes report the number of times something happened even though they do not grasp number concepts or have not engaged in the mental work needed to answer accurately. Inconsistent and incredulous answers ("Thousands of times," "Every day") populate transcripts, and even reasonable estimates cannot be taken at face value. For example, when Lindsay Wandrey and her colleagues asked 167 maltreated children to estimate the number of foster care placements and court visits they had had, three children in the sample (a 6-year-old, a 9-year-old, and a 10-year-old) gave wildly exaggerated estimates (Wandrey, Lyon, Quas, & Friedman, 2012). Error rates were troubling even when data from these children were excluded, however. Only a minority of the children reported the exact number of placements or court visits, and responses to questions about broad categories (more than one, more than five, more than 10) were also highly inaccurate. For example, only 67% of the older children correctly reported whether they had experienced more than five placements.

Children and adults usually reconstruct the time of an event by combining contextual memories of the event with knowledge of their usual patterns of daily, weekly, seasonal, and yearly activities (Friedman, 2014). For example, you might not immediately recall that a tree in your yard fell over in December, but you could reconstruct this fact by remembering that it happened a few days before a New Year's Eve party at your house. Because of the reconstructive nature of temporal memory, the ability to accurately report when something happened develops gradually throughout childhood and adolescence. Even 4-year-olds can usually specify which of two events occurred most recently and the general time of day (e.g., waking, eating lunch), but it is not until 6 to 8 years that children are above chance when asked to report the day of the week, month, or season of a staged event (Friedman, 1991). When investigators compute the percentage of correct identifications, understanding of time and dates is limited before 8 to 10 years. In one of William Friedman's (1991) studies, in which children reported when staged events had occurred, only 39% of the 6-year-olds and 63% of the 8-year-olds recalled the exact or adjacent day of the week (Experiment 3). Other skills, such as specifying the year of a long-ago event or realizing that a temporal memory is likely just an estimate, develop even later (Friedman, 2014).[2]

Despite how challenging it is to remember temporal location, some child witnesses give remarkably accurate information about personally significant events. These temporal reconstructions are likely supported by rich memories and, in some cases, the temporal proximity of the events to landmark activities. For instance, even 6-year-olds often remember the day of the week of salient, parent-nominated events from the past 3 months (Pathman, Larkina, Burch, & Bauer, 2013). In Lindsay Wandrey and colleagues' study (2012), older children often gave reports of foster care placements and court visits that were not far from the truth, even though few reports reflected the exact temporal locations. However, it is difficult to judge which children will be able to report temporal information accurately because events that seem highly significant to adults are not always remembered well by children.

Interviewers can improve children's accuracy by asking questions about time that match witnesses' cognitive abilities. For example, most first- and third-grade children in one of Friedman's (1991) studies accurately ruled out the morning as a possible time of an afternoon event at school, and even nursery-school children rarely identified Saturday or Sunday as the day. Thus, young children find it easier to express time in terms of meaningful markers, such as which television show they were watching when the event occurred or whether it happened on a school day or weekend. Asking whether a child remembers what was happening the day a particular event occurred can elicit information that might help specify the date (e.g., that the child had a special friend sleep over). Because it is difficult to ask about temporal issues,

---

[2]As with other concepts, interviewers should not assume children will be able to accurately report temporal location just because they use temporal terms in their speech, can recite cultural lists ("January, February, March . . ."), or can identify the current hour, day of the week, or month (A. G. Walker, 2013; Wandrey et al., 2012).

interviewers should obtain guidelines for their regions of practice regarding the degree of specificity required. (See Friedman, 2014, for a review of the development of memory for the time of past events.)

Clarifying Ambiguities and Inconsistencies

Throughout conversation, interviewers have to clearly establish the meaning of the names, places, actions, and objects children mention. For instance, I have been consulted about cases involving ambiguity concerning which of two uncles a child initially implicated, whether a child claimed abuse at home or a child care facility, and even whether an innocent description of playing with a toy had been misinterpreted as discussion about the child's penis. In all of these cases, interviewers had failed to question their assumptions and the meaning of children's reports.

Quick Guide 5.2 lists some ways to clarify ambiguities. An interviewer can identify key details by asking the child to provide information another way (e.g., "Does Mom have another name?"), by describing what referents look like (e.g., "You said he gave you a [child's word]. What does the [child's word] look like?"), or just by asking for more information about the ambiguous referent (e.g., "Tell me about the [child's word]"). When witnesses are young, details provided about ambiguous objects or locations can sometimes identify those objects and locations even though children are incapable of labeling them clearly. For example, information about which toys were in a room where a child played might clarify that the child was talking about something that happened in out-of-home care rather than in his or her own home. When children's reports are unclear, interviewers assist the broader investigation by eliciting details that can be confirmed by visiting children's caregiving environments or tracking down other relevant leads.

Children sometimes contradict their earlier responses even when questions are not explicitly misleading (Andrews, Lamb, & Lyon, 2015). Many phenomena produce these apparent changes in testimony. For example, literal use of language can cause a child to say that someone put a penis in her mouth but then say "no" to a question such as "Did you put your mouth on his penis?" (Berliner & Barbieri, 1984). Children also use words restrictively, so they might say "yes" to a question about poking but "no" to a question about touching. Some answers to yes/no questions are thoughtless and inconsistent, and questions involving the word *any* often elicit answers of "no" that conflict with earlier testimony (e.g., *Child*: "Because he told me not to tell" [Intervening conversation]. *Adult*: "After he did that, did he say anything to you?" *Child*: "No"). Even when interviewers ask open-ended questions, children's tendency to shift topics abruptly and without warning can produce narratives that seem inconsistent to adults.

Asking children to explain is one way to resolve inconsistencies (e.g., "You said [child's first words on the issue], but then you said [child's second words on the issue]. Was that the same time or different times?"; see Quick Guide 5.2). Inconsistencies caused by language usage issues can often be handled by asking the child to describe an object or an event a second time (e.g., "I want to make sure I understand what happened after class on Friday. Tell me again what happened"). Whenever a peculiarity in how a child uses a word or phrase might become an important issue, it is useful to document the child's explanation for that word or phrase (e.g., "You said he [child's word] your brother and your brother fell down. Show me what [child's word] is").

Repeating Questions

Most forensic interviews contain repeated questions, with one sample averaging about six repeated questions per interview (La Rooy & Lamb, 2011). Interviewers often repeat questions when they are trying to clarify previous responses, but they also do so to challenge earlier responses and, sometimes, for no obvious reason. Children typically respond by reiterating their initial answers or offering elaborations, but a minority of repeated questions elicits contradictions. For example, 11% of the answers to repeated questions in one sample of sexual abuse interviews contradicted children's initial responses (Andrews & Lamb, 2014).

Repeated questions can shift children from inaccurate to accurate answers, but undesirable shifts (from accurate to inaccurate) also occur (Krähenbühl, Blades, & Eiser, 2009). A number of mechanisms drive these response changes, including a belief that adults are seeking another answer (which is more common among older children) and poor memory monitoring (which is more common among younger children; Howie, Nash, Kurukulasuriya, & Bowman, 2012).

Undesired changes in answers occur more often among young children and when interviewers ask suggestive questions or fail to explain why they are repeating focused questions (Howie, Kurukulasuriya, Nash, & Marsh, 2009; Howie, Sheehan, Mojarrad, & Wrzesinska, 2004). Interviewers can therefore minimize unwanted inconsistencies by (a) using repeated questions sparingly, (b) repeating questions mostly to seek clarification or to encourage distracted children to answer, (c) using the most open-ended question form possible, and (d) providing a brief justification for repetitions (e.g., "I might have forgotten something you said. Who was at your house when your mom went to the store?").

Overview of a Successful Questioning and Clarifying Phase

The four characteristics of a forensic interview (Chapter 2) are in full play during a successful questioning and clarifying phase. Here the interviewer delivers prompts to achieve fact-finding goals with forensically defensible practices. Using a repeated cycle in which open-ended prompts often follow focused prompts (to keep conversation child centered), the interviewer probes for needed details, explores alternative hypotheses for allegations, and clarifies ambiguous testimony (tests hypotheses). The interviewer also asks developmentally appropriate questions to elicit information that could identify other witnesses and physical evidence that might be retrievable (assists the broader investigation). Guided by the scope of the interview and the nature of the case, the interviewer might repeat the free narrative and questioning/clarifying phases to explore multiple issues (is mindful of commander's intent).

BUILDING BREAKS INTO THE INTERVIEW

Interview breaks accomplish two goals. For interviewers, breaks are a time to review what children said and plan questions to clarify testimony and address new issues. For children, breaks are a chance to clear their thoughts and become more comfortable about making new disclosures. Depending on how the conversation has unfolded, interviewers might take a break after an unsuccessful attempt to raise the topic, after children have completed the free narrative phase, or after an initial questioning and clarifying phase.[3] Because witnesses often provide new information whenever they search memory another time, immediately after a short break is a natural time for interviewers to ask children to explain an experience again.

A planning break is especially helpful after children have made unexpected comments or raised new allegations. In these situations, the interviewer can introduce a break with instructions such as the following (Orbach & Pipe, 2011): "Now I want to make sure I understood everything and see if there is anything else I need to ask. I will just [think about what you told me/go over my notes/go and check with X]" (p. 156).

When interviews are being recorded, it is important to continue recording during breaks (lest critics claim that breaks were used to influence children's testimonies). Currently, there are no guidelines for how to structure children's activity during breaks, but well-learned tasks, such as coloring a printed page, are not very distracting (Poole & Dickinson, 2014).

---

[3]*Achieving Best Evidence* (Ministry of Justice, 2011, p. 71) suggests providing a "touch card" that children can point to when they would like a break.

CLOSING THE INTERVIEW

The purpose of an interview and local practice dictate how interviewers wind down and close conversations. A popular way to initiate this phase is to ask whether the child has anything else to say (e.g., "You've told me a lot today. Is there something else you'd like to tell me?") or has any questions (e.g., "Is there something you'd like to ask me?"). It is important not to reinforce the child for relaying specific information or to make false promises (e.g., that the child will not be interviewed again). Karen Saywitz and Lorinda Camparo (2014) suggested the following response when children ask whether they will be taken away from their families or whether someone will go to jail:

> I don't really know what will happen next. And I don't want to tell you something that is not true. That wouldn't be fair to you. So we will talk to the adults who are making the decisions and find out what will happen next as soon as we can. What I do know is that we are working on making sure you stay safe and healthy, that no one gets hurt. (p. 150)

When a child asks questions about the interviewer's life (e.g., "Did your dad hit your mom too?"), it is best to acknowledge the child's concerns without disclosing personal information. For example, the interviewer could say, "Everyone, including me, has had things happen that they did not like or things that were upsetting. If you want to talk more about your feelings, I will find someone for you to talk to" (Saywitz & Camparo, 2014, p. 151). Sometimes interviewers give children or accompanying adults a contact name and phone number in case they want to discuss something further, and many interviewers revert to neutral topics for a minute or so to defuse tension before returning children to their caregivers.

RECAP

After delivering the early interview phases (Chapter 4), the interviewer explores case issues with the following phases:

1. *Raising the topic of the interview.* The interviewer raises the matter under investigation by starting with a broad and open-ended invitation that might get the child talking. During this phase, the interviewer funnels down to more targeted prompts only if necessary and in ways that avoid repeating allegations.
2. *Eliciting a free narrative.* After the child clearly acknowledges the topic, the interviewer delivers a series of open-ended prompts that elicit descriptions in the child's own words. The initial

prompt is broad (e.g., "Tell me what happened") and followed by encouragement to continue (e.g., "What happened next?" "What else happened?"), with subsequent prompts asking the child to elaborate on various points (e.g., "Tell me more about [child's words]." "What happened when [child's words]?"). For cases involving repeated similar events, the interviewer repeats this process to explore each incident (e.g., "Tell me about the first time this happened"), using information provided by the child to label each event (or assigning labels). The interviewer uses generic language to follow up statements describing scripts (the typical features of repeated similar events) and episodic language to elicit information about individual incidents.

3. *Questioning and clarifying*. During this phase, the interviewer explores alternative hypotheses for allegations and clarifies ambiguous testimony (tests hypotheses) using developmentally appropriate language (has a child-centered perspective), delivers prompts that might elicit information leading to corroborative evidence (supports the broader investigation), and repeats the free narrative and questioning phases (when necessary) to explore multiple issues (is mindful of commander's intent).

4. *Closing the interview*. The interviewer closes conversation in a way that makes sense given the purpose of the interview. Common practices include asking whether the child has anything else to say or has any questions before turning to conversation about a neutral topic and returning the child to a caregiver.

A break in the conversation can help the interviewer plan how to proceed, give a reluctant child time to become more comfortable, and increase the chance that a disclosing child will recall new information. The interviewer can take a break after attempts to raise the topic fail, after the free narrative phase, after an initial round of questioning and clarifying, or whenever unexpected information emerges.

PRINCIPLES TO PRACTICE: HOW CAN I ENCOURAGE RETICENT CHILDREN TO PROVIDE DETAILS?

Supervisors sometimes share frequent questions from staff members with me. This composite of several related questions asks how to explore allegations from reticent children without straying into overly suggestive questioning.

Interviewer's Question

When interviewing a 12-year-old recently following allegations of sexual abuse by a stepparent, the child was vague about the alleged assaults. She seemed unsure of dates and specific locations (e.g., rooms in the house) and offered no details during open-ended questioning. What's the best way to elicit these details without tainting my interview?

My Response

The amount of detail provided by abused children depends on many factors, including the child's age, how long ago the abuse occurred, and whether the abuse was just a few incidents or a series of related incidents. For example, some victims disclose after the perpetrator is no longer part of the family. If this 12-year-old was abused, the abuse occurred several years ago, and abuse was repeated, it would not be unusual for her initial free narrative to be a sparsely detailed, generic description of what usually happened.

To advance the conversation, it could help to reassure the child that you talk about these types of things all the time and will not be surprised or upset by anything she tells you. Next, determine whether the alleged abuse occurred one time or more than one time, and use a generic, open-ended prompt if she is reporting a repeated event (e.g., "Tell me what usually happened when . . ."). Build subsequent prompts on her narrative (e.g., "You said [her words]. Tell me more about that") and then transition into episodic prompts (e.g., "Tell me about the time you remember [best, the first time, etc.]"). Do not expect her to directly retrieve information about temporal location, but ask questions about what her life was like at that time to help her reconstruct ages and locations (e.g., what she remembers about where she lived at various times, who her teachers were, or what her interests were).

Case features dictate how to explore alternatives to the victim hypothesis (e.g., Could she have made up the story to impress a friend? Is she in therapy for another issue and recently retrieved a vague memory of something that may not be sexual abuse?). To begin exploring alternatives, you can ask how long she has remembered the incident, how the report came to light (e.g., "What were you thinking when you decided to tell?"), and whether the adults she disclosed to understand what happened or there has been a misunderstanding.

6

CASE-SPECIFIC DECISIONS AND EXPLORATION

Mastering the conversational habits (see Chapter 3, this volume) and conventional content (Chapters 4 and 5) of child interviewing does not fully prepare professionals to walk into a room and do their jobs. Another skill set rounds out the three Cs of child forensic interviewing: case-specific decisions and exploration. This skill set includes the knowledge and habits that interviewers rely on to meet the needs of individual cases. Interviewers who have this skill set understand the dynamics of the type of case under investigation, know how to meet charging and/or documentation requirements, and can deliver phases of the interview in ways that take into account the characteristics of individual children and the features of individual cases.

The best ways to learn advanced interviewing skills are through inservice and national training workshops, conferences, ongoing supervision, and online resources from groups who review interviewing research, legislative changes, and other relevant topics (e.g., social media trends that affect case investigation). Books provide foundational knowledge but are not updated

http://dx.doi.org/10.1037/14941-007
Interviewing Children: The Science of Conversation in Forensic Contexts, by D. A. Poole
Copyright © 2016 by the American Psychological Association. All rights reserved.

frequently or tailored to the legal and cultural environments where interviewers work. For these reasons, this chapter cannot be a comprehensive guide for case-specific practice. Instead, in the following discussion I introduce a collection of information that is broadly relevant for interviewers, supervisors, and the professionals who review transcripts: interviewing young children, the benefits and risks of interview props, accommodating disabilities, developmental assessments, consensus about having a support person in the interview room, multiple interviews, mentioning or displaying physical evidence, and using checklists to improve thoroughness.

INTERVIEWING YOUNG CHILDREN

There is no fixed age when children suddenly become capable of providing information that has probative value. For example, spontaneous declarations from one insistent 2-year-old opened a case that uncovered videotapes documenting years of sexual abuse against patients by a pediatrician (Goodman, Ogle, McWilliams, Narr, & Paz-Alonso, 2014), and many 3-year-olds successfully complete all phases of a forensic interview. In one transcript I read, a 3-year-old responded with the short answers typical of this age but nonetheless talked for a practice interview, completed a ground rules phase in which she practiced saying "I don't know" and corrected the interviewer, correctly labeled statements as a lie or the truth, disclosed in response to an open-ended prompt about why she was being interviewed, and then described a great deal of useful information while periodically admitting lack of knowledge.

But despite their often remarkable abilities, young children are challenging to interview. Preschoolers' reports are often sparse, and accuracy suffers when interviewers probe for details (Peterson, 2011). Among children exposed to misleading conversations, negative stereotypes about people, or suggestive questioning, testimony from the youngest children is often the least reliable and the most impaired by inexpert interviewing (Leichtman & Ceci, 1995; Poole, Brubacher, & Dickinson, 2015). Because of these findings, many professionals approach these interviews with trepidation and heightened concern that their methods will be subject to scrutiny. Keeping the following principles in mind can help interviewers maintain realistic expectations for children and for themselves:

- An interview is only one part of an investigation. Interviewers are not responsible for memory contamination prior to interviews, spontaneous confabulations, and other sources of inaccuracy that are not the product of their questioning methods.

Regardless of how children respond, interviewers support investigations by building adequate rapport, getting as much information as possible with open-ended prompts, and double checking the meaning of children's utterances.

- Interview procedures can be modified. For example, interviewers can keep early phases short to avoid fatiguing children, extend the length of these phases when shy children need more warm-up time, and drop one or more ground rules for very young children.

- Most young children will provide some confusing answers and self-contradictions. Because of inattention and issues related to language development, conversations with young children sometimes circle around an issue before understanding is achieved. For instance, a child might say "no" to "Did you talk to an officer?" but "yes" to "Did you talk to the police?" "No" is a frequent answer to questions that are not understood and also the default response to questions with the word *any* in them, as this dialogue illustrates:[1]

Interviewer:	When you are at your mom's, do you share a bedroom with anybody?
Child:	No—with my sister.
Interviewer:	And Louis. Does he share a bedroom with anybody?
Child:	No. He shares with his girlfriend.

To minimize contradictions, it is best to base questions on children's remarks (by using open-ended breadth and depth questions; see Quick Guide 1.1) and to use their words for people, places, actions, and things.

- Young children do not always sit still or look at you when they talk. If a child is highly distracted or seems to be avoiding questions by exploring, it makes sense to remove concerning items and ask the child to sit. But some children are responsive and cooperative while roaming the room, so there is no need to insist that these children sit. Using children's names periodically is often enough to get their attention. When young children are uninterested in talking, it can be productive simply to interact with them for a while or let them explore something in the room.

---

[1]This dialogue is a composite from several interviews I have read, but the names and details do not match any particular case.

Extra time, familiarity with the interviewer, and boredom with the interview space sometimes help preschoolers latch onto the purpose of the visit and engage in conversation. (See this chapter's Principles to Practice for reasons why developmental norms can mislead professionals who work with young children.)

INTERVIEW PROPS

Some interviewers use objects or printed materials to help children communicate, with most prop-based techniques accomplishing one of four major purposes:

- *Comfort techniques* help children feel more relaxed. Examples of these practices are recording children's responses on a flip board while asking about family members and allowing children to draw whatever they like during interviews.
- *Assessment techniques* learn something about children. For instance, using body diagrams to explore the terms children use for various body parts is one type of brief assessment.
- *Communication techniques* use props to elicit disclosures or to give children a nonverbal way of describing events. Interviewers use props to elicit testimony when they ask children to point to the places on a body diagram where they were touched or to draw what happened.
- *Clarification and documentation techniques* use props to clarify something children said or to document that interviewers did not misunderstand comments. Asking children who have already reported touching to verify where touching occurred by pointing to a body diagram or doll is an example of clarification and documentation.

Debate about the appropriate roles for props in interviews is ongoing and often heated. There is a reason for this lack of consensus: Physical objects can cue memory and provide a nonverbal way to communicate, thereby increasing the amount of information obtained, but they can also be distractors and play objects that increase inaccuracies. As the following review explains, the likelihood that a technique will benefit or harm testimony depends on many factors, including the match between a child's cognitive abilities and the skills needed to use the prop, the child's exposure to false information outside the interview setting, the questioning techniques an interviewer pairs with props, and the degree to which other evidence and the case context help the interviewer disregard impulsive responses.

Comfort Techniques

One way some interviewers help children relax is by providing paper and crayons for free drawing. Supporters of this practice claim that drawing materials make conversations feel less confrontational because there is somewhere to look during pauses and while talking about sensitive issues. Developmental psychologists, however, have expressed concern that play activities are distracting and could encourage speculation and silly remarks. Two studies released within a year of each other found support for both views.

Jason Dickinson and I arranged for children who had already participated in an eyewitness study to return to our laboratories for follow-up interviews (Poole & Dickinson, 2014). One or 2 years earlier, the children had experienced a live event and also heard misinformation about that event. When they arrived for the new study, each of the 5- to 12-year-olds experienced a second event so interviewers could talk about something recent along with what happened a long time ago. Some children received paper and markers with instructions that they could draw during the interview, whereas others did not. Interviewers used a variety of question types to elicit reports of the long-ago event; for the recent event, they delivered free-narrative prompts and a set of forensically meaningful focused questions (e.g., "Did Bonnie take your picture?" "How many times did Bonnie take your picture?"). Despite the large number of performance measures, we found no evidence that comfort drawing harmed children's testimony, even among the younger children. Compared with nondrawing age-mates, more of the younger children who drew reported experiencing touches, but this finding requires replication because of the large number of analyses conducted. Perhaps because drawing is a highly familiar activity that children can start and stop at will, they were not particularly distracted by the materials.

Emily Macleod, Julien Gross, and Harlene Hayne (2014) arrived at a different conclusion, however. In their study, 5- and 6-year-olds described a recent school trip in one of three conditions: verbal reports alone, talking while drawing about the trip (draw-and-talk), or talking while comfort drawing. Contrasting with my team's findings, children who freely drew reported more than twice as much erroneous information as the nondrawing group, and errors comprised a disturbing 17% of the information reported by children who drew whatever they chose. Many of these errors were plausible but untrue confabulations (which interviewers would not spot as wrong) and fantastical information (strange reports that could discredit the child, such as "We saw a mermaid"). Because these problems occurred less frequently among children who drew the target event, the research team concluded that a "playful approach to drawing appears incompatible with the task of talking about a real event" (Macleod et al., 2014, p. 9).

More research is needed to explain this discrepancy in findings. The children in our youngest group were older, on average, than those in the second study; memories of our events were either very recent or very stale (which might discourage speculation about unknown details); the children in our study did not converse with each other during the event; and our interview protocol included a ground rules phase with practice demonstrating the rules. Also, we used performance in the prior study to assign children to groups, thereby ensuring that children who tended to invent details were equally distributed across conditions. Unfortunately, there is no way to know which (if any) of these differences explains why free drawing was innocuous in our study but detrimental in another. Future research that studies a range of events is needed before policy groups can confidently recommend free drawing for children who may be prone to confabulation and fantasy.

Assessment Techniques

Developmental assessments are usually seen only in clinical evaluations and extended forensic interviews (an approach involving multiple interviews), but it is common for interviewers to assess how children use key words. For example, some interviewers ask children to label sexual and nonsexual parts on a body diagram, which also conveys that it is all right to talk about these parts. But before using props for this purpose, it is important to consider whether the practice might attract criticism for suggesting desired answers. This is a concern because in laboratory studies, children's erroneous points most often revisited places they previously labeled (Poole & Dickinson, 2011). Thus, even when interviewers intermix nongenital and genital locations during body part labeling, critics could argue that requests later in the interview (e.g., "Did somebody touch you somewhere else?") merely encouraged pointing to places that sounded familiar rather than prompting memory-based responses. For this reason, it prevents criticism to clarify sensitive words after children have described an event rather than before. (See Developmental Assessments, in this chapter, for an example of using objects to test children's understanding of some basic words.)

Communication and Clarification Techniques

The majority of research on props has asked whether drawing materials, anatomical dolls, and body diagrams help children report key facts about the matters under investigation. The draw-and-talk technique has garnered some of the strongest support, with many studies finding that children report more information when encouraged to draw target issues (e.g., Gross & Hayne, 1999; Gross, Hayne, & Drury, 2009; Macleod, Gross, & Hayne, 2013; Patterson &

Hayne, 2011).[2] Furthermore, the information provided by drawing children is typically as accurate as that of children who only talk (Gross & Hayne, 1999), and this greater productivity encourages interviewers to deliver minimal encouragers rather than numerous questions (Woolford, Patterson, Macleod, Hobbs, & Hayne, 2015). The biggest limitations are that draw-and-talk is not helpful for very young children (3 and 4 years; Butler, Gross, & Hayne, 1995), is detrimental when interviewers question suggestively (Bruck, Melnyk, & Ceci, 2000; Strange, Garry, & Sutherland, 2003), and encourages children reinterviewed after long delays to insert new erroneous details (Salmon & Pipe, 2000). Many protocols avoid these problems by recommending only verbal techniques, but when draw-and-talk is used, experts caution interviewers to favor open-ended questions and not to interpret all content in drawings as memory reports. (See D. A. Brown, 2011, for a review.)

Controversy about props has focused mainly on whether anatomically detailed dolls and body diagrams (also called *human figure diagrams*) help interviewers reliably distinguish abused from nonabused children. The literature on these props, which is voluminous, includes studies that assessed the value of adding props to largely well-conducted interviews, as well as studies that did not exploit recommended practices, studies with and without suggestive influences, and studies involving a variety of target touches.

Regarding the type of touch, studies of memory for medical examinations permit questions about genital touching (e.g., Steward et al., 1996), but children may be more willing to report socially sanctioned than abusive touching, and these studies did not replicate the atmosphere of concern about touching that can propagate errors among nontouched children. Therefore, the design of existing medical studies tipped the scale in favor of finding benefits (because objects served as memory cues and reporting aids) with relatively low error rates. However, studies that questioned children about innocuous touching seem less informative (because touches to the arm, face, and so forth are not very memorable), but this touching was unexpected and sometimes paired with suggestive influences (e.g., Poole & Dickinson, 2011). As a result, the design of these studies tipped the scale toward greater risks. It is fair to say that the true picture probably lies somewhere in between and is context dependent: Whether props are overly risky or largely beneficial likely depends on the age and cognitive abilities of witnesses, the degree of prior contaminating influences, and the overall quality of interviews. (For a review, see Poole & Bruck, 2012.)

---

[2]For the sketch reinstatement of context technique, children sketch an event before interviewers ask them to describe what happened. In a study involving older children with autism spectrum disorder and typical children, children who sketched before talking reported more information without an increase in errors (Mattison, Dando, & Ormerod, 2015).

To understand why developmental psychologists are concerned about using props with young children or those with intellectual disability, consider the mental skills a child must have to report an event using props. Two foundational skills are dual representation (an understanding that props are simultaneously objects and symbols of something else; DeLoache, 2000, 2005) and awareness that the object represents the child. But more is involved. A child must also keep questions in mind while interacting with the prop, search memory for relevant information and gate out irrelevant memories, and then map memories onto the prop. To use an analogy, most teenagers are safe drivers, and most are skilled at using their phones, but we do not want teenagers (or anyone) to use phones when they drive because it is difficult to coordinate multiple tasks. In the same way, a child could understand the representational intent of an object and be able to recall salient information, but this tells us little about how that child will perform when we embed props in a challenging memory task.

The problem with props is that young children sometimes fail to keep the topic of questioning in mind, fail to inhibit irrelevant thoughts, and respond to what psychologists call the *affordances of objects* by pointing thoughtlessly to diagrams, putting fingers in the holes of dolls, and engaging in other behaviors made possible by the object. When the neural circuits that inhibit irrelevant behavior, hold information in mind, and flexibly juggle thoughts are still immature, it is challenging to map previous experiences onto objects. This proved true when Nicole Lytle's research team repeatedly placed a large sticker on children and then asked them to place a smaller sticker in the same location on a body diagram. Even though no memory was involved, 30% of 5-year-olds did not place all four stickers accurately (Lytle, London, & Bruck, 2015, Experiment 2). When assistants in another study asked children to report touching experiences by pointing to a diagram, a minority of children who were 7 years and younger displayed two behaviors found among some adults with brain damage: perseveration (repeatedly pointing to places on the body diagram) and confabulation (inventing stories about the erroneous points; Poole, Dickinson, Brubacher, Liberty, & Kaake, 2014). Thus, many children reliably use props as interviewers intend, but some do not. (For evidence that props significantly increase young children's false reports of forensically meaningful touches, see Bruck, Kelley, & Poole, in press.)

Because props elicit both true and false disclosures, reviews of research on props offer two different conclusions: Some claim support for their utility (e.g., Faller, 2007), whereas others claim that introducing props can be tantamount to divining testimony (Poole & Bruck, 2012). There are three reasons why some commentators are more critical of props than others: basic research (e.g., the sticker study) has shown that young children lack the cognitive machinery to reliably map experiences onto symbols (for a field study extending these findings, see Thierry, Lamb, Orbach, & Pipe, 2005), studies cited to support props did not reproduce the dynamics of complicated cases (e.g., an atmosphere of concern about abuse), and it is unclear how much value props add beyond questions alone (especially when early interview phases prepare children to talk; Lamb, Hershkowitz, Sternberg, Boat, & Everson, 1996; Poole & Dickinson, 2011). In 2015, the National Children's Advocacy Center responded to the evidence on body diagrams by concluding that this prop "should not be used as a matter of standard practice" and "should be introduced only if the child has made a verbal disclosure of maltreatment and other clarification options and approaches have been exhausted" (p. 2).

A less risky prop-based practice is to elicit statements using an open-ended approach but then to confirm the meaning of children's words (e.g., "my pee-pee"), if necessary, by introducing an interview aid (e.g., "Show me where your pee-pee is"). Alternatively, many interviewers use follow-up questions to clarify reports (e.g., *Interviewer*: "I want to understand what your bottom is. What do you use your bottom for?" *Child*: "For peeing"). (For discussions of other techniques and approaches, see D. A. Brown, 2011, and Burrows & Powell, 2014.)

ACCOMMODATING DISABILITIES

Children with disabilities have physical, cognitive, or emotional impairments that interfere with their ability to perform some activities in ways that are typical for children their age. Many conditions cause disabilities in one or more of the following categories:

- *Speech and language impairments* include problems speaking and understanding speech.
- *Cognitive disabilities* affect the ability to attend, remember, reason, or understand some types of information (e.g., text or mathematical expressions).
- *Emotional disturbances* produce inappropriate feelings or behavior.
- *Perceptual disorders* produce limitations in hearing and vision.
- *Movement disorders* hinder the ability to walk or control some body parts normally.
- *Chronic health problems* include medical conditions, such as epilepsy and diabetes.

Because definitions of disabilities vary across time and sources, frequency estimates also vary. According to the Centers for Disease Control and Prevention (CDC), about one in six children in the United States has a developmental disability or other developmental delay (CDC, 2013), and about 13% of 3- to 21-year-olds in the United States qualify for educational services under the Individuals with Disabilities Education Act (National Center for Education Statistics, 2015). Because children with disabilities are more likely to be victimized than peers and are over-represented in forensic samples (L. Jones et al., 2012), case-specific decisions often involve plans for talking to children whose interview performance might be affected by a disability.[3]

Understanding Disability Terminology

Disability terminology is confusing because there are numerous conditions, labels change over time, and the classification of conditions varies from source to source. There are three major systems for naming and classifying disabilities:

- The *International Classification of Diseases* is the international standard for medical and mental health diagnoses (World Health Organization, 2014).
- The *Diagnostic and Statistical Manual of Mental Disorders* (5th ed.; DSM–5) defines mental health terms used by psychiatrists, psychologists, and other mental health professionals in the United States (American Psychiatric Association, 2013). This reference work lists the characteristics of each condition and associated statistical information, such as each condition's prevalence (when known) and gender ratio.
- The *Individuals With Disabilities Education Act* (U.S. Department of Education, 2015) defines the disabilities that qualify U.S. children for special education services.

It is common for professionals to use several terms for a condition. For example, *fetal alcohol syndrome* is an older term for children who have cognitive limitations associated with prenatal alcohol exposure, and *fetal alcohol effect* has been used to describe subtle problems produced by maternal alcohol use. Currently, *fetal alcohol spectrum disorder* refers to a range of symptoms caused by prenatal alcohol exposure, from mild to severe (Bakoyiannis et al., 2014). Similarly, most parents use the term *autism*, whereas the *DSM–5* uses *autism spectrum disorder*.

---

[3]For a special issue on witnesses with disabilities, see the March 2013 issue of the *International Journal of Disability, Development and Education*.

Many professional organizations and government agencies post useful information about specific disabilities on the web:

- The CDC sponsors an A to Z list of diseases and conditions on their website (http://www.cdc.gov).
- Typing the name of a condition and *DSM* into an Internet search engine will pull up the defining characteristics of mental health diagnoses.
- An online resource about interviewing children with disabilities is available from CARES Northwest, a child abuse assessment center, through funding by Oregon's Children's Justice Act Task Force. Search for *Project Ability: Demystifying Disability in Child Abuse Interviewing* (Shelton, Bridenbaugh, Farrenkopf, & Kroeger, 2010).

Talking About Differences

Because the conditions children have do not define who they are, professionals typically use *person-first language* (also called *people-first language*) to talk about differences and disabilities. For example, they write "Amanda has autism" rather than "Amanda is autistic" and "She communicates with her eyes" rather than "She is nonverbal." Person-first language describes what a child *has*, not what a child *is*. But some members of difference communities identify with a label and point out that person-first language often describes liabilities (e.g., "She *has* cancer") rather than differences (e.g., "He *is* slender"). For this reason, many advocates in the autism community prefer *identity-first* language, such as "autistic person" or "[person's name] is autistic" (L. Brown, 2015). Consultation with a supervisor can help professionals use recommended terms in written reports, but parents and children may have their own preferences for one-on-one conversations.

When communicating with caregivers, it is appropriate to ask, "Does [child's name] have any conditions that might influence how he or she will participate in an interview?" The question, "Does [child's name] receive any special education services?" could start a conversation about what services the child receives and why.

Interviewing Children With Disabilities

When professionals work with typically developing children, they usually can estimate how long a child will maintain attention, how difficult it will be to understand the child's speech, and what types of questions the child will be able to answer. By contrast, children with language disorders, intellectual disability, autism spectrum disorder, and other conditions have a wider range of abilities, and many of these children have more than one condition. For instance, children with autism spectrum disorder have an elevated rate of hearing impairment, and those with attention-deficit disorder are more likely than peers to have other psychiatric conditions, including conduct, tic, and anxiety disorders. This means that information about a child's primary diagnosis may not give interviewers all the information needed to plan an interview.

Because of differences from child to child, interviewers should plan to interview a child—not a condition. Regardless of a child's diagnoses, it is important to ask, "What are this child's needs, difficulties, and abilities?" As summarized in *Project Ability* (Shelton et al., 2010), "Professionals . . . need to know how to interview children with disabilities, but it is unrealistic to expect them to develop expertise in the many disabilities themselves" (p. 3). Rather than basing case decisions on extensive knowledge of individual disabilities, forensic interviewers accommodate differences in one of two ways: (a) through heightened reliance on developmentally neutral techniques or (b) through a child-specific approach that considers individual children's challenges and strengths.

The Developmentally Neutral Interview

For a *developmentally neutral interview*, the interviewer communicates in ways that are most likely to be understood regardless of whether the child is 5 or 15 years old. The interviewer gets acquainted with the child's behavior and language patterns during the rapport-building phase; uses simple, direct questions even young children usually understand; avoids misunderstandings by asking questions to double check the meaning of answers; and gives the child ample time to respond. A developmentally neutral interview does not condescend by treating children as younger than they are; instead, this style follows practices that help people of all ages participate meaningfully in conversation. When children's ability levels are unknown, a developmentally neutral interview follows nine key practices:

- *Schedule the interview to maximize cooperation.* Care should be taken to interview children at times when they are usually alert and interviews will not conflict with highly valued or medically necessary activities, such as favorite television shows or nebulizer treatments.
- *Minimize distractions.* Because some children are unusually bothered by visual clutter and noise, interviewers should minimize sensory stimulation by selecting quiet, sparsely decorated rooms that are free of noisy heating ducts, air conditioners, and lights that buzz.

- *Gather information about strengths and difficulties during rapport building.* Interviewers use early rapport building to acclimate to how children speak (which will prevent misunderstandings) and to observe children's ability to pay attention, answer simple questions, and describe personally experienced events.
- *Keep children on topic.* Children who are distractible, eager to please, or confused by questioning are especially likely to stray from the topic of conversation by interjecting descriptions of unrelated events. Topic shifters (e.g., "I'm going to ask you about something else now") and topic markers (e.g., "Tell me everything about those pictures") are important when interviewing children with language, attention, or intellectual disorders.
- *Irrelevant behavior that can be ignored* is ignored. Some children have atypical mannerisms and behavior. For example, children with autism spectrum disorder may avoid eye contact, and some children with visual impairments rock and press their eyes. Interviewers should maintain focus on the conversation by ignoring behavior that does not interfere with asking questions and hearing the answers.
- *Emphasize open-ended questions and minimize recall-detail, multiple choice, and yes/no questions.* Children who have difficulty understanding language develop strategies that help them participate in conversations. These children may take a conversational turn by repeating the last words other people said and may respond to yes/no questions even when they do not know the answers. Because many disabilities produce heightened suggestibility to focused questions, interviewers should rely as much as possible on open-ended questions and follow focused questions with more open-ended prompts (Henry, Bettenay, & Carney, 2011).
- *Use simple, direct questions.* In general, language concepts that are harder for typically developing children to master develop later among some children with disabilities, including those with vision, hearing, and intellectual impairments (Lukomski, 2014; Sattler, 2002). Therefore, interviewers should ask short, concrete questions that avoid pronouns, ambiguous terms, and words with double meanings.
- *Double-check the meaning of children's answers.* Even typically developing children use words before they fully understand their meaning. For example, it is not unusual for young children to say "in" when they mean "between," and many children say "sex" before they know what sex is. Children with language and

intellectual impairments are especially likely to use language in unusual ways and to answer questions just to be cooperative. Therefore, it is important that interviewers confirm what they thought they heard children say and what answers mean. By asking children to describe actions and objects, interviewers can verify that the actions and objects they assumed are the actions and objects children intended (e.g., "What did the [child's word] look like?").

- *Give children ample time to respond.* Young children and children with disabilities that affect language and cognitive development may need more time than their peers to formulate thoughts and communicate.

In sum, developmentally neutral interviewing respects a child's age while talking in ways that help even young children understand. In this way, interviewers minimize misunderstandings regardless of a child's level of emotional, language, and cognitive development.

The Child-Specific Approach

Information from records and conversations with caregivers can help interviewers take a more child-specific approach to interview planning. For example, CARES Northwest designed this simple rubric for summarizing a child's strengths and challenges (Shelton et al., 2010):

- Does this child have a disability or difficulty with
  - Speaking, understanding, and using language?
  - Thinking and reasoning?
  - Socializing, feeling, and behaving?
  - Hearing, seeing, moving, or staying healthy?
- How does the disability affect him?
- What strengths or abilities does he have?
- What else is necessary to know about the child and the disability?
  - Are there medical or educational records available for review? For example, a child may have an Individual Education Plan (IEP) that can provide information on his strengths, weaknesses, and communication preferences.
  - Who might be available for a general consultation on this disability (e.g., the child's caseworker or an expert in the community)?
- How can the setting and questions be structured for a successful interview? (p. 4)

This chapter's Quick Guides illustrate how these basic questions can be incorporated into sheets for recording information about a child (Quick Guide 6.1) and developing an interview plan (Quick Guide 6.2). The following

Diagnoses: None. Concerns:
Educational Accommodations: None. Concerns:

Language
    Primary mode of communication: Speaking. Other:
    Home language: English. Other:
    English proficiency: Age-appropriate. Concerns:
    Problems speaking clearly: None. Concerns:
    Problems understanding speech and communicating (for age): None. Concerns:
    Can this child follow directions? Yes. Concerns:
    Can this child answer simple questions? Yes. Concerns:
    Can this child tell a story about something that happened? Yes. Concerns:
    Other language issues:

Cognition: Attending, Remembering, and Reasoning
    Attention problems (and severity): None. Concerns:
    Intellectual disability (and severity): None. Concerns:
    Autism-spectrum disorder (and severity): None. Concerns:
    Other cognitive issues:

Emotional and Behavioral Challenges
    Eye contact: Normal. Concerns:
    Verbal perseveration: None. Concerns:
    Self-abusive behavior: None. Concerns:
    Obsessions/compulsions: None. Concerns:
    Anxiety-related behavior and reactions: None. Concerns:
    Anxiety-reducing topics, activities, and comfort objects: None. Suggestions:
    Irritability, oppositional behavior, and aggression: None. Concerns:
    Other emotional/behavioral challenges:

Perception
    Hearing: Normal. Concerns:
    Vision: Normal. Concerns:
    Sensitivity to environmental stimuli (e.g., noise, bright light, crowded spaces):
        Normal. Concerns:
    Other perception issues:

Movement
    Limitations walking and adaptive devices (wheelchair, etc.): None. Concerns:
    Limitations using arms and hands: None. Concerns:
    Problems with swallowing or breathing: None. Concerns:
    Problems speaking clearly (see "Language"): None. Concerns:

Health
    Allergies (especially food allergies): None. Concerns:
    Seizure disorders/epilepsy: None. Concerns:
    Medications: None. Concerns:
    Limitations in stamina or alertness: None. Concerns:
    Other health issues:
    Other movement issues:

Other Considerations

QUICK GUIDE 6.2
Interview Plan Sheet

Child's name: _____   Age: _____

Interviewer: _____   Date: _____

1. Known conditions that may influence behavior during the interview:

   _____
   _____
   _____
   _____
   _____

2. Summary of interview-relevant strengths and challenges:

   Language:

   Cognition: Attending, remembering, and reasoning:

   Emotional and behavioral challenges:

   Perception:

   Movement:

   Health:

3. Plan for interview scheduling, the physical environment, and questioning:

---

examples illustrate some of the ways interviewers accommodate children with disabilities.[4]

Language

Primary Mode of Communication Is Not Typical Speech or Writing

Some children communicate by signing or by using a form of augmentative and alternative communication (AAC). A certified interpreter can assist

---

[4]I consulted numerous resources to assemble the information in this section. I recommend the *Oregon Interviewing Guidelines* (Oregon Department of Justice, 2012) and *Project Ability: Demystifying Disability in Child Abuse Interviewing* (Shelton et al., 2010) for more information about interviewing children with disabilities. In 2009, members of the Forensic Interview Subcommittee of Michigan's Governor's Task Force on Child Abuse and Neglect reviewed a longer draft of this section and offered suggestions, as did Dr. Sharon Bradley Johnson, cofounder of the Central Assessment Lending Library at Central Michigan University. Special thanks to Dr. Bradley Johnson and Jim Smith for their feedback.

when a witness communicates through sign. Interviewers should be aware that an interpreter will communicate anything said near the child (even a phone conversation to someone else). During one-on-one conversations, interviewers should speak to children (not interpreters) with a normal voice and pace. Because most children with hearing loss are very attentive to facial expressions and gestures, extra care is needed to avoid reinforcing particular responses with nonverbal behavior. Because of the role of expressions and gestures in signed communication, children who sign may appear especially animated when communicating.

With AAC, children express themselves in some way other than typical speech or writing, such as by using a picture board or a computer-based technology. A professional who is familiar with or developed a child's communication method is the best resource for preinterview planning. (Information obtained through facilitated communication, in which adults touch or support children's arms or hands to help them interact with a device, often reflects adults' knowledge and is not forensically defensible; American Psychological Association, 1994.)

Problems Speaking Clearly

Cerebral palsy, intellectual disability, hearing impairments, and phonological disorders are some of the conditions that produce unclear speech. Knowing the nature of a child's speech problems before an interview helps avoid misunderstandings. It is important not to guess what a child said or to finish sentences for a child who stutters.

Cognition: Attending, Remembering, and Reasoning

Attention Problems

Children with attention problems are impulsive, often fail to listen, and may skip from thought to thought, thereby creating more opportunities for interviewers to misunderstand their stories. It is easier to keep children on task when interviewers remove unnecessary distractions, use children's names and frequent topic markers to reorient them, and avoid yes/no and forced-choice questions (which permit impulsive responses).

Intellectual Disability

Because children with intellectual disability (formerly known as mental retardation) develop skills more slowly than most age-mates, their abilities to recall past events and answer questions are at the level of a younger child. Intellectual disability is associated with concrete thinking and a tendency to interpret language literally. Therefore, interviewers should avoid abstract words and props that require children to use objects (e.g., a body diagram or doll) as symbols to represent something else (e.g., themselves). (See Valenti-Hein, 2002, for examples of adults' mapping errors.)

Autism Spectrum Disorder

Children with autism spectrum disorder vary widely in language ability, social understanding, and general intellectual functioning. As a group, though, these children are concrete thinkers who have difficulty integrating multiple ideas into a concept. They also have problems understanding social cues and other people's intentions. These children may avoid eye contact, fail to shift their attention to where other people are looking, have difficulty transitioning from one activity to another, and insist on talking about topics that interest them. Some children display *echolalia*, which involves an immediate or delayed repetition of something another person said. Interviewers should not expect children with this disorder to look at them and should not assume that partial repetition of a question is a "yes" response. When working with children who *perseverate* (i.e., respond the same over and over again), interviewers should not ask a series of yes/no questions that pull for the same answer (because children might answer subsequent questions with the practiced response).

Emotional and Behavioral Challenges

Anxiety-Related Behavior and Reactions

It is useful to know whether children have difficulty separating from parents or have other fears that could make interviewing difficult. When anxiety is a concern, it is helpful to take children and their caregivers on a stroll around the facility to give them extra time with a neutral activity. Interviewers can ask in advance about topics that calm children.

Irritability, Oppositional (Antiauthority) Behavior, and Aggression

Adults who live or work with irritable, aggressive children may have information that can help with interview preparation. For example, crayons and other objects may provide opportunities for conduct-disordered children to break and throw objects.

Health

Seizure Disorders and Epilepsy

Seizure activity could be mistaken for misbehavior or inattention. For example, some seizures manifest as brief periods of staring, whereas others involve vocalizations or purposeless actions (e.g., picking at clothing). (For an overview, consult online information from the Epilepsy Foundation.)

Limitations in Stamina or Alertness

Knowing how long a child can participate in an interview helps interviewers plan what can be accomplished in a single interview. Children with vision, hearing, or motor problems often become fatigued much sooner than their peers without disabilities.

Perception

Hearing Loss

Most children with hearing impairments have losses that are unilateral (in one ear), slight or mild, or corrected by a hearing aid. Interviewers can ask whether a child's hearing is better in one ear and position chairs appropriately, but it is necessary to directly face children who rely partly on speech reading. When talking, interviewers should avoid exaggerated mouth movements (which make speech reading more difficult), use a normal voice level, and respond to children's requests to repeat a question with phrases or sentences (which are easier to comprehend than single words).

Vision Loss

To reduce the anxiety associated with severe vision loss, it is helpful to provide time for children to explore the room so they have the same information sighted children would have. To assist, the interviewer can walk around the room while describing it (e.g., "Windows are on this wall, a chair for you is here and one for me here"). During conversation, interviewers should tell children when they will be handing them something (to avoid evoking a startle) and describe what they are doing during pauses. Because some children with vision loss echo phrases or sentences they have heard but do not understand, it is important to probe ambiguous responses. Interviewers and center staff members should not pet service animals.

Sensitivity to Environmental Stimuli

Some children are more relaxed if they wait for a few minutes in a calm environment (e.g., without noise, bright light, crowded spaces) before the interview begins.

Movement

Cerebral palsy and muscular dystrophy are two of the many conditions that affect children's ability to move their bodies normally. Interviewers should be prepared to fit a wheelchair into interviewing rooms, if necessary. Children with Tourette's disorder display motor tics and/or spontaneous vocalizations, which can increase in frequency during stressful situations. Interviewers should ignore irrelevant behavior, realize that speech clarity is not a reliable indicator of children's intellectual levels, and allow adequate time for children to respond.

DEVELOPMENTAL ASSESSMENTS

In Chapter 2, I discussed why most guidelines do not include a separate phase for assessing children's developmental levels. In current models, early rapport building gives interviewers a chance to document how children respond to simple questions, and the practice narrative provides a sense of how children describe past events (which is useful for countering claims that abuse reports were sparser than expected). By front-loading interviews with practices that encourage children to talk and privileging open-ended prompts, interviewers eliminate the need to deliver many difficult questions. When interviewers adopt these best practices and avoid repeating questions, young children and those with mild to moderate intellectual disability perform quite well (D. A. Brown, Lewis, Lamb, & Stephens, 2012; Henry et al., 2011; Henry & Gudjonsson, 2003).

When there are concerns about whether a child will understand words in planned questions, the interviewer can ask the child to demonstrate knowledge. For example, two empty pencil boxes and a pencil permit the following prompts:

- Put this pencil *on top of* a box.
- Put this pencil *in* a box.
- Put this pencil *between* the boxes.
- Is there *one* box or *more than one* box? Good. Look at this. Is there *more than one* pencil or *one* pencil? (The second question tests whether the child is simply repeating the last words mentioned by the interviewer.)

Because children can pass simple requests without reliably answering similar questions about past events, there are limits to the value of such questions. Still, investigative teams can explore children's answers when doing so might shed light on an important issue. For example, the concern that a young child might have been mimicking an adult when she said that "white goo" came out of a suspect's penis could be explored by testing her knowledge of the word *white* (which is not one of the first color words children usually learn; Franklin, Clifford, Williamson, & Davies, 2005). In a similar way, a team facing an airtight alibi from a suspect because a young child said that abuse occurred "yesterday" could explore the child's use of this word. (See Grant & Suddendorf, 2011, for evidence of a prolonged time frame for mastery of *yesterday*.)

CONSENSUS ABOUT A SUPPORT PERSON IN THE INTERVIEWING ROOM

There is little evidence that children cope better with a support person in the room. For example, the presence of a parent is associated with more crying among children anticipating blood draws (Gross, Stern, Levin, Dale, & Wojnilower, 1983) and has no impact on the behavior or heart rate of children experiencing dental procedures (Afshar, Baradaran Nakhjavani, Mahmoudi-Gharaei, Paryab, & Zadhoosh, 2011). Perhaps because most child witnesses are attentive and show few emotional behaviors without a support person, eyewitness studies have also found no conclusive evidence that a companion improves the quality of children's testimony (Poole & Lamb, 1998).

There are many concerns about unwanted side effects from having a support person in the interviewing room. For example, a familiar person could inhibit children from talking about sensitive issues, such as sexual experiences or underage drinking that was encouraged by a suspect. Also, the presence of someone who had preinterview conversations with a child could trigger claims that the child merely repeated what was expected during the interview. The following guidance from the Oregon Interviewing Guidelines Workgroup (Oregon Department of Justice, 2012) summarizes consensus on the issue:

> The presence of parents, school personnel, private therapists, caretakers, or other family members in the interview room is strongly discouraged. Even supportive adults can intentionally or unintentionally coach or nonverbally cue a child, thereby contaminating the interview. There are possible exceptions to the standard of excluding a support person; these should be discussed on a case-by-case basis by the multidisciplinary team (MDT) members participating in the interview process. For example, children with disabilities or extremely traumatized children who cannot separate from a supportive caregiver may be an exception or may need additional rapport building prior to the formal forensic interview. (p. 9)

In rare cases when a companion is necessary, it is important to seat this person out of the child's sight (but within the field of view of the video recording) to avoid criticism that the child was responding to nonverbal feedback or reactions from a trusted adult. During the opening introduction, the adult and child should be warned that only the child is allowed to answer questions (e.g., "Mrs. Nelson can't talk now—this is your special time to talk").

MULTIPLE INTERVIEWS

There are many reasons why child witnesses sometimes participate in more than one interview: they were too distressed to participate fully in the first, the case is too complicated to explore in a single session, new information emerges, and evidence suggests that a witness may be concealing information (La Rooy, Katz, Malloy, & Lamb, 2010). Because children and adults alike typically recall new information across repeated retellings of an event (which is a phenomenon called *reminiscence*), investigative teams also reinterview witnesses when additional information could help solve a case. For example, in an analysis of interviews with a child who witnessed her sister's abduction, most of the unique details the child reported across six interviews were elicited during the second and subsequent interviews (Orbach, Lamb, La Rooy, & Pipe, 2012).

Whether repeated interviews are productive or problematic depends on the features of the case, including the length of time between interviews, the quality of the interviews, and the motivations of people in children's lives to influence their testimony through threats, intentional coaching, or inadvertent influences (e.g., overheard conversations). When external influence is not an issue and interviews are nonsuggestive, children's reports across repeated interviews generally contain few explicit contradictions. In the aforementioned abduction case, for example, only four of the 809 details reported in the second through sixth interviews contradicted earlier reports (Orbach et al., 2012). Additional interviews are most likely to elicit unreliable testimony when conversation occurs long after the event and witnesses are very young (Peterson, 2002), when interviewers' techniques are more suggestive than simple yes/no questions (La Rooy, Lamb, & Pipe, 2009), and when other influences have contaminated children's reports. (For discussions of how children typically report personally significant events in the absence of misleading information, see Peterson, 2002, 2011, 2012; for information about confusions among multiple instances of a repeated event, see H. L. Price, Connolly, & Gordon, 2015.)

Because of the potential benefits of another interview, research does not support a blanket prohibition against multiple interviews. The decision to reinterview a child should be made after careful consideration of possible risks and expected benefits. A second or third interview can benefit the prosecution when children do not contradict central details and new, valuable information emerges, but subsequent interviews are invaluable to the defense when these conversations document significantly changed stories, a pattern of adult influence (e.g., the infiltration of changing adult beliefs into children's reports), and expanding stories with obvious confabulations.[5]

PHYSICAL EVIDENCE

It is well known that children do not always disclose during abuse-focused interviews (for reviews, see Pipe, Lamb, Orbach, & Cederborg, 2007), and it is typical for disclosing children to report only a portion of the relevant events that occurred (Dickinson, Del Russo, & D'Urso, 2008). When attempts to raise an issue fail and physical evidence exists, some protocols permit interviewers to mention or display that evidence. Examples of physical evidence include such things as video recorders, belts, photographs of the condition of a home (in neglect cases), items of clothing, and images of the child allegedly taken by a suspect.

The decision to use physical evidence is best made by an investigative team that has carefully considered the necessity of introducing this evidence and determined whether items or images have to be sanitized (e.g., masked to cover abusive material). The State of Michigan Governor's Task Force on Child Abuse and Neglect and Department of Human Services (2011, p. 40) protocol suggested that interviewers "be up-front" early in interviews by saying something such as, "I have some pictures I may want to show you and talk about today, but first I want to get to know you better." This approach leaves open the option of showing or not showing evidence without blindsiding children later in an interview. When images depict sexually abusive activity, investigative teams should know the laws and procedures in their jurisdictions that govern who can possess this material, the required procedures for maintaining chain of custody, who is allowed to make copies of digital evidence, and whether special permissions are required before using images in interviews.

---

[5]Some children who do not disclose sexual abuse during a first interview are referred for a multi-session procedure that was initially called Extended Forensic Evaluation. Later renamed the National Children's Advocacy Center Extended Forensic Interview Protocol (National Children's Advocacy Center, 2010), this procedure begins with a focus on rapport building, developmental assessment, and other issues before transitioning to abuse exploration in later sessions (or earlier if a disclosure occurs). Although additional opportunities to disclose does increase disclosure rates (Carnes, Nelson-Gardell, Wilson, & Orgassa, 2001) and changes to the protocol have addressed some concerns (see Connell, 2009, for issues in early versions of the model), updated research is needed on the types of cases referred for multiple sessions and the interviewing practices being implemented in the field.

USING CHECKLISTS TO IMPROVE THOROUGHNESS

Each case comes packaged with a set of issues the interviewer has to address. In sexual abuse investigations, for instance, the interviewer may be expected to ask whether anyone else has touched the child inappropriately, whether the child has knowledge of other children who have been touched inappropriately, who else knows what happened, and so forth. In child protective services interviews, the interviewer may be charged to explore for all forms of abuse and ask questions that assess the impact of maltreatment on the child.

Failing to cover expected topics is a common problem that leads to a loss of corroborative evidence, testimony that is too sketchy to support a case, and a failure to protect the witness or other children affected by a dangerous situation. Policies that provide expert interviewers minimize missing information, yet there is always a risk of lack of thoroughness because our cognitive machinery is not advanced enough to juggle the information in some complex cases. Like an airplane design that is too unwieldy for pilots to manage, an interview can simply be "too much to fly."[6]

Checklists have long been used by the aviation industry to reduce pilot errors and are a familiar tool among builders, medical personnel, and many other professionals. According to famed physician Atul Gawande (2009), "Checklists seem able to defend anyone, even the experienced, against failure in many more tasks than we realized" (p. 48). When thoughtfully constructed, checklists provide a "cognitive net" that can catch errors in memory, attention, and thoroughness.

In *The Checklist Manifesto: How to Get Things Right* (2009), Gawande summarized what he learned about error prevention after the World Health Organization recruited him for an initiative to reduce preventable harm from surgery. Regardless of the purpose of a checklist, it is usually constructed with input from the professionals who will use it and developed through an iterative process of drafting, testing, and revision. According to Gawande, successful lists have four important features:

- *Brevity*. No rule fits every situation, but individual checklists typically run from five to nine items, with complex tasks broken into separate checklists for different stages of tasks and different situations. Overly long checklists distract professionals from the

---

[6]I borrowed this analogy from Atul Gawande (2009) who illustrated the problem of extreme complexity with a story about the crash of Boeing Company's Model 299 test plane in 1935. After the cause of the crash was determined to be pilot error, a newspaper reported that the equipment was "too much airplane for one man to fly" (p. 33).

task at hand and encourage them to mindlessly check off items. For maximal impact, checklists include what Daniel Boorman called "the killer items"—steps that are critically important but sometimes skipped (Gawande, 2009, p. 123).

- *Transparent wording.* The wording of checklist items should be simple, precise, and in language familiar to those who will use the list.
- *Uncluttered formatting.* Adherence is better when checklists fit on one page and are visually uncluttered (without unnecessary verbiage, colors, and graphics).
- *Links to clear pause points or event triggers.* The two types of lists—*do-confirm* (check off after you have completed a task) and *read-do* (work through list items one item at a time)— must be linked to defined pause points in the task or specific event triggers. In an interview, a pause point could be the end of a particular interview phase, whereas an event trigger could be an unexpected recantation. In other fields, checklist usage is high when professionals are trained to use them and the situations that prompt workers to consult the list have become automatic.

It is easy to link do-confirm lists to planned breaks during interviews. For example, a break after initial questioning and clarifying is a natural time to consult a hypothesis-testing plan sheet to identify unexplored issues, and before closing the interview is another natural time for a checklist review. Partly because interviewers avoid interrupting children, it is easy to forget to explore new allegations that emerge unexpectedly, but interviewers can keep track of these issues by jotting children's comments down at the top of columns that appear next to frequently overlooked checklist items (e.g., Who else may have allegedly harmed the child? How was the child affected by what happened? Are there other sources of evidence related to what happened?; State of Maine Child and Family Services, 2010, p. 50). Before closing conversation, the interviewer may realize that although the primary allegation was thoroughly explored (e.g., sexual abuse by a neighbor), a new disclosure was not. If the interviewer is charged to explore this disclosure, the checklist could prompt questions about how often this has occurred, whether the child knows someone who might be able to confirm this situation, and so forth.

The decision to use checklists should be based on need, feasibility, and with a consideration of the benefits and risks. Because checklists document what should be covered, they could promote criticism of interviewers who fail to use them effectively. On the flip side, carefully constructed checklists can promote more thorough exploration and serve as valuable training and supervision tools. Interview scripts (i.e., example dialogue), which are another strategy for alleviating the cognitive strains of interviewing, are discussed in Chapter 7.

RECAP

Professionals customize interviews when they decide which issues to explore and which interviewing strategies to use. These decisions are based on information about the dynamics of the type of case (e.g., physical abuse, sexual abuse, arson), the evidence needed to meet charging and/or documentation needs, and case features. Expert interviewers deliver the conventional content of forensic interviews in ways that accommodate children's ages, levels of cognitive ability, and temperaments.

With young witnesses, interviewers can shorten early interview phases to avoid fatiguing communicative children, extend the length of these phases for children needing more time to warm up, and drop one or more ground rules. Interview props can be helpful for assessing children's linguistic knowledge and clarifying reports, but a subset of young witnesses respond thoughtlessly with props.

A disability can affect a child witness's ability to talk about past events. Interviewers can maximize the performance of children with disabilities by adhering to best-practice standards and using information about children's strengths and challenges to design settings and questioning strategies. Comprehensive developmental assessments are rarely necessary, but interviewers can test children's understanding of critical words when doing so will test an alternative hypothesis or clarify children's intent. The presence of parents, school personnel, and other companions in the interview room is discouraged; when a support person is necessary, it is best to seat the adult on camera but out of the child's sight.

Whether repeated interviews are productive or problematic depends on the length of time between interviews, the quality of the interviews, and the potential for people in children's lives to influence their testimony. When external influence is not an issue and interviewing is nonsuggestive, children's reports across repeated interviews generally contain few explicit contradictions. Some protocols permit interviewers to mention or display physical evidence, such as a belt or photographs. As with repeated interviews, the decision to encourage more complete reports by using physical evidence should be made on a case-by-case basis. Checklists encourage thoroughness by helping interviewers catch unexplored issues before they close interviews.

PRINCIPLES TO PRACTICE: SHOULD THE CHILD BE ABLE TO ANSWER THIS QUESTION?

Psychologists and attorneys sometimes wonder whether the inability to answer seemingly simple questions is evidence of a fabricated report. Often, these professionals are aware that children typically master particular words or concepts by a certain age and are concerned because an older child floundered in the face of these words or concepts. To evaluate the significance of such trip-ups, it is important to understand developmental norms.

Example Questions About Children's Cognitive Abilities[7]

I have a case in which a 6-year-old boy said the event happened "yesterday," but the suspect has an airtight alibi for that day. I thought only younger children misunderstand that word. Is this evidence that the child's allegation was coached?

I have a case in which a 7-year-old said the abuse happened 20 times when this is implausible. Does this mean the child is simply making things up?

My Response

Authors who write about development often report the age of acquisition (AoA) of particular concepts and skills. In tables of developmental norms and research articles, AoA could be the age when 50% of children have mastered a skill, 75% have mastered a skill, or something else. Regardless of the definition used, AoA is the age when children show good—but not errorless—performance. In research articles, for example, passing three out of four trials might qualify a child as having mastered a skill. Thus, statements about skill mastery do not always mean what professionals think these statements mean. For example, William Friedman and his colleagues summarized results from a study about children's temporal reports by saying that "4-year-olds could reconstruct the time of day if the event happened 7 weeks ago" (Friedman, Reese, & Dai, 2011, p. 156). The fact that some of the nursery-school children were not 4-years-old (4 years was the average age) and only 76% passed the task did not violate conventions for summarizing results in the developmental literature.

Because AoA describes the age when most children can do something most of the time, we cannot assume that children older than a stated AoA have mastered a skill. For example, most 5-year-olds know the word *yesterday*,

---

[7]These questions are typical of ones I have been asked but do not represent any particular cases.

but in one study over 40% of parents said their 5-year-olds were not reliably using this word correctly (Grant & Suddendorf, 2011). Similarly, most 7-year-olds can count to 20 and perform simple addition, but they do not always accurately report the number of times something has happened. (My own memory of telling priests during confession that I lied and disobeyed my mother 300 to 400 times per week illustrates how children sometimes use large numbers to mean "a lot" or—as in my case—to cover their bases; Poole & Lamb, 1998, p. 161.) When analyzing transcripts, experts flag concerning comments that could have a developmental explanation, place case information on a timeline that allows them to track the context and evolution of a child's testimony, and consider what the overall picture looks like when common language and memory errors are removed from the picture.

7

PROTOCOLS AND INTERVIEWER TRAINING

The basic principles of talking to children are simple. Adults should start by introducing themselves and engaging in some relaxed chitchat. While they are becoming familiar with children's speech patterns and behavioral rhythms, they should also display a patient and engaged demeanor that conveys that this is the children's time to talk. It is useful to set expectations by explaining that interviewers do not know what has happened in the children's lives, that they are interested in things that really happened, that it is OK to say "I don't know" when answers are unknown, and that children can correct mistakes the interviewers make (although children's ages and the type of conversation will influence decisions about the need for these instructions). Using transition comments that flag topic shifts, and topic markers that make individual prompts unambiguous, interviewers can complete rapport building by steering conversation through a practice narrative before transitioning to the matters under investigation by delivering the initial open-ended

http://dx.doi.org/10.1037/14941-008
Interviewing Children: The Science of Conversation in Forensic Contexts, by D. A. Poole

topic opener. The purpose of conversation and children's reports dictate how interviewers cycle between prompts that elicit free narrative descriptions and questions requesting specific information. Throughout conversations, interviewers give children ample time to reply, use minimal encouragers to turn conversation back to the children, and try to follow focused questions with more open-ended prompts. The exact nature of this process will depend on children's ages and abilities, the purpose of conversations, and case features.

Some professionals believe this description applies only to formal investigative interviews, but nothing is further from the truth. If you have ever noticed your physician greeting you at the start of an appointment or chatting briefly about a recent news story, you know that physicians are being encouraged to get their conversational ducks in a row (Gillian & Sekeres, 2014). When helping professionals tell me that forensic interviewing is irrelevant for the type of work they do, I ask whether they introduce themselves to children or say "hi" to familiar children (they say "of course"), whether they take time to build rapport ("of course"), and whether they encourage children to talk, use developmentally appropriate questions, and confirm children's intents (rather than taking answers at face value—"of course," "of course," "of course"). Informal and repeated conversations seem different from investigative interviews on the surface, but the same principles—in modified forms—still apply.

Interview protocols are descriptions of how these conversational practices can be played out to achieve various goals. This chapter reviews some characteristics of protocols, describes some well-known protocols, and reviews the components of effective training programs and supervision.

PROTOCOL CHARACTERISTICS

Interview protocols range from short lists of basic principles to lengthy documents with information about child development and legal and procedural requirements. Although there is no taxonomy for categorizing protocols, it is helpful when faced with an unfamiliar one to ask whether it is primarily a conventional or practice-based protocol, proprietary or publicly available, less structured or highly structured, and generic or jurisdiction specific.

Conventional Versus Practice-Based Protocols

Interest in interview protocols surged in the 1980s and early 1990s when researchers studying adult and child eyewitnesses released the early protocols that inspired a generation of scholars. The protocols described later in this chapter shared core recommendations derived from basic principles of memory retrieval and social influence, such as the benefits of eliciting freely recalled narratives, following witnesses' trains of thought, and avoiding suggestive questions. Because these principles infused most subsequent protocols, I refer to guidelines inspired by psychological research—including the Memorandum of Good Practice (Home Office and the Department of Health in England and Wales, 1992), the Step-Wise Interview (Yuille, Hunter, Joffe, & Zaparniuk, 1993), the cognitive interview (Fisher & Geiselman, 1992),[1] and their descendants—as conventional protocols.

While researchers were exploring eyewitness performance in laboratory studies, front-line interviewers and clinicians were translating on-the-job experiences into their own approaches to interviewing. More so than researchers, practitioners placed high value on techniques that were easy to train and produced more disclosures. As a result, practice-based protocols were generally more supportive of direct questions and props than were conventional protocols. (For discussions of early examples, see Anderson et al., 2010, and Morgan, 1995.) Today, some guidelines from advocacy organizations occupy a middle ground by recommending the well-researched principles in conventional protocols while also permitting cautious use of techniques that have become popular among practitioners. (For histories of the protocol movement, see Faller, 2015, and Poole & Dickinson, 2013.)

Proprietary Versus Publicly Available Protocols

It is remarkable how often people ask me about interviewing approaches I have never heard of and cannot find referenced in research databases. The reason is that anyone can invent a technique, give it a name, and then offer training for a fee. When techniques are proprietary rather than publicly available, workshop attendees are sometimes required to sign confidentiality agreements to prevent unwanted dissemination (which protects the developers' financial interests). Because the scientific community does not have the information needed to test these techniques, compelling evidence for the superiority of proprietary techniques is typically sparse or nonexistent.

To promote transparency in the legal system and foster the research that improves our ability to serve children, families, and communities, it is critical for policymakers to insist that the protocols they adopt be publicly available. This recommendation does not prevent professionals or organizations from holding copyright to their research reviews and training materials, but it does send a message that interview procedures should be available for the

---

[1]Because *cognitive interview* usually appears in lower case letters rather than being flagged as a proper noun, I followed that convention here.

asking and, therefore, testable. A testable protocol is reproduced with sufficient details for research teams to recreate them in the laboratory. Overly general descriptions and frequently changing protocols do not support evidence-based practice, especially when protocol creators claim that any deviations from their current recommendations void study findings.

Less Structured Versus Highly Structured Protocols

All protocols are structured in the sense that they guide interviewers through a set of interview phases, but protocols vary widely in how much guidance they provide regarding what interviewers might actually say. Compared with less structured protocols, highly structured protocols provide scripted dialogue blocks to illustrate how interviewers might deliver instructions and word prompts. Early interview phases are especially suited for scripting because interviewers usually settle on a fixed procedure for delivering these phases. For instance, it is helpful to have a prepared script with introductions for younger and older children, prompts for opening chitchat, remarks for transitioning between phases, and instructions for conducting the practice narrative and ground rules phases.

Especially helpful are scripts that suggest ways of handling snags in conversation. For example, in my research the percentage of 5-year-olds who correctly answered the "Tell me if I say something wrong" ground rules question jumped from 50% to 81% after we added scripted dialogue to help interviewers continue instruction whenever children failed the first practice question (Dickinson, Brubacher, & Poole, 2015). Interviewers who used the less effective protocol were expected to continue instruction after wrong answers and had been trained to do so, but in the absence of a script they often became flustered and moved on prematurely.

There is no doubt that highly structured protocols improve interviewing performance and simplify training (Lamb, 2014; Lamb, Hershkowitz, Orbach, & Esplin, 2008). One reason for the popularity of less structured protocols is that interviewers tend to be deeply attached to their individual approaches to introductions, ground rules, and other specifics. In addition, there is concern that providing example dialogue will make it easier to challenge interviewers who did not adhere strictly to printed suggestions. Finally, when protocols are used for diverse purposes or by highly trained interviewers, policymakers tend to gravitate toward the flexibility of less structured approaches (Poyer, n.d.). Child advocacy centers and agencies that chose a less structured protocol can provide an outline with suggested transition comments, which makes it easier for interviewers to create customized scripts consistent with protocol guidelines, as in this excerpt of the case issues phases from the State of Maine Child and Family Services' *Fact-Finding Child Interview* (2010):

5. Explore child-directed perceptions and concerns

   "Now it's time to talk about something else." (For example, "I'm interested in how things are going for you at home, with your family, and at school.")

   The purpose of this step is to ask the child about three topics:
   (i) positive qualities of caregiving environments (strengths; e.g., "When you think about ___, what makes you happy? What do you like about living here?")
   (ii) negative qualities of caregiving environments (concerns; e.g., "What do you worry about? What do you not like about living here?")
   (iii) possible solutions for concerns; (e.g., "What would help you to worry less? If you could change something about living here, what would you change?")

   Follow three steps for each topic:
   a. Introduce the topic with an open-ended prompt.
   b. Elicit a free narrative about perceptions/concerns mentioned by the child.
   c. Ask follow-up questions to explore perceptions/concerns mentioned by the child. If the child makes an abuse allegation, test alternative hypotheses and explore for other sources of evidence (witnesses, physical, medical, etc.). Assess for impact on the child.

6. Explore interviewer-directed topics of concern (e.g., relevant checklist topics)

   "Now there are some other things I'd like to talk about."

   a. Introduce a topic of concern (e.g., sexual, physical, or emotional abuse, neglect) using the least suggestive prompts possible (e.g., "I'm here to talk with you because ___ is worried about you. What do you think s/he is worried about?"). Avoid using suggestive words like *bad*, *hurt*, *abuse*, and *wrong*.
   b. Elicit a free narrative about the first topic of concern. (e.g., Child: "I got a bruise on my face." Interviewer: "What happened to your face?" or Child: "Bill has been touching me." Interviewer: "What happened with Bill?").
   c. Ask follow-up questions to explore the first topic of concern. Test alternative hypotheses and explore for other sources of evidence (witnesses, physical, medical, etc.). Assess for impact on the child.
   d. Repeat a–c for other interviewer-directed topics.
   e. Pause to review checklists or the interview plan; identify and explore missed issues. (p. 49)

Generic Versus Jurisdiction-Specific Protocols

Because generic protocols are designed for portability across jurisdictions, these documents package interviewing advice without details about local practices. Jurisdiction-specific protocols are often longer because of content about local policies and procedures.

A BRIEF TOUR OF PROTOCOLS

The proliferation of interview protocols creates frequent confusion about how protocols relate to each other. In fact, the field is dominated by a few parent models that spawned offspring as policy groups stripped irrelevant material from jurisdiction-specific protocols, added jurisdiction-specific material to generic protocols, and combined techniques from two or more models into hybrid approaches. This tour of some well-known protocols can help professionals who are new to the field understand many of the numerous protocols currently in use.

The Memorandum of Good Practice

The Memorandum of Good Practice (Great Britain; updated as Achieving Best Evidence in Criminal Proceedings) and the Step-Wise Guidelines for Child Interviews (Canada) were motivated by legislative changes that allowed recordings of child interviews to supplement children's courtroom testimony. In Great Britain, the Criminal Justice Act of 1991 permitted courts to reject improperly conducted interviews or portions of interviews, which created pressure for a code of practice (Bull & Barnes, 1995). Responding to a request from the Home Office, Ray Bull and Di Birch drafted the Memorandum of Good Practice, which was released in 1992.[2]

Inspired by work conducted in Germany (e.g., Steller & Köhnken, 1989; Trankell, 1972; Undeutsch, 1982) and recommendations from child psychiatrist David Jones (D. P. H. Jones & McQuiston, 1988), the team adopted the phased structure of rapport building, free narrative, questioning, and closure that has organized most subsequent protocols (R. Bull, personal communication, June 15, 2011). Also influential was the notion of a question hierarchy, with open-ended questions at the top followed by specific yet nonleading questions, closed questions, and leading questions (with the recommendation to avoid leading questions). *Achieving Best Evidence in Criminal Proceedings* (Ministry of Justice, 2011), which is available online, includes

---

[2]See Bull and Davies (1996) for more information about the development process.

helpful appendices that discuss children with disabilities, suggestions for navigating ground rules, and enhanced cognitive interview techniques.

The Step-Wise Interview

Canadian researcher John Yuille developed the Step-Wise Interview (now the Step-Wise Guidelines for Child Interviews) to help interviewers elicit the high-quality narratives needed for *statement validity analysis* (Steller & Köhnken, 1989; Undeutsch, 1982), a technique that evaluates credibility by tallying characteristics typical of memory reports (Yuille, 1988). The major phases of the initial Step-Wise protocol have survived remarkably well as a general template for forensic interviews: "1. Rapport building, 2. Requesting recall of two specific events, 3. Telling the truth, 4. Introducing the topic of concern, 5. Free narrative, 6. General questions, 7. Specific questions (if necessary), 8. Interview aids (if necessary), and Concluding the interview" (Yuille, Hunter, Joffe, & Zaparniuk, 1993, p. 99).

In the late 1990s, Yuille changed the protocol's name to the Step-Wise Guidelines for Child Interviews to emphasize the goal of maintaining a flexible approach that takes children's developmental levels into account (Yuille, Cooper, & Hervé, 2009). Other changes included the option to assess linguistic concepts early in interviews, the deletion of early and extensive ground rules discussion, and a more cautious stance on anatomical dolls while incorporating a broader range of interview tools (e.g., cognitive interview techniques for preadolescents and adolescents). A field test confirmed that training in the Step-Wise Guidelines reduced the frequency of leading and suggestive questions, increased workers' satisfaction with their interviews, and improved children's and families' perceptions of the investigative process (Yuille, 1996, as cited in Yuille et al., 2009).

The Cognitive Interview

While cross-country collaborations were promoting the development of child-oriented protocols in Great Britain and Canada, an effort was under way in the United States to improve interviews with cooperative adult witnesses. Years later, cognitive psychologist Ron Fisher (2014) described how he and a colleague, Ed Geiselman, stumbled into the field of interviewing research:

> Shortly after a friend left from visiting my apartment, he called me and indicated that he couldn't find his wallet. (The idea, I assume, was that if I found the wallet, I was supposed to return it to him.) I looked for the wallet, did not find it in my apartment, and then spoke to my friend on the telephone for a few minutes. About 15 min into the conversation,

my friend remembered where he left his wallet. That was the end of the experience, and I did not think about it much, except that the experience repeated itself about 2 weeks later, this time with another friend who couldn't find her eyeglasses, but who remembered after our 15-min telephone conversation. Naturally, I wondered whether anything I had said during the telephone conversations prompted these newly-found recollections. And then I realized that I was simply incorporating into the telephone conversations the principles of memory that I was lecturing about in my Memory course. Shortly thereafter, I spoke with Ed Geiselman (who was conducting excellent research in applied cognition), and we started to consider who could use this skill of assisting other people to remember. Ed's immediate response was "police investigators," as they solve crimes mainly by eliciting information from witnesses. Ed and I then met with the head of the Behavioral Sciences Division of the Los Angeles Police Department (LAPD) to see what kind of training they provided to police investigators for interviewing cooperative witnesses. Ed and I were surprised, to say the least, when we heard that the LAPD—and almost all other police departments—provided only minimal training (closer to none) to investigators on how to interview cooperative witnesses. (pp. 615–616)

The resulting approach was a flexible set of strategies to address the social dynamics of conversations, the need for clear communication during interviews, and the cognitive realities of memory retrieval (Fisher & Geiselman, 1992; Fisher, Schreiber Compo, Rivard, & Hirn, 2014). For example, interviewers can facilitate recall by asking witnesses to mentally recreate the context of crimes and to recall events multiple times and in varied ways, such as by focusing on visual information for one recall attempt and auditory information for another.

Many studies have tested various combinations of cognitive interview techniques, with child studies sometimes dropping techniques requiring more advanced mental machinery (e.g., Memon, Holley, Wark, Bull, & Köhnken, 1996). Overall, cognitive interviews retrieve significantly more details from child and adult witnesses than structured protocols and existing practices in the field (Fisher, Brennan, & McCauley, 2002). Although some studies have found higher inaccuracy rates in child samples (Köhnken, Milne, Memon, & Bull, 1999), this is not a typical finding for modified protocols (Memon, Meissner, & Fraser, 2010), even when interviewing young children (Verkampt, Ginet, & Colomb, 2014) and children with an intellectual disability (Gentle, Milne, Powell, & Sharman, 2013; Milne, Sharman, Powell, & Mead, 2013). As with any protocol, it is best to select a package of techniques, compatible with children's abilities, that will not result in overly lengthy (and, therefore, fatiguing) interviews (Verkampt & Ginet, 2010). In recognition of the success of this approach, many child protocols include cognitive interview components or mention that cognitive interview techniques are useful interviewing tools (e.g., Ministry of Justice, 2011).

The National Institute of Child Health and Human Development Protocol

The most widely researched child interview protocol, the National Institute of Child Health and Human Development (NICHD) Investigative Interview Protocol, is continually updated to reflect new findings (consult http://www.nichdprotocol.com). This protocol took shape in the 1990s when developmental psychologist Michael Lamb and his colleagues entered into an agreement with a government agency in Israel to provide interviewing workshops in exchange for access to transcripts and case information for research (Lamb, 2014). Lamb (2014) later recalled,

> We were quite surprised and disappointed when detailed examination of the interviews conducted by the youth investigators showed that, in the main, these interviewers used few of the widely recommended practices we had described and explained at length—in particular, they asked very few open-ended questions—and they were far more likely to use the types of closed-ended questions that we had sought to discourage (Lamb et al., 1996 [Lamb, Hershkowitz, Sternberg, Esplin, et al., 1996]). The results of this first study therefore made us question the value or utility of the types of training that we had embraced and our concerns resonated with the conclusions being reached by colleagues around the world engaged in similar efforts to train interviewers and to improve the quality of investigative practice. (p. 609)

The team responded to these disappointing findings by developing a highly structured protocol and initiating a program of research to better understand the needs of child witnesses and interviewers. Consistently, studies have found that the NICHD protocol improves interviewing (Lamb et al., 2008) and produces tangible benefits in the field. For example, the richer narratives associated with protocol interviews improve credibility judgments (Hershkowitz, Fisher, Lamb, & Horowitz, 2007) and increase the likelihood of charging and convicting suspects (Pipe, Orbach, Lamb, Abbott, & Stewart, 2013).

The Ten Step Investigative Interview

Many abbreviated guidelines reflect the general structure and practices of one or more parent protocols. A well-known example comes from Thomas Lyon, a child maltreatment scholar with a dual background in psychology and law. Lyon's Ten Step Investigative Interview is an adaptation of the NICHD protocol that separates instructions into 10 topics, with example prompts that illustrate each interview phase: (a) don't know instruction, (b) don't understand instruction, (c) you're wrong instruction, (d) ignorant interviewer instruction, (e) promise to tell the truth, (f) practice narratives, (g) allegation, (h) allegation follow-up, (i) follow up with Tell Me More and What Happened Next questions, and (j) exploration of multiple incidents (Lyon, 2005). Abbreviated guidelines such as this one provide a useful overview of conventional practice, are less overwhelming for new interviewer training than longer documents, and are well suited for jurisdictions that prefer the flexibility of a less structured approach.

The Narrative Elaboration Technique

Karen Saywitz and her colleagues developed the narrative elaboration technique to help children communicate the information that makes a coherent narrative: the people involved, where events happened, what happened, and what children heard (conversations) and felt. Core features of the technique are instructions that encourage detailed reports and training that teaches children to respond to reminder cards representing the four categories of information. In an early demonstration, extensive training greatly increased the amount of information children recalled during a subsequent interview, bringing the performance of younger children (7–8 years old) to the level of older children (10–11 years old) who had not received narrative elaboration training (Saywitz & Snyder, 1996). Subsequent studies showed that briefer training also encourages more complete memory reports (Bowen & Howie, 2002; Camparo, Wagner, & Saywitz, 2001).

In an interview guide, Saywitz and Camparo (2014) embedded narrative elaboration techniques in a broader discussion of evidence-based interviewing practices. Particularly helpful are separate instructions for younger and older children, lists of suggested questions for addressing important topics during abuse investigations, and reproducible reminder cards. As with most ancillary techniques, more research is needed to determine which features of narrative elaboration contribute most to improved recall and how the technique affects the testimonies of children exposed to misleading stereotypes and misinformation.

Guidelines From Professional Organizations and Policy Committees

Practice recommendations from the parent protocols described in this chapter have been repackaged in numerous ways to produce two types of documents: guidelines from professional organizations and protocols from policy committees tasked with developing local standards of practice. Two examples of guidelines from professional organizations are *Forensic Interviewing in Cases of Suspected Child Abuse* from the American Professional Society on the Abuse of Children (2012) and the National Children's Advocacy Center Child Forensic Interview Structure (National Children's Advocacy Center, 2012). These guidelines, which continually evolve to reflect new findings, are the basis for training programs in the United States serving a national audience. Across the world, many jurisdictions have crafted practice standards by merging recommendations from one or more parent protocols with information about local procedures and legal considerations. (For examples, see Oregon Department of Justice, 2012; Scottish Government, 2011.)

INTERVIEWER TRAINING

Years ago, a humbling experience increased my appreciation for the skills involved in interviewing. Back then, we offered parents the option of coming into the laboratory for final interviews or receiving a research assistant in their homes, which decreased study attrition and maintained a diverse participant sample. After an assistant called in sick just minutes before an interview, I grabbed an interviewing kit and confidently headed out to serve as her substitute. My confidence was misplaced. I was not accustomed to walking into a stranger's home, and I was even less accustomed to setting up the recording equipment my assistants usually managed. I felt flustered as I sat on the floor to deliver a set of scripted questions to an adorable little girl, and it was only after reviewing my interview when I noticed my numerous mistakes. That day I was, quite frankly, a horrible interviewer.

How had this happened? I had lived and breathed the protocol for months. I had written it with a colleague, edited it, and trained my team to use it. I had reviewed dozens of transcripts to provide ongoing feedback to assistants, and I could easily have reproduced the entire protocol from memory. But critically, what I did not have was extensive experience actually doing interviews in novel and emotionally arousing situations.

Today, we know that expert skill develops as several forms of learning build gradually over time through repeated practice with feedback. As a laboratory manager, my experiences had been restricted to a type of learning called *explicit* learning—facts and principles I could consciously think about and articulate. What I lacked was the type of practice that builds *implicit* (nonconscious) learning—those automatic responses that are the building blocks of well-learned habits. Because I worked mainly in my laboratory, I was not conditioned to relax in novel environments, and I lacked the well-honed procedural skills in which one interviewing behavior triggers the next without thought. As a result, the slightest interruption caused me to lose my place, and I lacked the ability to move without conscious thought to one question when a child said "no" but to a different question when the child said "yes." Instead of conducting an interview the way one prepares coffee in the morning, my brain had only been programmed to move through an interview deliberately—by reading and thinking in a situation that could not be navigated by reading and thinking.

Today, the failures and successes of training programs around the world have taught us valuable lessons about kinds of experiences that advance skills on the job. Providing supportive environments where interviewers can encounter these experiences is an ongoing goal in the field of forensic interviewing.

Characteristics of Effective Training Programs

Eduardo Salas and his colleagues drew two conclusions after reviewing the research on training and development in organizations: "(a) training works, and (b) the way training is designed, delivered, and implemented matters" (Salas, Tannenbaum, Kraiger, & Smith-Jentsch, 2012, p. 74). On the basis of studies of diverse on-the-job skills, these experts penned five recommendations for initial training programs:

- *Include information, demonstration, practice, and feedback.* It is well known that informational lectures build knowledge but have little influence on what workers actually do on the job. Therefore, it is not surprising that lecture-oriented interviewer training usually has little or no impact on how professionals conduct interviews. In an early example, Amye Warren and her colleagues (1999) found no increase in the number of open-ended questions delivered by experienced interviewers after a 10-day program, and training sessions in the United Kingdom also produced disappointing results. By contrast, successful training in cognitive interview techniques included recorded examples of good and poor interviewing behaviors along with role-playing exercises involving practice and feedback. (For a review of these and other early training studies, see Powell, Fisher, & Wright, 2005.)
- *Use behavioral modeling practices to demonstrate and describe desired behaviors.* Phrasing learning points as action-oriented statements, which are called *rule codes*, often produces the best performance. For example, a trainer who just showed a video of an expert interviewer asking many open-ended questions might review the rule code "Deliver a long series of open-ended prompts." Verb-based statements (e.g., "Deliver," "Tolerate silence") clearly tell trainees what *they* should do. Training effectiveness is also increased

when trainers provide contrasting positive and negative models (rather than just positive models), provide immediate opportunities for trainees to practice skills (using some examples generated by the trainees), follow practice with feedback, and encourage trainees to set individualized goals for how they will use new skills on the job (P. J. Taylor, Russ-Eft, & Chan, 2005).

■ *Provide the cognitive challenges encountered at work.* The training conditions associated with rapid initial learning are not always those that promote skill use in the varied environments workers encounter after training (Soderstrom & Bjork, 2015). For example, it is easier to learn single skills faster when learners master one type of problem before tackling another. However, people who learn with this type of "blocked" practice often struggle after training, when real-life problems require them to use the right skills at the right times (Rohrer & Taylor, 2007). The alternative approach is to structure learning that requires people to work through diverse examples, which slows initial learning but increases people's ability to transfer skills to new situations. As Salas and his colleagues explained (2012), "Practice opportunities should require trainees to engage in the same cognitive processes they will need to engage in when they return to work. Often, that will mean designing sufficient challenge into the training" (p. 86). For interviewers, sufficient challenge could include opportunities to conduct an entire interview rather than role-playing only individual phases.

■ *Build some errors into training.* Because people learn more when they make and correct mistakes (Huelser & Metcalfe, 2012), it is helpful to construct training activities that will produce some errors. (For an example training exercise, see this chapter's Principles to Practice.) Do not, however, make training activities so difficult that interviewers rehearse bad habits.

■ *Encourage self-reflection.* To benefit fully from training, professionals have to accurately assess how their performance compares to a standard and adjust their learning strategies and behaviors when necessary. These higher level cognitions are often called *self-regulatory* processes or *metacognitions*. Simple practices that engage self-regulatory processes include asking trainees to set individual goals and asking whether they are ready for a test or role-play (Sitzmann, Bell, Kraiger, & Kanar, 2009).

Even with a well-constructed curriculum, the benefits of training are typically realized only after students return for additional training after time in the field. For example, one training team measured the performance of child protection workers and police officers before training and then delivered a 2-day program that included practice asking open-ended questions and giving children time to talk. During the next 2 months, workers submitted interviews weekly and received written feedback in addition to a telephone feedback session. The trainers then delivered a 2-day refresher course and interview feedback for 2 more months, after which they sent feedback on a by-request basis. Despite a great deal of individualized attention, significant improvement occurred only after the refresher course. As this example illustrates, it usually takes multiple learning opportunities, spaced over time, to produce durable changes in behavior (Rischke, Roberts, & Price, 2011).

Today, it is understood that initial workshops only provide a foundation for learning to occur on the job (Tannenbaum, 1997). Therefore, successful interviewer training combines well-constructed learning modules with opportunities for practice and feedback that continue for many months after introductory programs. (See Benson & Powell, 2015, for a review of interviewer training evaluations, a list of core training topics, and evidence for the efficacy of a predominantly computer-based interviewing training program.)

Technology-Based Training

When instructional content is held constant, web-based training is just as effective as classroom-based training (Salas et al., 2012). Especially promising are simulations that allow workers to practice new skills and receive feedback. For example, Sonja Brubacher and her colleagues dramatically increased teachers' use of open questions by asking them to read a short article about the characteristics of good free narrative prompts and arranging for them to repeatedly "interview" a child avatar (Brubacher, Powell, Skouteris, & Guadagno, 2015). During these online sessions, trainees selected which of four prompts to deliver for each conversational turn, the avatar responded in a typical way for that question type, and trainees received feedback about why their choice was or was not the best. In a subsequent face-to-face interview with an assistant who role-played a child, the percentage of open-ended questions increased from 13% during a baseline interview to 51% after training. Similarly, forensic interviewers experienced marked improvements from using a computer-based curriculum that provided practice and feedback (Benson & Powell, 2015; see also Pompedda, Zappalà, & Santtila, 2015).

Ongoing Supervision and Feedback

It is easier to become an effective learning coach when you understand the nature of expertise, how learning unfolds over time, and the characteristics of effective performance feedback. Collectively, this information helps supervisors understand why novice interviewers make errors, why learning is usually slow, and how to craft feedback that promotes skill development.

It is self-evident that experts have a large storehouse of task-specific knowledge, but they also differ from novices in the following ways (Donovan, Bransford, & Pellegrino, 2015):

- *Expert knowledge is organized in terms of "big ideas" or concepts.* Instead of paying attention to unimportant details, experts have conceptual understanding that focuses their attention on critical information. For example, novice interviewers often think of forensic interviewing in terms of fixed questions or interview phases, whereas experts think in terms of the overarching goals of an interview, such as the need to assess for safety. As a result, expert interviewers are more likely than novices to respond flexibly when unexpected information emerges during interviews.
- *Expert knowledge is conditionalized.* More so than novices, experts know when specific knowledge is relevant and when it is not. Because expert interviewers do not have to mentally search through everything they have learned to find necessary information, they are more likely than novices to ask good questions.
- *Experts retrieve relevant information quickly, with little effort.* Once good interviewing habits are deeply engrained, the mental resources needed to deliver basic instructions decreases. As a result, expert interviewers are more likely than novices to react productively to changes in children's behavior and to realize when answers are potentially ambiguous.
- *Experts notice meaningful patterns.* Because expert knowledge is well organized and easy to retrieve, experienced professionals perceive details and patterns that nonexperts miss. For example, an expert interviewer would notice that a child becomes upset when discussing a particular individual or uses words that are atypical for the child's age. As a result of observing such things, expert interviewers are more likely to explore concerns their nonexpert peers fail to notice.

This brief compendium of the expert mind explains why initial workshops cannot produce skilled interviewers: It takes repeated experiences and feedback before knowledge has the efficient organization that supports skilled perception and action.

This journey toward expertise is best described as "slow and hard" (Fischer, Schwartz, & Connell, 2004, p. 1). Newly acquired knowledge is often inert, which means that workers tend not to use new knowledge when relevant situations arise (Renkl, Mandl, & Gruber, 1996). For example, an interviewer could know it is best to follow a generically worded response (e.g., "Grandpa keeps touching me") with a generically worded follow-up prompt (e.g., "Tell me what Grandpa does") yet repeatedly fail to use generic prompts. It might take repeated feedback and practice before generically worded prompts are so strongly associated with relevant interview situations that these prompts come readily to mind.

Another reason learning is slow and hard is that there is no delete button to erase old ways of performing a task from memory. Because old strategies continually compete with new strategies, less desirable habits periodically reappear (Siegler, 2006). With experience and feedback, the proportion of time interviewers use a new strategy will gradually increase, but improvement is not always evident over short periods of time. Instead, learning trajectories are irregular while people are mastering new skills, with periods of improvement punctuated by collapses of skill as knowledge expands and reorganizes (Fischer & Bidell, 2006). By helping interviewers understand that new knowledge is not put to use fresh out of the training gate, that performance will fluctuate over time, and that skills often collapse in new contexts, supervisors establish supportive learning environments that help interviewers set realistic goals, stay motivated, and plan strategies for improving.

Armed with a realistic view of the learning process, interviewers and supervisors can meet periodically to engage in a powerful development process: reviewing an interview to discuss "what went well and where improvement is possible" through a process called *debriefing* (Salas et al., 2012, p. 90). Debriefing sessions have the most impact on skill when trainees' professional environments celebrate learning, instill confidence that everyone can learn, and point out how skill improvement benefits workers. It is best if the instructional objectives of post-training feedback are based on information about which performance gaps most affect case outcomes, and these will differ depending on workers' levels of experience and the nature of their jobs. To illustrate, Quick Guide 7.1 lists a set of objectives for evaluating interviewers' conversational habits, and similar lists can describe key goals for delivering conventional content and engaging in case-specific exploration.

After defining a set of learning objectives, supervisors should establish a format for feedback sessions that is consistent with evidence-based practice. Central to feedback intervention theory is the notion that the cues embedded in feedback direct workers' attention to one of three levels of cognition that regulate task performance: a level higher than the task itself (involving concepts of the self), an intermediate level (involving motivations to engage in the task), and a lower level (focusing on details of performing the task; Kluger & DeNisi, 1996, 1998). Although workers usually attend at the intermediate level, the nature of feedback can shift their attention to a higher or

QUICK GUIDE 7.1
Learning Points for Training Exercises and Feedback Sessions:
Conversational Habits

Tables of learning points, like this example for conversational habits, can guide interview critiques. During training workshops, audience members can observe interviews and take notes to prepare for group discussion. For feedback sessions, supervisors can develop separate lists that address their development goals for novice versus experienced interviewers.

	Interview examples	
Standard	Met the standard	Missed opportunities
Act relaxed and friendly. Ignore behavior that is not impeding the interview.		
Use still-your-turn feedback. Show interest and turn conversation back to the child with comments such as "OK" or by repeating part of what the child said.		
Give the child adequate time to think and add more.		
Privilege open-ended prompts. Deliver a series of open-ended prompts and continually cycle back to open-ended prompts after asking focused questions.		
Use topic shifters and topic markers. Use transition statements before changing topics (e.g., "I'm going to ask about something different now") and repeat the names of people/ actions in questions.		
Use developmentally appropriate language. Use age-appropriate words and simple questions. Ask one question at a time.		

lower level. Cues that direct attention to the self—even when this feedback is praise—often reduce feedback effectiveness. Alternatively, effective feedback shifts attention to the learning process, helps workers perceive discrepancies between standards and current levels of performance, conveys concrete strategies for how to improve, presents information in manageable units that are not overwhelming, and encourages workers to generate solutions and solve problems (rather than passively providing solutions; see Shute, 2008, for useful summaries of feedback dos and don'ts). The following debriefing template illustrates one way of incorporating these findings into practice:

- *Introduce the case.* Start by asking the interviewer to talk about the challenges of this particular child or case. This process focuses discussion on ways to overcome challenges rather than on limitations in interviewing skill.

- *Identify two behaviors that meet standards.* The interviewer and the supervisor (or peer) each nominates a strength of this interview, which is a behavior the interviewer should continue or could do more often. For each nomination, it is best to score a short section of the interview to compare behavior against the standard. For example, timing a few delays between child responses and interviewer's speech will show typical pause lengths. This verification process provides opportunities to revise overly optimistic perceptions and correct misunderstandings about the meaning of a standard.

- *Identify one or two opportunities for improvement.* The interviewer and the supervisor (or peer) each nominates a challenge that arose during the interview or a skill that could be refined with practice. The pair then discusses how the challenge could have been handled and how the skill could be practiced in daily conversations or through other strategies (e.g., online simulations). During early feedback sessions, it is best to select skills that improve rapidly because early improvement rates predict investment in the feedback process (Salas et al., 2012).

Effective debriefs are associated with large performance gains in military teams, and developmentally focused performance reviews are playing an increasing role in other fields, including public safety and health care (Salas et al., 2012). In the field of forensic interviewing, four pillars support skilled performance: a protocol that sets clear performance standards, mandatory training for new interviewers, periodic refresher training, and ongoing performance feedback focusing on well-defined interviewing skills.

EMBRACING CHANGE: MATT'S STORY

I started this book by introducing Matt Sonders, a police officer who trains law enforcement personnel to respond when active shooters threaten lives. As in many fields, expert responding in Matt's world involves an orchestrated set of behaviors that are strikingly different from how people naturally react. As our interview continued, Matt talked about his experiences as a trainer, where new guidelines come from, and the importance of staying open to change.

Poole: Your students participate in realistic simulations. Why is this so important?

Sonders: You can't train one way and then say, "But if this was an actual gun fight then do this." Under pressure, people will do what they did in training. We call it muscle memory or, when something goes wrong, training scars.

Poole: Do you get any resistance when teaching new approaches?

Sonders: There is a lot of it. An example is something as simple as how you hold your firearm. If you are moving through a building, we often train to carry our weapons in the "low ready position." Well, the old low ready position was always here—arms extended out but down, locked at the elbows, and this was how you walked around, ready to engage a target. The idea was that all you had to do to engage a target is bring the gun up quickly.

Then we started training with guys from Special Forces, and these guys didn't do that—they were holding their pistols close to their chest and down like this. So now we don't project pistols out where someone can grab them if we are cornering. If you're in a stack with a firearm extended, you may end up pointing your gun at an officer in front of you; if you are facing sideways, you may not be squared off to your target. So the new way is optimal. I have control.

Poole: When you first tell someone about that, don't they say, "Oh, yeah, that makes sense . . . that's what I should be doing"?

Sonders: The guys who do it the old way say, "That's nonsense. If I have to shoot someone I want to be able to raise my weapon quickly and shoot them." But the difference in time is negligible. The new way builds in a fraction of a second of additional time, but that time can be used to make a decision about whether you are making a good shoot.

Poole: Do you have experienced people who continue to position weapons the old way, even after training?

Sonders: Yes, they flat out refuse. They say, "I'm not going to be not ready to shoot." [But] the new way is not not ready to shoot. It is ready to shoot. It's just better.

Poole: What do officers say to you after they train and see other people having more success than they are having?

Sonders: That's usually what it takes to change their tactics.

Poole: People used older techniques for a long time before they figured out that something else was going to work better. What did it take to finally change guidelines?

Sonders: People coming back from the military—Special Forces, Marine units doing this on a daily basis, and the statistics-driven results from analyzing combat situations overseas. Also, a lot of raids and police shootings are captured on in-car dash cam videos now, where you can see the results. We also train more with simulated munitions, and that gives us an opportunity to test—outside of actual combat—how people tend to react because there is a pain penalty involved. On our SWAT team, if we are going to change any techniques, we get a house, we get training ammunition, and we try it and see how it works.[3] Approaches are constantly evolving.

Poole: What are the characteristics of people who perform better in training than their peers?

Sonders: The only thing I've seen is that the people from departments that train regularly usually perform best. It's a skill . . . it's perishable.

As I said goodbye to Matt, I marveled at the similarity of our experiences: how information about what works and does not work floods in from multiple sources, the pattern of guideline revisions followed by initial resistance, and the challenges of developing enduring behaviors that are highly automatic yet flexible. Regardless of our backgrounds and day-to-day challenges, today our professional worlds are worlds of constant change.

RECAP

Four pillars support skilled interviewing of children: a protocol that guides practice, mandatory training for new interviewers, periodic refresher training, and ongoing performance feedback. Interview protocols describe standards for directing interviews from opening introductions through interview closure. Laboratory research on memory and cognition, augmented by practitioners' experiences, inspired current protocols, which can be proprietary or publicly available, less structured or highly structured, and generic or jurisdiction specific. A handful of protocols, including the Memorandum of Good Practice (now Achieving Best Evidence), the Step-Wise Interview (now the Step-Wise Guidelines for Child Interviews), the cognitive interview, and the NICHD Investigative Interview Protocol, inspired many of the other protocols currently in use.

Regardless of whether training occurs in person or is technology-based, effective programs (a) include information, demonstration, practice, and

---

[3]Matt also pointed out how the techniques chosen for training depend on context. For example, techniques that work well in one context may not work well in another, and easy-to-learn but nonoptimal techniques may work better if superior techniques require too many training hours for professionals to become proficient.

feedback; (b) use behavioral modeling practices by phrasing learning points as action-oriented statements (rule codes), modeling desired behaviors, providing immediate opportunities for practice and feedback, and encouraging trainees to set individualized goals; (c) provide the cognitive challenges encountered at work; (d) build some errors into training; and (e) encourage self-reflection. Successful interviewer training combines learning modules with opportunities for practice and feedback that continue for many months after introductory programs.

Learning is slow because new knowledge is often inert, old strategies compete with new strategies, and performance collapses periodically. A powerful learning activity is debriefing, which is the process of reviewing a work example to discuss strengths and opportunities for improvement. Supervisors increase the effectiveness of feedback sessions when they keep attention on the learning process, help workers perceive discrepancies between standards and current levels of performance, convey concrete strategies for how to improve, present information in manageable units that are not overwhelming, and encourage workers to generate solutions and solve problems. Because practice standards continually evolve, training and development opportunities should be part of the fabric of interviewers' professional lives.

PRINCIPLES TO PRACTICE: HOW CAN I ENCOURAGE WORKERS TO EXPLORE NARRATIVES MORE FULLY?

Supervisors and trainers sometimes struggle to address gaps in workers' interviewing skills. This query targets a difficult interview phase: questioning and clarifying.

Question From a Department of Human Services Training Manager

On the basis of what we are seeing in reports, my staff is struggling with the questioning and clarifying part of the protocol. They seem to especially struggle with allowing the time to clarify the child's comments and seek legally relevant information. Do you have any suggestions?

My Response

Interviewers will be less likely to skip important topics if there is a short break in every interview when they pause to complete a checklist of needed information. But even with a checklist, interviewers need practice making decisions under pressure. To help develop this skill, in my laboratory the last experience new interviewers have before practicing with children is role plays, which we call *throwing*, in which assistants posing as children try to derail trainees by delivering unexpected answers and generally acting uncooperatively. At first the trainees become flustered, lose their places, and fail to act in ways that conform to the principles guiding each interview phase. Eventually they gain confidence and can keep overarching goals in mind to flexibly work through difficulties. Trainees greatly enjoy these exercises, perhaps because the process is fun, builds deep understanding of the rationale behind each interview phase, and dramatically increases their confidence in their ability to handle whatever situations might arise after training.

REFERENCES

Afshar, H., Baradaran Nakhjavani, Y., Mahmoudi-Gharaei, J., Paryab, M., & Zadhoosh, S. (2011). The effect of parental presence on the 5-year-old children's anxiety and cooperative behavior in the first and second dental visit. *Iranian Journal of Pediatrics, 21,* 193–200.

Almerigogna, J., Ost, J., Akehurst, L., & Fluck, M. (2008). How interviewers' non-verbal behaviors can affect children's perceptions and suggestibility. *Journal of Experimental Child Psychology, 100,* 17–39. http://dx.doi.org/10.1016/j.jecp.2008.01.006

Almerigogna, J., Ost, J., Bull, R., & Akehurst, L. (2007). A state of high anxiety: How nonsupportive interviewers can increase the suggestibility of child witnesses. *Applied Cognitive Psychology, 21,* 963–974. http://dx.doi.org/10.1002/acp.1311

American Professional Society on the Abuse of Children. (2012). *Practice guidelines: Forensic interviewing in cases of suspected child abuse.* Chicago, IL: Author.

American Psychiatric Association. (2013). *Diagnostic and statistical manual of mental disorders* (5th ed.). Washington, DC: Author.

American Psychological Association. (1994). *Resolution on facilitated communication.* Retrieved from http://www.apa.org/about/policy/chapter-11.aspx

Anderson, J., Ellefson, J., Lashley, J., Miller, A. L., Olinger, S., Russell, A., . . . Weigman, J. (2010). The CornerHouse forensic interview protocol: RATAC®. *Thomas M. Cooley Journal of Practical and Clinical Law, 12,* 193–331.

Andrews, S. J., & Lamb, M. E. (2014). The effects of age and delay on responses to repeated questions in forensic interviews with children alleging sexual abuse. *Law and Human Behavior, 38,* 171–180. http://dx.doi.org/10.1037/lhb0000064

Andrews, S. J., Lamb, M. E., & Lyon, T. D. (2015). Question types, responsiveness, and self-contradictions when prosecutors and defense attorneys question alleged victims of child sexual abuse. *Applied Cognitive Psychology, 29,* 253–261. http://dx.doi.org/10.1002/acp.3103

APA Presidential Task Force on Evidence-Based Practice. (2006). Evidence-based practice in psychology. *American Psychologist, 61,* 271–285. http://dx.doi.org/10.1037/0003-066X.61.4.271

Argyle, M. (1986). Rules for social relationships in four cultures. *Australian Journal of Psychology, 38,* 309–318. http://dx.doi.org/10.1080/00049538608259017

Bakoyiannis, I., Gkioka, E., Pergialiotis, V., Mastroleon, I., Prodromidou, A., Vlachos, G. D., & Perrea, D. (2014). Fetal alcohol spectrum disorders and cognitive functions of young children. *Reviews in the Neurosciences, 25,* 631–639. http://dx.doi.org/10.1515/revneuro-2014-0029

Beall, P. M., Moody, E. J., McIntosh, D. N., Hepburn, S. L., & Reed, C. L. (2008). Rapid facial reactions to emotional facial expressions in typically developing

191

children and children with autism spectrum disorder. *Journal of Experimental Child Psychology, 101*, 206–223. http://dx.doi.org/10.1016/j.jecp.2008.04.004

Bello, A., Sparaci, L., Stefanini, S., Boria, S., Volterra, V., & Rizzolatti, G. (2014). A developmental study on children's capacity to ascribe goals and intentions to others. *Developmental Psychology, 50*, 504–513. http://dx.doi.org/10.1037/a0033375

Benson, M. S., & Powell, M. B. (2015). Evaluation of a comprehensive interactive training system for investigative interviewers of children. *Psychology, Public Policy, and Law, 21*, 309–322. http://dx.doi.org/10.1037/law0000052

Berliner, L., & Barbieri, M. K. (1984). The testimony of the child victim of sexual assault. *Journal of Social Issues, 40*, 125–137. http://dx.doi.org/10.1111/j.1540-4560.1984.tb01097.x

Bishop, G., Spence, S. H., & McDonald, C. (2003). Can parents and teachers provide a reliable and valid report of behavioral inhibition? *Child Development, 74*, 1899–1917. http://dx.doi.org/10.1046/j.1467-8624.2003.00645.x

Bjorklund, D. F. (2007). *Why youth is not wasted on the young: Immaturity in human development.* Malden, MA: Wiley-Blackwell.

Borsutzky, S., Fujiwara, E., Brand, M., & Markowitsch, H. J. (2008). Confabulations in alcoholic Korsakoff patients. *Neuropsychologia, 46*, 3133–3143. http://dx.doi.org/10.1016/j.neuropsychologia.2008.07.005

Bottoms, B. L., Quas, J. A., & Davis, S. L. (2007). The influence of the interviewer-provided social support on children's suggestibility, memory, and disclosures. In M.-E. Pipe, M. E. Lamb, Y. Orbach, & A.-C. Cederborg (Eds.), *Child sexual abuse: Disclosure, delay, and denial* (pp. 135–157). New York, NY: Routledge.

Bouquard, T. L. (2004). *Arson investigation: The step-by-step procedure* (2nd ed.). Springfield, IL: Charles C Thomas.

Bowen, C. J., & Howie, P. M. (2002). Context and cue cards in young children's testimony: A comparison of brief narrative elaboration and context reinstatement. *Journal of Applied Psychology, 87*, 1077–1085.

Broaders, S. C., & Goldin-Meadow, S. (2010). Truth is at hand: How gesture adds information during investigative interviews. *Psychological Science, 21*, 623–628. http://dx.doi.org/10.1177/0956797610366082

Brown, D. A. (2011). The use of supplementary techniques in forensic interviews with children. In M. E. Lab, D. J. La Rooy, L. C. Malloy, & C. Katz (Eds.), *Children's testimony: A handbook of psychological research and forensic practice* (2nd ed., pp. 217–249). http://dx.doi.org/10.1002/9781119998495.ch12

Brown, D. A., Lamb, M. E., Lewis, C., Pipe, M.-E., Orbach, Y., & Wolfman, M. (2013). The NICHD Investigative Interview Protocol: An analogue study. *Journal of Experimental Psychology: Applied, 19*, 367–382. http://dx.doi.org/10.1037/a0035143

Brown, D. A., Lewis, C. N., Lamb, M. E., & Stephens, E. (2012). The influences of delay and severity of intellectual disability on event memory in children. *Journal of Consulting and Clinical Psychology, 80,* 829–841. http://dx.doi.org/10.1037/a0029388

Brown, L. (2015). *Identity-first language.* Retrieved from Autistic Self Advocacy Network website: http://autisticadvocacy.org/home/about-asan/identity-first-language/

Brubacher, S. P., & La Rooy, D. J. (2014). Witness recall across repeated interviews in a case of repeated abuse. *Child Abuse & Neglect, 38,* 202–211. http://dx.doi.org/10.1016/j.chiabu.2013.06.010

Brubacher, S. P., Malloy, L. C., Lamb, M. E., & Roberts, K. P. (2013). How do interviewers and children discuss individual occurrences of alleged repeated abuse in forensic interviews? *Applied Cognitive Psychology, 27,* 443–450. http://dx.doi.org/10.1002/acp.2920

Brubacher, S. P., Poole, D. A., & Dickinson, J. J. (2015). The use of ground rules in investigative interviews with children: A synthesis and call for research. *Developmental Review, 36,* 15–33. http://dx.doi.org/10.1016/j.dr.2015.01.001

Brubacher, S. P., Powell, M. B., & Roberts, K. P. (2014). Recommendations for interviewing children about repeated experiences. *Psychology, Public Policy, and Law, 20,* 325–335. http://dx.doi.org/10.1037/law0000011

Brubacher, S. P., Powell, M. B., Skouteris, H., & Guadagno, B. (2014). An investigation of the question-types teachers use to elicit information from children. *The Australian Educational and Developmental Psychologist, 31,* 125–140. http://dx.doi.org/10.1017/edp.2014.5

Brubacher, S. P., Powell, M. B., Skouteris, H., & Guadagno, B. (2015). The effects of e-simulation interview training on teachers' use of open-ended questions. *Child Abuse & Neglect, 43,* 95–103. http://dx.doi.org/10.1016/j.chiabu.2015.02.004

Brubacher, S. P., Roberts, K. P., & Powell, M. B. (2011). Effects of practicing episodic versus scripted recall on children's subsequent narratives of a repeated event. *Psychology, Public Policy, and Law, 17,* 286–314. http://dx.doi.org/10.1037/a0022793

Brubacher, S. P., Roberts, K. P., & Powell, M. B. (2012). Retrieval of episodic versus generic information: Does the order of recall affect the amount and accuracy of details reported by children about repeated events? *Developmental Psychology, 48,* 111–122. http://dx.doi.org/10.1037/a0025864

Bruck, M., Ceci, S. J., & Francoeur, E. (1999). The accuracy of mothers' memories of conversations with their preschool children. *Journal of Experimental Psychology: Applied, 5,* 89–106. http://dx.doi.org/10.1037/1076-898X.5.1.89

Bruck, M., Kelley, K., & Poole, D. (in press). Children's reports of body touching in medical examinations: The benefits and risks of using body diagrams. *Psychology, Public Policy, & Law.*

Bruck, M., Melnyk, L., & Ceci, S. J. (2000). Draw it again Sam: The effect of drawing on children's suggestibility and source monitoring ability. *Journal of Experimental Child Psychology, 77,* 169–196. http://dx.doi.org/10.1006/jecp.1999.2560

Buda, M., Fornito, A., Bergström, Z. M., & Simons, J. S. (2011). A specific brain structural basis for individual differences in reality monitoring. *The Journal of Neuroscience, 31*, 14308–14313. http://dx.doi.org/10.1523/JNEUROSCI. 3595-11.2011

Bull, R., & Barnes, P. (1995). Children as witnesses. In D. Bancroft & R. Carr (Eds.), *Influencing children's development* (pp. 116–149). Oxford, England: Blackwell.

Bull, R., & Davies, G. (1996). The effect of child witness research on legislation in Great Britain. In B. L. Bottoms & G. S. Goodman (Eds.), *International perspectives on child abuse and children's testimony: Psychological research and law* (pp. 96–113). Thousand Oaks, CA: Sage.

Burrows, K. S., & Powell, M. B. (2014). Prosecutor's perspectives on clarifying terms for genitalia in child sexual abuse interviews. *Australian Psychologist, 49*, 297–304. http://dx.doi.org/10.1111/ap.12068

Butler, S., Gross, J., & Hayne, H. (1995). The effect of drawing on memory performance in young children. *Developmental Psychology, 31*, 597–608. http://dx.doi.org/10.1037/0012-1649.31.4.597

Camparo, L. B., Wagner, J. T., & Saywitz, K. J. (2001). Interviewing children about real and fictitious events: Revisiting the narrative elaboration procedure. *Law and Human Behavior, 25*, 63–80. http://dx.doi.org/10.1023/A:1005691926064

Cantlon, J., Payne, G., & Erbaugh, C. (1996). Outcome-based practice: Disclosure rates of child sexual abuse comparing allegation blind and allegation informed structured interviews. *Child Abuse & Neglect, 20*, 1113–1120. http://dx.doi.org/10.1016/0145-2134(96)00100-7

Carnes, C. N., Nelson-Gardell, D., Wilson, C., & Orgassa, U. C. (2001). Extended forensic evaluation when sexual abuse is suspected: A multisite field study. *Child Maltreatment, 6*, 230–242. http://dx.doi.org/10.1177/1077559501006003004

Carter, C. A., Bottoms, B. L., & Levine, M. (1996). Linguistic and socioemotional influences on the accuracy of children's reports. *Law and Human Behavior, 20*, 335–358. http://dx.doi.org/10.1007/BF01499027

Ceci, S. J., & Bruck, M. (1995). *Jeopardy in the courtroom: A scientific analysis of children's testimony.* http://dx.doi.org/10.1037/10180-000

Ceci, S. J., Kulkofsky, S., Klemfuss, J. Z., Sweeney, C. D., & Bruck, M. (2007). Unwarranted assumptions about children's testimonial accuracy. *Annual Review of Clinical Psychology, 3*, 311–328. http://dx.doi.org/10.1146/annurev.clinpsy.3.022806.091354

Centers for Disease Control and Prevention. (2013). *Developmental disabilities.* Retrieved from http://www.cdc.gov/ncbddd/developmentaldisabilities/index.html

Chapman, L. J., & Chapman, J. P. (1967). Genesis of popular but erroneous psychodiagnostic observations. *Journal of Abnormal Psychology, 72*, 193–204. http://dx.doi.org/10.1037/h0024670

Child Advocacy Center. (2014). *Forensic interviews.* Retrieved from http://www.smvoices.org/what_we_do/forensic_interviews.html

Churchland, P. S. (2008). The impact of neuroscience on philosophy. *Neuron, 60,* 409–411. http://dx.doi.org/10.1016/j.neuron.2008.10.023

Ciaramelli, E., Ghetti, S., & Borsotti, M. (2009). Divided attention during retrieval suppresses false recognition in confabulation. *Cortex, 45,* 141–153. http://dx.doi.org/10.1016/j.cortex.2007.10.006

Clark, C. R. (2009). Professional roles: Key to accuracy and effectiveness. In K. Kuehnle & M. Connell (Eds.), *The evaluation of child sexual abuse allegations: A comprehensive guide to assessment and testimony* (pp. 69–79). Hoboken, NJ: Wiley.

Connell, M. (2009). The extended forensic evaluation. In K. Kuehnle & M. Connell (Eds.), *The evaluation of child sexual abuse allegations: A comprehensive guide to assessment and testimony* (pp. 451–487). Hoboken, NJ: Wiley.

Connolly, D. A., & Gordon, H. M. (2014). Can order of general and specific memory prompts help children to recall an instance of a repeated event that was different from the others? *Psychology, Crime & Law, 20,* 852–864. http://dx.doi.org/10.1080/1068316X.2014.885969

Connolly, D. A., Hockley, W. E., & Pratt, M. W. (1996). A developmental evaluation of frequency memory for actions presented in lists, scripts, and stories. *Memory, 4,* 243–264. http://dx.doi.org/10.1080/096582196388942

Connolly, D. A., Price, H. L., & Gordon, H. M. (2009). Judging the credibility of historic child sexual abuse complainants: How judges describe their decisions. *Psychology, Public Policy, and Law, 15,* 102–123. http://dx.doi.org/10.1037/a0015339

Connolly, D. A., Price, H. L., & Gordon, H. M. (2010). Judicial decision making in timely and delayed prosecutions of child sexual abuse in Canada: A study of honesty and cognitive ability in assessments of credibility. *Psychology, Public Policy, and Law, 16,* 177–199. http://dx.doi.org/10.1037/a0019050

Connolly, D. A., Price, H. L., Lavoie, J. A., & Gordon, H. M. (2008). Perceptions and predictors of children's credibility of a unique event and an instance of a repeated event. *Law and Human Behavior, 32,* 92–112. http://dx.doi.org/10.1007/s10979-006-9083-3

Cowan, N. (2010). The magical mystery four: How is working memory capacity limited, and why? *Current Directions in Psychological Science, 19,* 51–57. http://dx.doi.org/10.1177/0963721409359277

Cross, T. P., Whitcomb, D., & De Vos, E. (1995). Criminal justice outcomes of prosecution of child sexual abuse: A case flow analysis. *Child Abuse & Neglect, 19,* 1431–1442. http://dx.doi.org/10.1016/0145-2134(95)00106-2

Danby, M. C., Brubacher, S. P., Sharman, S. J., & Powell, M. B. (2015). The effects of practice on children's ability to apply ground rules in a narrative interview. *Behavioral Sciences & the Law, 33,* 446–458. http://dx.doi.org/10.1002/bsl.2194

Davies, G. M., Wilson, C., Mitchell, R., & Milsom, J. (1995). *Videotaping children's evidence: An evaluation.* London, England: Home Office.

Davis, S. L., & Bottoms, B. L. (2002). Effects of social support on children's eyewitness reports: A test of the underlying mechanism. *Law and Human Behavior, 26,* 185–215. http://dx.doi.org/10.1023/A:1014692009941

DeLoache, J. S. (2000). Dual representation and young children's use of scale models. *Child Development, 71,* 329–338. http://dx.doi.org/10.1111/1467-8624.00148

DeLoache, J. S. (2005). Mindful of symbols. *Scientific American, 293,* 72–77. http://dx.doi.org/10.1038/scientificamerican0805-72

Dent, H. (1982). The effects of interviewing strategies on the results of interviews with child witnesses. In A. Trankell (Ed.), *Reconstructing the past: The role of psychologists in criminal trials* (pp. 278–297). Deventer, Netherlands: Kluwer.

de Villiers, J. G., & de Villiers, P. A. (1978). *Language acquisition.* Cambridge, MA: Harvard University Press.

Dickinson, J. J., Brubacher, S. P., & Poole, D. A. (2015). Children's performance on ground rules questions: Implications for forensic interviewing. *Law and Human Behavior, 39,* 87–97. http://dx.doi.org/10.1037/lhb0000119

Dickinson, J. J., Del Russo, J. A., & D'Urso, A. (2008, March). *Children's disclosure of sex abuse: A new approach to answering elusive questions.* Paper presented at the annual conference of the American Psychology and Law Society, Jacksonville, FL.

Dilalla, L. F., Kagan, J., & Reznick, J. S. (1994). Genetic etiology of behavioral inhibition among 2-year-old children. *Infant Behavior and Development, 17,* 405–412. http://dx.doi.org/10.1016/0163-6383(94)90032-9

Dodge, K. A. (1983). Behavioral antecedents of peer social status. *Child Development, 54,* 1386–1399. http://dx.doi.org/10.2307/1129802

Donovan, M. S., Bransford, J. D., & Pellegrino, J. W. (Eds.). (2015). *How people learn: Brain, mind, experience, and school.* Washington, DC: National Academies Press.

Drummey, A. B., & Newcombe, N. S. (2002). Developmental changes in source memory. *Developmental Science, 5,* 502–513. http://dx.doi.org/10.1111/1467-7687.00243

DuPre, D. P., & Sites, J. (2015). *Child abuse investigation field guide.* Oxford, England: Elsevier.

Erskine, A., Markham, R., & Howie, P. (2001). Children's script-based inferences: Implications for eyewitness testimony. *Cognitive Development, 16,* 871–887. http://dx.doi.org/10.1016/S0885-2014(01)00068-5

Evans, A. D., Lee, K., & Lyon, T. D. (2009). Complex questions asked by defense lawyers but not prosecutors predicts convictions in child abuse trials. *Law and Human Behavior, 33,* 258–264. http://dx.doi.org/10.1007/s10979-008-9148-6

Evans, A. D., & Roberts, K. P. (2009). The effects of different paraphrasing styles on the quality of reports from young child witnesses. *Psychology, Crime & Law, 15,* 531–546. http://dx.doi.org/10.1080/10683160802385398

Evans, A. D., Roberts, K. P., Price, H. L., & Stefek, C. P. (2010). The use of paraphrasing in investigative interviews. *Child Abuse & Neglect, 34,* 585–592. http://dx.doi.org/10.1016/j.chiabu.2010.01.008

Evans, A. D., Stolzenberg, S. N., Lee, K., & Lyon, T. D. (2014). Young children's difficulty with indirect speech acts: Implications for questioning child witnesses. *Behavioral Sciences & the Law, 32,* 775–788. http://dx.doi.org/10.1002/bsl.2142

Evarts, B. (2011, November). *Children playing with fire*. Retrieved from National Fire Protection Association website: http://www.nfpa.org/research/reports-and-statistics/fire-causes/arson-and-juvenile-firesetting/children-playing-with-fire

Faller, K. C. (2003). *Understanding and assessing child sexual maltreatment* (2nd ed.). Thousand Oaks, CA: Sage.

Faller, K. C. (2007). *Interviewing children about sexual abuse: Controversies and best practice*. http://dx.doi.org/10.1093/acprof:oso/9780195311778.001.0001

Faller, K. C. (2015). Forty years of forensic interviewing of children suspected of sexual abuse, 1974–2014: Historical benchmarks. *Social Sciences, 4*, 34–65. http://dx.doi.org/10.3390/socsci4010034

Farran, D. C., & Kasari, C. (1990). A longitudinal analysis of the development of synchrony in mutual gaze in mother–child dyads. *Journal of Applied Developmental Psychology, 11*, 419–430. http://dx.doi.org/10.1016/0193-3973(90)90018-F

Fawcett, C., & Liszkowski, U. (2012). Mimicry and play initiation in 18-month-old infants. *Infant Behavior and Development, 35*, 689–696. http://dx.doi.org/10.1016/j.infbeh.2012.07.014

Feltovich, P. J., Spiro, R. J., & Coulson, R. L. (1997). Issues of expert flexibility in contexts characterized by complexity and change. In P. J. Feltovich, K. M. Ford, & R. R. Hoffman (Eds.), *Expertise in context: Human and machine* (pp. 125–146). Menlo Park, CA: MIT Press.

Fischer, K. W., & Bidell, T. R. (2006). Dynamic development of action and thought. In W. Damon & R. M. Lerner (Eds.), *Handbook of child psychology: Vol. 1. Theoretical models of human development* (6th ed., pp. 313–399). New York, NY: Wiley.

Fischer, K. W., Schwartz, M., & Connell, M. W. (2004, October). *Analyzing the building of skills in classrooms and neural systems*. Paper presented at the Useable Knowledge Conference, Harvard Graduate School of Education, Cambridge, MA.

Fisher, R. P. (2014). How I got started: Intellectual challenges, excellent colleagues, and some serendipity. *Applied Cognitive Psychology, 28*, 615–616. http://dx.doi.org/10.1002/acp.2992

Fisher, R. P., Brennan, K. H., & McCauley, M. R. (2002). The cognitive interview method to enhance eyewitness recall. In M. L. Eisen, J. A. Quas, & G. S. Goodman (Eds.), *Memory and suggestibility in the forensic interview* (pp. 265–286). Mahwah, NJ: Erlbaum.

Fisher, R. P., & Geiselman, R. E. (1992). *Memory-enhancing techniques for investigative interviewing: The cognitive interview*. Springfield, IL: Charles C Thomas.

Fisher, R. P., Schreiber Compo, N., Rivard, J., & Hirn, D. (2014). Interviewing witnesses. In T. Perfect & D. S. Lindsay (Eds.), *The Sage handbook of applied memory* (pp. 559–578). http://dx.doi.org/10.4135/9781446294703.n31

Fivush, R., Berlin, L., Sales, J. M., Mennuti-Washburn, J., & Cassidy, J. (2003). Functions of parent–child reminiscing about emotionally negative events. *Memory, 11*, 179–192. http://dx.doi.org/10.1080/741938209

Flavell, J. H., Botkin, P. T., Fry, C. L., Jr., Wright, J. W., & Jarvis, P. E. (1975). *The development role-taking and communication skills in children.* Huntington, NY: Robert E. Krieger.

Foley, M. A. (2014). Children's memory for source. In P. J. Bauer & R. Fivush (Eds.), *The Wiley handbook on the development of children's memory* (Vol. 1, pp. 427–452). Sommerset, NJ: Wiley-Blackwell.

Fox, N. A., Nichols, K. E., Henderson, H. A., Rubin, K., Schmidt, L., Hamer, D., . . . Pine, D. S. (2005). Evidence for a gene–environment interaction in predicting behavioral inhibition in middle childhood. *Psychological Science, 16,* 921–926. http://dx.doi.org/10.1111/j.1467-9280.2005.01637.x

Franklin, A., Clifford, A., Williamson, E., & Davies, I. (2005). Color term knowledge does not affect categorical perception of color in toddlers. *Journal of Experimental Child Psychology, 90,* 114–141. http://dx.doi.org/10.1016/j.jecp.2004.10.001

Friedman, W. J. (1991). The development of children's memory for the time of past events. *Child Development, 62,* 139–155. http://dx.doi.org/10.2307/1130710

Friedman, W. J. (2014). The development of memory for the times of past events. In P. J. Bauer & R. Fivush (Eds.), *The Wiley handbook on the development of children's memory* (Vol. 1, pp. 394–407). Chichester, England: Wiley.

Friedman, W. J., Reese, E., & Dai, X. (2011). Children's memory for the times of events from the past years. *Applied Cognitive Psychology, 25,* 156–165. http://dx.doi.org/10.1002/acp.1656

Fusaro, M., & Harris, P. L. (2008). Children assess informant reliability using bystanders' nonverbal cues. *Developmental Science, 11,* 771–777. http://dx.doi.org/10.1111/j.1467-7687.2008.00728.x

Garven, S., Wood, J. M., Malpass, R. S., & Shaw, J. S., III. (1998). More than suggestion: The effect of interviewing techniques from the McMartin Preschool case. *Journal of Applied Psychology, 83,* 347–359. http://dx.doi.org/10.1037/0021-9010.83.3.347

Gawande, A. (2009). *The checklist manifesto: How to get things right.* New York, NY: Metropolitan Books.

Gaynor, J. (2002). *The juvenile firesetter intervention handbook* (ERIC No. ED449407). Washington, DC: Federal Emergency Management System. Retrieved from http://eric.ed.gov/?id=ED449407

Gentle, M., Milne, R., Powell, M. B., & Sharman, S. J. (2013). Does the Cognitive Interview promote the coherence of narrative accounts in children with and without an intellectual disability? *International Journal of Disability, Development and Education, 60,* 30–43. http://dx.doi.org/10.1080/1034912X.2013.757138

Ghetti, S., & Angelini, L. (2008). The development of recollection and familiarity in childhood and adolescence: Evidence from the dual-process signal detection model. *Child Development, 79,* 339–358. http://dx.doi.org/10.1111/j.1467-8624.2007.01129.x

Gillian, T. D., & Sekeres, M. A. (2014, February 14). Can doctors be taught how to talk to patients? *The New York Times*. Retrieved from http://well.blogs.nytimes.com/2014/02/27/can-doctors-be-taught-how-to-talk-to-patients/

Goldman, J. G. (2010, October 18). The thoughtful animal: Ed Tronick and the "Still Face Experiment" [Web log post]. Retrieved from http://scienceblogs.com/thoughtfulanimal/2010/10/18/ed-tronick-and-the-still-face/

Gomes, D. M., Sheahan, C., Fitzgerald, R. J., Connolly, D. A., & Price, H. L. (2015, March). *A meta-analysis examining differences in children's memory for single and repeat events*. Paper session presented at the American Psychology–Law Society Conference, San Diego, CA.

Goodman, G. S., Aman, C., & Hirschman, J. (1987). Child sexual and physical abuse: Children's testimony. In S. J. Ceci, M. P. Toglia, & D. F. Ross (Eds.), *Children's eyewitness memory* (pp. 1–23). http://dx.doi.org/10.1007/978-1-4684-6338-5_1

Goodman, G. S., Ogle, C. M., McWilliams, K., Narr, R. K., & Paz-Alonso, P. (2014). Memory development in the forensic context. In P. J. Bauer & R. Fivush (Eds.), *The Wiley handbook on the development of children's memory* (Vol. 2, pp. 920–941). Chichester, England: Wiley.

Goodman, G. S., Sharma, A., Thomas, S. F., & Considine, M. G. (1995). Mother knows best: Effects of relationship status and interviewer bias on children's memory. *Journal of Experimental Child Psychology, 60*, 195–228. http://dx.doi.org/10.1006/jecp.1995.1038

Goodman, G. S., Taub, E. P., Jones, D. P., England, P., Port, L. K., Rudy, L., . . . Melton, G. B. (1992). Testifying in criminal court: Emotional effects on child sexual assault victims. *Monographs of the Society for Research in Child Development, 57*(5), i, iii, v, 1–142. http://dx.doi.org/10.2307/1166127

Grant, J. B., & Suddendorf, T. (2011). Production of temporal terms by 3-, 4-, and 5-year-old children. *Early Childhood Research Quarterly, 26*, 87–95. http://dx.doi.org/10.1016/j.ecresq.2010.05.002

Gross, A. M., Stern, R. M., Levin, R. B., Dale, J., & Wojnilower, D. A. (1983). The effect of mother–child separation on the behavior of children experiencing a diagnostic medical procedure. *Journal of Consulting and Clinical Psychology, 51*, 783–785. http://dx.doi.org/10.1037/0022-006X.51.5.783

Gross, J., & Hayne, H. (1999). Drawing facilitates children's verbal reports after long delays. *Journal of Experimental Psychology: Applied, 5*, 265–283. http://dx.doi.org/10.1037/1076-898X.5.3.265

Gross, J., Hayne, H., & Drury, T. (2009). Drawing facilitates children's reports of factual and narrative information: Implications for educational contexts. *Applied Cognitive Psychology, 23*, 953–971. http://dx.doi.org/10.1002/acp.1518

Gueguen, M., Jacob, C., & Martin, A. (2009). Mimicry in social interaction: Its effect on human judgment and behavior. *European Journal of Soil Science, 8*, 253–259.

Heath, C., & Heath, D. (2007). *Made to stick: Why some ideas survive and others die.* New York, NY: Random House.

Henry, L. A., Bettenay, C., & Carney, D. P. J. (2011). Children with intellectual disabilities and developmental disorders. In M. E. Lamb, D. J. La Rooy, L. C. Malloy, & C. Katz (Eds.), *Children's testimony: A handbook of psychological issues and forensic practice* (pp. 251–283). http://dx.doi.org/10.1002/9781119998495.ch13

Henry, L. A., & Gudjonsson, G. H. (2003). Eyewitness memory, suggestibility, and repeated recall sessions in children with mild and moderate intellectual disabilities. *Law and Human Behavior, 27,* 481–505. http://dx.doi.org/10.1023/A:1025434022699

Herman, S. (2010). The role of corroborative evidence in child sexual abuse evaluations. *Journal of Investigative Psychology and Offender Profiling, 7,* 189–212. http://dx.doi.org/10.1002/jip.122

Hershkowitz, I. (2002). The role of facilitative prompts in interviews of alleged sex and abuse victims. *Legal and Criminological Psychology, 7,* 63–71. http://dx.doi.org/10.1348/135532502168388

Hershkowitz, I., Fisher, S., Lamb, M. E., & Horowitz, D. (2007). Improving credibility assessment in child sexual abuse allegations: The role of the NICHD Investigative Interview Protocol. *Child Abuse & Neglect, 31,* 99–110. http://dx.doi.org/10.1016/j.chiabu.2006.09.005

Hershkowitz, I., Lamb, M. E., & Katz, C. (2014). Allegation rates in forensic child abuse investigations: Comparing the revised and standard NICHD protocols. *Psychology, Public Policy, and Law, 20,* 336–344. http://dx.doi.org/10.1037/a0037391

Hershkowitz, I., Lamb, M. E., Katz, C., & Malloy, L. (2015). Does enhanced rapport-building alter the dynamics of investigative interviews with suspected victims of intrafamilial abuse? *Journal of Police and Criminal Psychology, 30,* 6–14. http://dx.doi.org/10.1007/s11896-013-9136-8

Hershkowitz, I., Lamb, M. E., Orbach, Y., Katz, C., & Horowitz, D. (2012). The development of communicative and narrative skills among preschoolers: Lessons from forensic interviews about child abuse. *Child Development, 83,* 611–622.

Hershkowitz, I., Orbach, Y., Lamb, M. E., Sternberg, K. J., & Horowitz, D. (2006). Dynamics of forensic interviews with suspected abuse victims who do not disclose abuse. *Child Abuse & Neglect, 30,* 753–769. http://dx.doi.org/10.1016/j.chiabu.2005.10.016

Hoff, E. (2014). *Language development.* Belmont, CA: Wadsworth Cengage Learning.

Home Office and the Department of Health in England and Wales. (1992). *Memorandum of Good Practice on video recorded interviews with child witnesses for criminal proceedings.* London, England: Author.

Howie, P., Kurukulasuriya, N., Nash, L., & Marsh, A. (2009). Inconsistencies in children's recall of witnessed events: The role of age, question format and perceived reason for question repetition. *Legal and Criminological Psychology, 14,* 311–329. http://dx.doi.org/10.1348/135532508X383879

Howie, P., Nash, L., Kurukulasuriya, N., & Bowman, A. (2012). Children's event reports: Factors affecting responses to repeated questions in vignette scenarios and event recall interviews. *The British Journal of Developmental Psychology, 30*, 550–568. http://dx.doi.org/10.1111/j.2044-835X.2011.02064.x

Howie, P., Sheehan, M., Mojarrad, T., & Wrzesinska, M. (2004). 'Undesirable' and 'desirable' shifts in children's responses to repeated questions: Age differences in the effect of providing a rationale for repetition. *Applied Cognitive Psychology, 18*, 1161–1180. http://dx.doi.org/10.1002/acp.1049

Hrdy, S. B. (2009). *Mothers and others: The evolutionary origins of mutual understanding*. Cambridge, MA: Harvard University Press.

Huelser, B. J., & Metcalfe, J. (2012). Making related errors facilitates learning, but learners do not know it. *Memory & Cognition, 40*, 514–527. http://dx.doi.org/10.3758/s13421-011-0167-z

Hulse, D. A. (1994). *Linguistic complexity in child abuse interviews* (Unpublished master's thesis). University of Tennessee at Chattanooga.

Hunt, J. S., & Borgida, E. (2001). Is that what I said?: Witnesses' responses to interviewer modifications. *Law and Human Behavior, 25*, 583–603. http://dx.doi.org/10.1023/A:1012754207074

Hupbach, A., Gomez, R., Hardt, O., & Nadel, L. (2007). Reconsolidation of episodic memories: A subtle reminder triggers integration of new information. *Learning & Memory, 14*, 47–53. http://dx.doi.org/10.1101/lm.365707

Imhoff, M. C., & Baker-Ward, L. (1999). Preschoolers' suggestibility: Effects of developmentally appropriate language and interviewer supportiveness. *Journal of Applied Developmental Psychology, 20*, 407–429. http://dx.doi.org/10.1016/S0193-3973(99)00022-2

Jefferson, G. (1989). Notes on a possible metric which provides for a 'standard maximum' silence of approximately one second in conversation. In D. Roger & P. Bull (Eds.), *Conversation: An interdisciplinary perspective* (pp. 166–192). Clevedon, England: Multilingual Matters.

Johnson, M. K., Hashtroudi, S., & Lindsay, D. S. (1993). Source monitoring. *Psychological Bulletin, 114*, 3–28. http://dx.doi.org/10.1037/0033-2909.114.1.3

Jones, C. H., & Powell, M. B. (2005). The effect of event context on children's recall of nonexperienced events across multiple interviews. *Legal and Criminological Psychology, 10*, 83–101.

Jones, D. P. H., & McQuiston, M. G. (1988). *Interviewing the sexually abused child* (3rd ed.). London, England: Gaskell.

Jones, L., Bellis, M. A., Wood, S., Hughes, K., McCoy, E., Eckley, L., . . . Officer, A. (2012, September 8). Prevalence and risk of violence against children with disabilities: A systematic review and meta-analysis of observational studies. *The Lancet, 380*, 899–907. http://dx.doi.org/10.1016/S0140-6736(12)60692-8

Kagan, J., Reznick, S., Clarke, C., Snidman, N., & Garcia-Coll, C. (1984). Behavioral inhibition to the unfamiliar. *Child Development, 55*, 2212–2225. http://dx.doi.org/10.2307/1129793

Kahneman, D. (2011). *Thinking, fast and slow.* New York, NY: Farrar, Straus & Giroux.

Kalichman, S. C. (1999). *Mandated reporting of suspected child abuse: Ethics, law, & policy* (2nd ed.). http://dx.doi.org/10.1037/10337-000

Kassin, S. M., Dror, I. E., & Kukucka, J. (2013). The forensic confirmation bias: Problems, perspectives, and proposed solutions. *Journal of Applied Research in Memory and Cognition, 2,* 42–52. http://dx.doi.org/10.1016/j.jarmac.2013.01.001

Kassin, S. M., & Gudjonsson, G. H. (2004). The psychology of confessions: A review of the literature and issues. *Psychological Science in the Public Interest, 5,* 33–67. http://dx.doi.org/10.1111/j.1529-1006.2004.00016.x

Katz, C., Hershkowitz, I., Malloy, L. C., Lamb, M. E., Atabaki, A., & Spindler, S. (2012). Non-verbal behavior of children who disclose or do not disclose child abuse in investigative interviews. *Child Abuse & Neglect, 36,* 12–20. http://dx.doi.org/10.1016/j.chiabu.2011.08.006

Kaye, K., & Charney, R. (1981). Conversational asymmetry between mothers and children. *Journal of Child Language, 8,* 35–49. http://dx.doi.org/10.1017/S0305000900002993

Kim, G., Walden, T. A., & Knieps, L. J. (2010). Impact and characteristics of positive and fearful emotional messages during infant social referencing. *Infant Behavior and Development, 33,* 189–195. http://dx.doi.org/10.1016/j.infbeh.2009.12.009

Kluger, A. M., & DeNisi, A. (1996). The effects of feedback interventions on performance: A historical review, a meta-analysis, and a preliminary feedback intervention theory. *Psychological Bulletin, 119,* 254–284. http://dx.doi.org/10.1037/0033-2909.119.2.254

Kluger, A. M., & DeNisi, A. (1998). Feedback interventions: Toward the understanding of a double-edged sword. *Current Directions in Psychological Science, 7,* 67–72. http://dx.doi.org/10.1111/1467-8721.ep10772989

Köhnken, G., Milne, R., Memon, A., & Bull, R. (1999). The cognitive interview: A meta-analysis. *Psychology, Crime & Law, 5,* 3–27. http://dx.doi.org/10.1080/10683169908414991

Koocher, G. P. (2009). Ethical issues in child sexual abuse evaluations. In K. Kuehnle & M. Connell (Eds.), *The evaluation of child sexual abuse allegations: A comprehensive guide to assessment and testimony* (pp. 81–98). Hoboken, NJ: Wiley.

Krähenbühl, S., Blades, M., & Eiser, C. (2009). The effect of repeated questioning on children's accuracy and consistency in eyewitness testimony. *Legal and Criminological Psychology, 14,* 263–278. http://dx.doi.org/10.1348/135532508X398549

Kuczaj, S. A., II, & Lederberg, A. R. (1977). Height, age, and function: Differing influences on children's comprehension of 'younger' and 'older.' *Journal of Child Language, 4,* 395–416. http://dx.doi.org/10.1017/S0305000900001768

Kuehnle, K., & Connell, M. (Eds,). (2009). *The evaluation of child sexual abuse allegations: A comprehensive guide to assessment and testimony.* Hoboken, NJ: Wiley.

Kuehnle, K., & Connell, M. (2010). Child sexual abuse suspicions: Treatment considerations during investigation. *Journal of Child Sexual Abuse, 19,* 554–571. http://dx.doi.org/10.1080/10538712.2010.512554

Lamb, M. E. (2014). How I got started: Drawn into the life of crime: Learning from, by, and for child victims and witnesses. *Applied Cognitive Psychology, 28,* 607–611. http://dx.doi.org/10.1002/acp.3031

Lamb, M. E., Hershkowitz, I., Orbach, Y., & Esplin, P. W. (2008). *Tell me what happened: Structured investigative interviews of child victims and witnesses.* http://dx.doi.org/10.1002/9780470773291

Lamb, M. E., Hershkowitz, I., Sternberg, K. J., Boat, B., & Everson, M. D. (1996). Investigative interviews of alleged sexual abuse victims with and without anatomical dolls. *Child Abuse & Neglect, 20,* 1251–1259. http://dx.doi.org/10.1016/S0145-2134(96)00121-4

Lamb, M. E., Hershkowitz, I., Sternberg, K. J., Esplin, P. W., Hovav, M., Manor, T., & Yudilevitch, L. (1996). Effects of investigative utterance types on Israeli children's responses. *International Journal of Behavioral Development, 19,* 627–637. http://dx.doi.org/10.1177/016502549601900310

Lamb, M. E., & Malloy, L. C. (2013). Child development and the law. In R. M. Lerner, M. A. Easterbrooks, & J. Mistry (Eds.), *Handbook of psychology: Vol. 6. Developmental psychology* (2nd ed., pp. 571–593). Hoboken, NJ: Wiley.

Lamb, M. E., Orbach, Y., Hershkowitz, I., Esplin, P. W., & Horowitz, D. (2007). A structured forensic interview protocol improves the quality and informativeness of investigative interviews with children: A review of research using the NICHD Investigative Interview Protocol. *Child Abuse & Neglect, 31,* 1201–1231. http://dx.doi.org/10.1016/j.chiabu.2007.03.021

Lamb, M. E., Orbach, Y., Hershkowitz, I., Horowitz, D., & Abbott, C. B. (2007). Does the type of prompt affect the accuracy of information provided by alleged victims of abuse in forensic interviews? *Applied Cognitive Psychology, 21,* 1117–1130. http://dx.doi.org/10.1002/acp.1318

Lamb, M. E., Orbach, Y., Sternberg, K. J., Hershkowitz, I., & Horowitz, D. (2000). Accuracy of investigators' verbatim notes of their forensic interviews with alleged child abuse victims. *Law and Human Behavior, 24,* 699–708. http://dx.doi.org/10.1023/A:1005556404636

La Rooy, D. J., Brown, D., & Lamb, M. E. (2012). Suggestibility and witness interviewing using the Cognitive Interview and NICHD protocol. In A. M. Ridley, F. Gabbert, & D. J. La Rooy (Eds.), *Suggestibility in legal contexts: Psychological research and forensic implications* (pp. 197–216). http://dx.doi.org/10.1002/9781118432907.ch10

La Rooy, D. J., Katz, C., Malloy, L. C., & Lamb, M. E. (2010). Do we need to rethink guidance on repeated interviews? *Psychology, Public Policy, and Law, 16,* 373–392. http://dx.doi.org/10.1037/a0019909

La Rooy, D., & Lamb, M. E. (2011). What happens when interviewers ask repeated questions in forensic interviews with children alleging abuse? *Journal of Police and Criminal Psychology, 26,* 20–25. http://dx.doi.org/10.1007/s11896-010-9069-4

La Rooy, D., Lamb, M. E., & Pipe, M.-E. (2009). Repeated interviewing: A critical evaluation of the risks and potential benefits. In K. Kuehnle & M. Connell (Eds.), *The evaluation of child sexual abuse allegations: A comprehensive guide to assessment and testimony* (pp. 327–361). Hoboken, NJ: Wiley.

Leander, N. P., Chartrand, T. L., & Bargh, J. A. (2012). You give me the chills: Embodied reactions to inappropriate amounts of behavioral mimicry. *Psychological Science, 23,* 772–779. http://dx.doi.org/10.1177/0956797611434535

Leichtman, M. D., & Ceci, S. J. (1995). The effects of stereotypes and suggestions on preschoolers' reports. *Developmental Psychology, 31,* 568–578. http://dx.doi.org/10.1037/0012-1649.31.4.568

Lilienfeld, S. O. (2007). Psychological treatments that cause harm. *Perspectives on Psychological Science, 2,* 53–70. http://dx.doi.org/10.1111/j.1745-6916.2007.00029.x

Loftus, E. F., Garry, M., & Feldman, J. (1994). Forgetting sexual trauma: What does it mean when 38% forget? *Journal of Consulting and Clinical Psychology, 62,* 1177–1181. http://dx.doi.org/10.1037/0022-006X.62.6.1177

London, K., Bruck, M., Wright, D. B., & Ceci, S. J. (2008). Review of the contemporary literature on how children report sexual abuse to others: Findings, methodological issues, and implications for forensic interviewers. *Memory, 16,* 29–47. http://dx.doi.org/10.1080/09658210701725732

Lowenstein, J. A., Blank, H., & Sauer, J. D. (2010). Uniforms affect the accuracy of children's eyewitness identification decisions. *Journal of Investigative Psychology and Offender Profiling, 7,* 59–73. http://dx.doi.org/10.1002/jip.104

Lukomski, J. (2014). Best practices in planning effective instruction for children who are deaf or hard of hearing. In P. Harrison & A. Thomas (Eds.), *Best practices in school psychology* (pp. 367–376). Bethesda, MD: National Association of School Psychologists.

Lum, J. A. G., Powell, M. B., Timms, L., & Snow, P. (2015). A meta-analysis of cross sectional studies investigating language in maltreated children. *Journal of Speech, Language, and Hearing Research, 58,* 961–976. http://dx.doi.org/10.1044/2015_JSLHR-L-14-0056

Lyon, T. D. (2005). *Ten step investigative interview.* Retrieved from http://works.bepress.com/thomaslyon/5

Lyon, T. D. (2011). Assessing the competency of child witnesses: Best practice informed by psychology and law. In M. E. Lamb, D. J. La Rooy, L. C. Malloy, & C. Katz (Eds.), *Children's testimony: A handbook of psychological research and forensic practice* (pp. 69–85). http://dx.doi.org/10.1002/9781119998495.ch4

Lyon, T. D., & Ahern, E. C. (2011). Disclosure of child sexual abuse. In J. E. B. Myers (Ed.), *The APSAC handbook on child maltreatment* (3rd ed., pp. 233–252). Los Angeles, CA: Sage.

Lyon, T. D., Carrick, N., & Quas, J. A. (2010). Young children's competency to take the oath: Effects of task, maltreatment, and age. *Law and Human Behavior*, *34*, 141–149. http://dx.doi.org/10.1007/s10979-009-9177-9

Lyon, T. D., & Evans, A. D. (2014). Young children's understanding that promising guarantees performance: The effects of age and maltreatment. *Law and Human Behavior*, *38*, 162–170. http://dx.doi.org/10.1037/lhb0000061

Lyon, T. D., Malloy, L. C., Quas, J. A., & Talwar, V. A. (2008). Coaching, truth induction, and young maltreated children's false allegations and false denials. *Child Development*, *79*, 914–929. http://dx.doi.org/10.1111/j.1467-8624.2008.01167.x

Lyon, T. D., Quas, J. A., & Carrick, N. (2013). Right and righteous: Children's incipient understanding and evaluation of true and false statements. *Journal of Cognition and Development*, *14*, 437–454. http://dx.doi.org/10.1080/15248372.2012.673187

Lyon, T. D., & Saywitz, K. J. (1999). Young maltreated children's competence to take the oath. *Applied Developmental Science*, *3*, 16–27. http://dx.doi.org/10.1207/s1532480xads0301_3

Lyon, T. D., Scurich, N., Choi, K., Handmaker, S., & Blank, R. (2012). "How did you feel?": Increasing child sexual abuse witnesses' production of evaluative information. *Law and Human Behavior*, *36*, 448–457. http://dx.doi.org/10.1037/h0093986

Lyon, T. D., Wandrey, L., Ahern, E., Licht, R., Sim, M. P. Y., & Quas, J. A. (2014). Eliciting maltreated and nonmaltreated children's transgression disclosures: Narrative practice rapport building and a putative confession. *Child Development*, *85*, 1756–1769. http://dx.doi.org/10.1111/cdev.12223

Lytle, N., London, K., & Bruck, M. (2015). Young children's ability to use two-dimensional and three-dimensional symbols to show placements of body touches and hidden objects. *Journal of Experimental Child Psychology*, *134*, 30–42. http://dx.doi.org/10.1016/j.jecp.2015.01.010

Macleod, E., Gross, J., & Hayne, H. (2013). The clinical and forensic value of information that children report while drawing. *Applied Cognitive Psychology*, *27*, 564–573.

Macleod, E., Gross, J., & Hayne, H. (2014). Drawing conclusions: The effect of instructions on children's confabulation and fantasy errors. *Memory*, *24*, 21–31. http://dx.doi.org/10.1080/09658211.2014.982656

Malloy, L. C., Shulman, E. P., & Cauffman, E. (2014). Interrogations, confessions, and guilty pleas among serious adolescent offenders. *Law and Human Behavior*, *38*, 181–193. http://dx.doi.org/10.1037/lhb0000065

Matsumoto, D. (2006). Culture and nonverbal behavior. In V. Manusov & M. L. Patterson (Eds.), *The Sage handbook of nonverbal communication* (pp. 219–236). http://dx.doi.org/10.4135/9781412976152.n12

Mattison, M. L. A., Dando, C. J., & Ormerod, T. C. (2015). Sketching to remember: Episodic free recall task support for child witnesses and victims with autism spectrum disorder. *Journal of Autism and Developmental Disorders, 45*, 1751–1765. http://dx.doi.org/10.1007/s10803-014-2335-z

Memon, A., Holley, A., Wark, L., Bull, R., & Köhnken, G. (1996). Reducing suggestibility in child witness interviews. *Applied Cognitive Psychology, 10*, 503–518. http://dx.doi.org/10.1002/(SICI)1099-0720(199612)10:6<503::AID-ACP416>3.0.CO;2-R

Memon, A., Meissner, C. A., & Fraser, J. (2010). The cognitive interview: A meta-analytic review and study space analysis of the past 25 years. *Psychology, Public Policy, and Law, 16*, 340–372. http://dx.doi.org/10.1037/a0020518

Mesman, J., van IJzendoorn, M. K., & Bakermans-Kranenburg, M. K. (2009). The many faces of the Still-Face Paradigm: A review and meta-analysis. *Developmental Review, 29*, 120–162. http://dx.doi.org/10.1016/j.dr.2009.02.001

Miller, G. (2012). Mysteries of the brain. How are memories retrieved? *Science, 338*, 30–31. http://dx.doi.org/10.1126/science.338.6103.30-b

Milne, R., Sharman, S. J., Powell, M. B., & Mead, S. (2013). Assessing the effectiveness of the cognitive interview for children with severe intellectual disabilities. *International Journal of Disability, Development and Education, 60*, 18–29. http://dx.doi.org/10.1080/1034912X.2013.757137

Ministry of Justice. (2011). *Achieving best evidence in criminal proceedings: Guidance on interviewing victims and witnesses, and guidance on using special measures.* Retrieved from https://www.cps.gov.uk/publications/docs/best_evidence_in_criminal_proceedings.pdf

Moody, E. J., McIntosh, D. N., Mann, L. J., & Weisser, K. R. (2007). More than mere mimicry? The influence of emotion on rapid facial reactions to faces. *Emotion, 7*, 447–457. http://dx.doi.org/10.1037/1528-3542.7.2.447

Moore, D. K. (1998). Prosecuting child sexual abuse in rural Kentucky: Factors influencing case acceptance by prosecuting attorneys. *American Journal of Criminal Justice, 22*, 207–234. http://dx.doi.org/10.1007/BF02887258

Morgan, M. (1995). *How to interview sexual abuse victims: Including the use of anatomical dolls.* http://dx.doi.org/10.4135/9781483326849

Nahum, L., Bouzerda-Wahlen, A., Guggisberg, A., Ptak, R., & Schnider, A. (2012). Forms of confabulation: Dissociations and associations. *Neuropsychologia, 50*, 2524–2534. http://dx.doi.org/10.1016/j.neuropsychologia.2012.06.026

National Association of Certified Child Forensic Interviewers. (2014). *The child centered approach to investigative child forensic interviewing.* Retrieved from http://www.naccfi.com/2014%20Course%20Curriculum%20%20FEB%20No%20Live%20Links.pdf

National Center for Education Statistics. (2015). *The condition of education: Children and youth with disabilities.* Retrieved from http://nces.ed.gov/programs/coe/indicator_cgg.asp

National Center for Prosecution of Child Abuse. (1993). *Investigation and prosecution of child abuse* (2nd ed.). Alexandria, VA: American Prosecutors Research Institute.

National Center for Prosecution of Child Abuse. (2004). *Investigation and prosecution of child abuse* (3rd ed.). Thousand Oaks, CA: Sage.

National Children's Advocacy Center. (2010). *NCAC renames the extended forensic evaluation protocol*. Retrieved from http://www.nationalcac.org/professionals/ images/stories/pdfs/final%20-%20ncac%20renames%20extended%20forensic %20evaluation%20training-revised.pdf

National Children's Advocacy Center. (2012). *National Children's Advocacy Center Child Forensic Interview structure*. Huntsville, AL: Author.

National Children's Advocacy Center. (2014). *Update to the National Children's Advocacy Center's Child Forensic Interview structure*. Retrieved from http://www. nationalcac.org/ncac-training/update-to-ncac-cfis-2014.html

National Children's Advocacy Center. (2015). *Position paper on the use of human figure drawings in forensic interviews*. Retrieved from http://calio.org/images/ position-paper-human-figure-drawings.pdf

Nelson, N. W. (1976). Comprehension of spoken language by normal children as a function of speaking rate, sentence difficulty, and listener age and sex. *Child Development, 47*, 299–303. http://dx.doi.org/10.2307/1128319

Newcombe, N. S., Lloyd, M. E., & Balcomb, F. (2012). Contextualizing the development of recollection: Episodic memory and binding in young children. In G. Simona & P. Bauer (Eds.), *Origins and development of recollection: Perspectives from psychology and neuroscience* (pp. 73–100). http://dx.doi.org/10.1093/acprof: oso/9780195340792.003.0004

Newcombe, N. S., Lloyd, M. E., & Ratliff, K. R. (2007). Development of episodic and autobiographical memory: A cognitive neuroscience perspective. In N. S. Newcombe, M. E. Lloyd, & K. R. Ratliff (Eds.), *Advances in child development and behavior* (Vol. 35, pp. 37–85). http://dx.doi.org/10.1016/B978-0-12-009735- 7.50007-4

Niec, L. N., Eyberg, S., & Chase, R. M. (2012). Parent–child interaction therapy: Implementing and sustaining a treatment program for families of young children with disruptive behavior disorders. In A. Rubin (Ed.), *Programs and interventions for maltreated children and families at risk* (pp. 61–69). Hoboken, NJ: Wiley.

Orbach, Y., Lamb, M. E., La Rooy, D. J., & Pipe, M.-E. (2012). A case study of witness consistency and memory recovery across multiple investigative interviews. *Applied Cognitive Psychology, 26*, 118–129. http://dx.doi.org/10.1002/acp.1803

Orbach, Y., & Pipe, M.-E. (2011). Investigating substantive issues. In M. E. Lamb, D. J. La Rooy, L. C. Malloy, & C. Katz (Eds.), *Children's testimony: A handbook of psychological research and forensic practice* (2nd ed., pp. 147–164). http://dx.doi. org/10.1002/9781119998495.ch8

Orbach, Y., Shiloach, H., & Lamb, M. E. (2007). Reluctant disclosers of child sexual abuse. In M.-E. Pipe, M. E. Lamb, Y. Orbach, & A.-C. Cederborg (Eds.), *Child sexual abuse: Disclosure, delay, and denial* (pp. 115–134). New York, NY: Routledge.

Oregon Department of Justice. (2012). *Oregon interviewing guidelines* (3rd ed.). Retrieved from http://www.doj.state.or.us/victims/pdf/oregon_interviewing_guidelines.pdf

Over, H., Carpenter, M., Spears, R., & Gattis, M. (2013). Children selectively trust individuals who have imitated them. *Social Development, 22*, 215–224. http://dx.doi.org/10.1111/sode.12020

Pathman, T., Larkina, M., Burch, M., & Bauer, P. J. (2013). Young children's memory for the times of personal past events. *Journal of Cognition and Development, 14*, 120–140. http://dx.doi.org/10.1080/15248372.2011.641185

Patterson, T., & Hayne, H. (2011). Does drawing facilitate older children's reports of emotionally laden events? *Applied Cognitive Psychology, 25*, 119–126. http://dx.doi.org/10.1002/acp.1650

Perry, N. W., McAuliff, B. D., Tam, P., Claycomb, L., Dostal, C., & Flanagan, C. (1995). When lawyers question children: Is justice served? *Law and Human Behavior, 19*, 609–629. http://dx.doi.org/10.1007/BF01499377

Perry, N. W., & Teply, L. (1985). Interviewing, counseling, and in-court examination of children: Practical approaches for attorneys. *Creighton Law Review, 18*, 1369–1426.

Peterson, C. (2002). Children's long-term memory for autobiographical events. *Developmental Review, 22*, 370–402. http://dx.doi.org/10.1016/S0273-2297(02)00007-2

Peterson, C. (2011). Children's memory reports over time: Getting both better and worse. *Journal of Experimental Child Psychology, 109*, 275–293. http://dx.doi.org/10.1016/j.jecp.2011.01.009

Peterson, C. (2012). Children's autobiographical memories across the years: Forensic implications of childhood amnesia and eyewitness memory for stressful events. *Developmental Review, 32*, 287–306. http://dx.doi.org/10.1016/j.dr.2012.06.002

Peterson, C., & Biggs, M. (1997). Interviewing children about trauma: Problems with "specific" questions. *Journal of Traumatic Stress, 10*, 279–290. http://dx.doi.org/10.1002/jts.2490100208

Peterson, C., & Rideout, R. (1998). Memory for medical emergencies experienced by 1- and 2-year-olds. *Developmental Psychology, 34*, 1059–1072. http://dx.doi.org/10.1037/0012-1649.34.5.1059

Piaget, J. (1928). *Judgment and reasoning in the child.* http://dx.doi.org/10.4324/9780203207260

Pipe, M.-E., Lamb, M. E., Orbach, Y., & Cederborg, A.-C. (Eds.). (2007). *Child sexual abuse: Disclosure, delay, and denial.* New York, NY: Routledge.

Pipe, M.-E., Orbach, Y., Lamb, M. E., Abbott, C. B., & Stewart, H. (2013). Do case outcomes change when investigative interviewing practices change? *Psychology, Public Policy, and Law, 19*, 179–190. http://dx.doi.org/10.1037/a0030312

Pipe, M.-E., & Wilson, J. C. (1994). Cues and secrets: Influences on children's event reports. *Developmental Psychology, 30*, 515–525. http://dx.doi.org/10.1037/0012-1649.30.4.515

Pompedda, F., Zappalà, A., & Santtila, P. (2015). Simulations of child sexual abuse interviews using avatars paired with feedback improves interview quality. *Psychology, Crime & Law, 21*, 28–52. http://dx.doi.org/10.1080/1068316X. 2014.915323

Poole, D. A., Brubacher, S. P., & Dickinson, J. J. (2015). Children as witnesses. In B. L. Cutler & P. A. Zapf (Eds.), *APA handbook of forensic psychology: Vol. 2. Criminal investigation, adjudication, and sentencing outcomes* (pp. 3–31). Washington, DC: American Psychological Association.

Poole, D. A., & Bruck, M. (2012). Divining testimony? The impact of interviewing props on children's reports of touching. *Developmental Review, 32*, 165–180. http://dx.doi.org/10.1016/j.dr.2012.06.007

Poole, D. A., & Dickinson, J. J. (2011). Evidence supporting restrictions on uses of body diagrams in forensic interviews. *Child Abuse & Neglect, 35*, 659–669. http://dx.doi.org/10.1016/j.chiabu.2011.05.004

Poole, D. A., & Dickinson, J. J. (2013). Investigative interviews of children. In R. Holliday & T. Marche (Eds.), *Child forensic psychology: Victim and eyewitness memory* (pp. 157–178). New York, NY: Palgrave Macmillan.

Poole, D. A., & Dickinson, J. J. (2014). Comfort drawing during investigative interviews: Evidence of the safety of a popular practice. *Child Abuse & Neglect, 38*, 192–201. http://dx.doi.org/10.1016/j.chiabu.2013.04.012

Poole, D. A., Dickinson, J. J., & Brubacher, S. P. (2014). Sources of unreliable testimony from children. *Roger Williams University Law Review, 19*, 382–410.

Poole, D. A., Dickinson, J. J., Brubacher, S. P., Liberty, A. E., & Kaake, A. M. (2014). Deficient cognitive control fuels children's exuberant false allegations. *Journal of Experimental Child Psychology, 118*, 101–109. http://dx.doi.org/10.1016/j.jecp. 2013.08.013

Poole, D. A., & Lamb, M. E. (1998). *Investigative interviews of children: A guide for helping professionals.* http://dx.doi.org/10.1037/10301-000

Poole, D. A., & Lindsay, D. S. (2001). Children's eyewitness reports after exposure to misinformation from parents. *Journal of Experimental Psychology: Applied, 7*, 27–50. http://dx.doi.org/10.1037/1076-898X.7.1.27

Poole, D. A., & Lindsay, D. S. (2002). Reducing child witnesses' false reports of misinformation from parents. *Journal of Experimental Child Psychology, 81*, 117–140. http://dx.doi.org/10.1006/jecp.2001.2648

Poole, D. A., & White, L. T. (1991). Effects of question repetition on the eyewitness testimony of children and adults. *Developmental Psychology, 27*, 975–986. http://dx.doi.org/10.1037/0012-1649.27.6.975

Powell, M. B. (2003, December). A guide to introducing the topic of an interview about abuse with a child. *Australian Police Journal*, 259–263.

Powell, M. B., Fisher, R. P., & Wright, R. (2005). Investigative interviewing. In N. Brewer & K. D. Williams (Eds.), *Psychology and law: An empirical perspective* (pp. 11–42). New York, NY: Guilford Press.

Powell, M. B., & Guadagno, B. (2008). An examination of the limitations in investigative interviewers' use of open-ended questions. *Psychiatry, Psychology and Law, 15,* 382–395. http://dx.doi.org/10.1080/13218710802101621

Powell, M. B., Hughes-Scholes, C. H., & Sharman, S. J. (2012). Skill in interviewing reduces confirmation bias. *Journal of Investigative Psychology and Offender Profiling, 9,* 126–134. http://dx.doi.org/10.1002/jip.1357

Powell, M. B., Hughes-Scholes, C. H., Smith, R., & Sharman, S. J. (2014). The relationship between investigative interviewing experience and open-ended question usage. *Police Practice and Research: An International Journal, 15,* 283–292. http://dx.doi.org/10.1080/15614263.2012.704170

Powell, M. B., & Snow, P. C. (2007). Guide to questioning children during the free-narrative phase of an investigative interview. *Australian Psychologist, 42,* 57–65. http://dx.doi.org/10.1080/00050060600976032

Poyer, K. L. (n.d.). *Investigative interviews of children.* Washington, DC: U.S. Department of Justice, Federal Bureau of Investigation, Office for Victim Assistance.

Pozzulo, J. D. (2007). Person description and identification by child witnesses. In R. C. L. Lindsay, D. F. Ross, J. D. Read, & M. P. Toglia (Eds.), *Handbook of eyewitness psychology: Vol. 2. Memory for people* (pp. 283–307). Mahwah, NJ: Erlbaum.

Pozzulo, J. D. (2013). Child eyewitness person descriptions and lineup identifications. In R. Holliday & T. Marche (Eds.), *Child forensic psychology: Victim and eyewitness memory* (pp. 209–240). New York, NY: Palgrave Macmillan.

Pratt, C. (1990). On asking children—and adults—bizarre questions. *First Language, 10,* 167–175. http://dx.doi.org/10.1177/014272379001002905

Price, G. R., Mazzocco, M. M. M., & Ansari, D. (2013). Why mental arithmetic counts: Brain activation during single digit arithmetic predicts high school math scores. *The Journal of Neuroscience, 33,* 156–163. http://dx.doi.org/10.1523/JNEUROSCI.2936-12.2013

Price, H. L., Connolly, D. A., & Gordon, H. M. (2015). *Children who have experienced a repeated event only appear less consistent than those who experienced a unique event.* Manuscript submitted for publication.

Price, H. L., Ornstein, P. A., & Poole, D. A. (2015). *The influence of prior "knowledge" on inexperienced interviewers' questioning.* Manuscript in preparation.

Price, H. L., Roberts, K. P., & Collins, A. (2013). The quality of children's allegations of abuse in investigative interviews containing practice narratives. *Journal of Applied Research in Memory and Cognition, 2,* 1–6. http://dx.doi.org/10.1016/j.jarmac.2012.03.001

Principe, G. F., DiPuppo, J., & Gammel, J. (2013). Effects of mothers' conversation style and receipt of misinformation on children's event reports. *Cognitive Development, 28,* 260–271. http://dx.doi.org/10.1016/j.cogdev.2013.01.012

Principe, G. F., Greenhoot, A. F., & Ceci, S. J. (2014). Young children's eyewitness memory. In T. J. Perfect & D. S. Lindsay (Eds.), *The Sage handbook of applied memory* (pp. 633–653). http://dx.doi.org/10.4135/9781446294703.n35

Principe, G. F., & Schindewolf, E. (2012). Natural conversations as a source of false memories in children: Implications for the testimony of young witnesses. *Developmental Review, 32*, 205–223. http://dx.doi.org/10.1016/j.dr.2012.06.003

Putallaz, M., & Gottman, J. M. (1981). An interactional model of children's entry into peer groups. *Child Development, 52*, 986–994. http://dx.doi.org/10.2307/1129103

Quas, J. A., Bauer, A., & Boyce, W. T. (2004). Physiological reactivity, social support, and memory in early childhood. *Child Development, 75*, 797–814. http://dx.doi.org/10.1111/j.1467-8624.2004.00707.x

Quas, J. A., & Lench, H. C. (2007). Arousal at encoding, arousal at retrieval, interviewer support, and children's memory for a mild stressor. *Applied Cognitive Psychology, 21*, 289–305. http://dx.doi.org/10.1002/acp.1279

Raj, V., & Bell, M. A. (2010). Cognitive processes supporting episodic memory formation in childhood: The role of source memory, binding, and executive functioning. *Developmental Review, 30*, 384–402. http://dx.doi.org/10.1016/j.dr.2011.02.001

Reich, P. A. (1986). *Language development.* Englewood Cliffs, NJ: Prentice-Hall.

Renkl, A., Mandl, H., & Gruber, H. (1996). Inert knowledge: Analyses and remedies. *Educational Psychologist, 31*, 115–121. http://dx.doi.org/10.1207/s15326985ep3102_3

Rischke, A. E., Roberts, K. P., & Price, H. L. (2011). Using spaced learning principles to translate knowledge into behavior: Evidence from investigative interviews of alleged child abuse victims. *Journal of Police and Criminal Psychology, 26*, 58–67. http://dx.doi.org/10.1007/s11896-010-9073-8

Roberts, K. P., Brubacher, S. P., Powell, M. B., & Price, H. L. (2011). Practice narratives. In M. E. Lamb, D. J. La Rooy, L. Malloy, & C. Katz (Eds.), *Children's testimony: A handbook of psychological research and forensic practice* (pp. 129–145). http://dx.doi.org/10.1002/9781119998495.ch7

Roberts, K. P., & Duncanson, S. (2011, March). *Enhancing children's testimony with the facilitative interview technique.* Paper presented at the annual meeting of the American Psychology–Law Society, Miami, FL.

Roberts, K. P., & Lamb, M. E. (1999). Children's responses when interviewers distort details during investigative interviews. *Legal and Criminological Psychology, 4*, 23–31. http://dx.doi.org/10.1348/135532599167752

Roberts, K. P., & Lamb, M. E. (2010). Reality-monitoring characteristics in confirmed and doubtful allegations of child sexual abuse. *Applied Cognitive Psychology, 24*, 1049–1079. http://dx.doi.org/10.1002/acp.1600

Roberts, K. P., Lamb, M. E., & Sternberg, K. J. (2004). The effects of rapport-building style on children's reports of a staged event. *Applied Cognitive Psychology, 18*, 189–202. http://dx.doi.org/10.1002/acp.957

Rogers, M. A. (2009, June). What are the phases of intervention research? *Access Academics and Research.* Retrieved from http://asha.org/academic/questions/PhasesClinicalResearch/

Rohrer, D., & Taylor, K. (2007). The shuffling of mathematics problems improves learning. *Instructional Science, 35,* 481–498. http://dx.doi.org/10.1007/s11251-007-9015-8

Rotenberg, K. J., Eisenberg, N., Cumming, C., Smith, A., Singh, M., & Terlicher, E. (2003). The contribution of adults' nonverbal cues and children's shyness to the development of rapport between adults and preschool children. *International Journal of Behavioral Development, 27,* 21–30. http://dx.doi.org/10.1080/01650250143000571

Rush, E. B., Quas, J. A., Yim, I. S., Nikolayev, M., Clark, S. E., & Larson, R. P. (2014). Stress, interviewer support, and children's eyewitness identification accuracy. *Child Development, 85,* 1292–1305. http://dx.doi.org/10.1111/cdev.12177

Salas, E., Tannenbaum, S. I., Kraiger, K., & Smith-Jentsch, K. A. (2012). The science of training and development in organizations: What matters in practice. *Psychological Science in the Public Interest, 13,* 74–101. http://dx.doi.org/10.1177/1529100612436661

Salmon, K., & Pipe, M.-E. (2000). Recalling an event one year later: The impact of props, drawing and a prior interview. *Applied Cognitive Psychology, 14,* 99–120. http://dx.doi.org/10.1002/(SICI)1099-0720(200003/04)14:2<99::AID-ACP639>3.0.CO;2-5

San Diego Child Protection Team. (2013). *Child victim witness checklists.* Retrieved from http://www.chadwickcenter.org/Documents/Checklist-%20Online%20version%20-%2001.2013.pdf

Sattler, J. M. (2002). *Assessment of children: Behavioral and clinical applications* (4th ed.). La Mesa, CA: Author.

Saywitz, K. J. (1988). The credibility of child witnesses. *Family Advocate, 10*(3), 38–41.

Saywitz, K. J., & Camparo, L. B. (2014). *Evidence-based child forensic interviewing: The developmental narrative elaboration interview.* Oxford, England: Oxford University Press.

Saywitz, K. J., & Moan-Hardie, S. (1994). Reducing the potential for distortion of childhood memories. *Consciousness and Cognition, 3,* 408–425. http://dx.doi.org/10.1006/ccog.1994.1023

Saywitz, K. J., & Snyder, L. (1996). Narrative elaboration: Test of a new procedure for interviewing children. *Journal of Consulting and Clinical Psychology, 64,* 1347–1357. http://dx.doi.org/10.1037/0022-006X.64.6.1347

Saywitz, K. J., Snyder, L., & Nathanson, R. (1999). Facilitating the communicative competence of the child witness. *Applied Developmental Science, 3,* 58–68. http://dx.doi.org/10.1207/s1532480xads0301_7

Schacter, D. L., Kagan, J., & Leichtman, M. D. (1995). True and false memories in children and adults: A cognitive neuroscience perspective. *Psychology, Public Policy, and Law, 1,* 411–428. http://dx.doi.org/10.1037/1076-8971.1.2.411

Schneider, L., Price, H. L., Roberts, K. P., & Hedrick, A. M. (2011). Children's episodic and generic reports of alleged abuse. *Applied Cognitive Psychology, 25,* 862–870. http://dx.doi.org/10.1002/acp.1759

Schnider, A. (2003). Spontaneous confabulation and the adaptation of thought to ongoing reality. *Nature Reviews Neuroscience*, *4*, 662–671. http://dx.doi.org/10.1038/nrn1179

Schofield, T. J., Parke, R. D., Castañeda, E. K., & Coltrane, S. (2008). Patterns of gaze between parents and children in European American and Mexican American families. *Journal of Nonverbal Behavior*, *32*, 171–186. http://dx.doi.org/10.1007/s10919-008-0049-7

Scoboria, A., & Fisico, S. (2013). Encouraging and clarifying "don't know" responses enhances interview quality. *Journal of Experimental Psychology: Applied*, *19*, 72–82. http://dx.doi.org/10.1037/a0032067

Scoboria, A., Mazzoni, G., & Kirsch, I. (2008). "Don't know" responding to answerable and unanswerable questions during misleading and hypnotic interviews. *Journal of Experimental Psychology: Applied*, *14*, 255–265. http://dx.doi.org/10.1037/1076-898X.14.3.255

The Scottish Government. (2011). *Guidance on joint investigative interviewing of child witnesses in Scotland*. Retrieved from www.gov.scot/Resource/Doc/365398/0124263.pdf

Shapiro, L. R. (2009). Eyewitness testimony for a simulated juvenile crime by male and female criminals with consistent or inconsistent gender-role characteristics. *Journal of Applied Developmental Psychology*, *30*, 649–666. http://dx.doi.org/10.1016/j.appdev.2009.07.007

Shelton, K., Bridenbaugh, H., Farrenkopf, M., & Kroeger, K. (2010). *Project Ability: Demystifying disability in child abuse interviewing*. Retrieved from http://www.oregon.gov/DHS/CHILDREN/ADVISORY/CJA/Documents/Project-Ability.pdf

Shute, V. J. (2008). Focus on formative feedback. *Review of Educational Research*, *78*, 153–189. http://dx.doi.org/10.3102/0034654307313795

Siegler, R. S. (2006). Microgenetic analyses of learning. In D. Kuhn & R. S. Siegler (Eds.), *Handbook of child psychology: Vol. 2. Cognition, perception, and language* (6th ed., pp. 464–510). Hoboken, NJ: Wiley.

Sitzmann, T., Bell, B. S., Kraiger, K., & Kanar, A. M. (2009). A multilevel analysis of the effect of prompting self-regulation in technology-delivered instruction. *Personnel Psychology*, *62*, 697–734. http://dx.doi.org/10.1111/j.1744-6570.2009.01155.x

Smith, K., & Milne, R. (2011). Planning the interview. In M. E. Lamb, D. J. La Rooy, L. C. Malloy, & K. Carmit (Eds.), *Children's testimony: A handbook of psychological research and forensic practice* (pp. 87–107). http://dx.doi.org/10.1002/9781119998495.ch5

Smith, R. M., Powell, M. B., & Lum, J. (2009). The relationship between job status, interviewing experience, gender, and police officers' adherence to open-ended questions. *Legal and Criminological Psychology*, *14*, 51–63. http://dx.doi.org/10.1348/135532507X262360

Soderstrom, N. C., & Bjork, R. A. (2015). Learning versus performance: An integrative review. *Perspectives on Psychological Science, 10*, 176–199. http://dx.doi.org/10.1177/1745691615569000

Spiro, R. J., Feltovich, P. J., & Coulson, R. L. (1996). Two epistemic world-views: Prefigurative schemas and learning in complex domains. *Applied Cognitive Psychology, 10*, 51–61. http://dx.doi.org/10.1002/(SICI)1099-0720(199611)10:7<51::AID-ACP437>3.0.CO;2-F

Staller, K. M., & Faller, K. C. (Eds.). (2010). *Seeking justice in child sexual abuse: Shifting burdens and sharing responsibilities.* New York, NY: Columbia University Press.

State of Maine Child and Family Services. (2010). *State of Maine Child and Family Services fact-finding child interview protocol.* Augusta, ME: Author.

State of Michigan Governor's Task Force on Child Abuse and Neglect and Department of Human Services. (2011). *Forensic interviewing protocol.* Retrieved from https://www.michigan.gov/documents/dhs/DHS-PUB-0779_211637_7.pdf

Steller, M., & Köhnken, G. (1989). Criteria-based statement analysis. In D. C. Raskin (Ed.), *Psychological methods in criminal investigation and evidence* (pp. 217–245). New York, NY: Springer.

Sternberg, K. J., Lamb, M. E., Hershkowitz, I., Esplin, P. W., Redlich, A., & Sunshine, N. (1996). The relationship between investigative utterance types and the informativeness of child witnesses. *Journal of Applied Developmental Psychology, 17*, 439–451. http://dx.doi.org/10.1016/S0193-3973(96)90036-2

Sternberg, K. J., Lamb, M. E., Hershkowitz, I., Yudilevitch, L., Orbach, Y., Esplin, P. W., & Hovav, M. (1997). Effects of introductory style on children's abilities to describe experiences of sexual abuse. *Child Abuse & Neglect, 21*, 1133–1146. http://dx.doi.org/10.1016/S0145-2134(97)00071-9

Sternberg, K. J., Lamb, M. E., Orbach, Y., Esplin, P. W., & Mitchell, S. (2001). Use of a structured investigative protocol enhances young children's responses to free-recall prompts in the course of forensic interviews. *Journal of Applied Psychology, 86*, 997–1005.

Steward, M. S., Steward, D. S., Farquhar, L., Myers, J. E. B., Reinhart, M., Welker, J., . . . Morgan, J. (1996). Interviewing young children about body touch and handling. *Monograph of the Society for Research in Child Development, 61* (4–5, Serial No. 248).

St. Jacques, P. L., & Schacter, D. L. (2013). Modifying memory: Selectively enhancing and updating personal memories for a museum tour by reactivating them. *Psychological Science, 24*, 537–543. http://dx.doi.org/10.1177/0956797612457377

Strange, D., Garry, M., & Sutherland, R. (2003). Drawing out children's false memories. *Applied Cognitive Psychology, 17*, 607–619. http://dx.doi.org/10.1002/acp.911

Stuart, R. B., & Lilienfeld, S. O. (2007). The evidence missing from evidence-based practice. *American Psychologist, 62*, 615–616. http://dx.doi.org/10.1037/0003-066X62.6.615

Tannen, D. (1990). *You just don't understand: Men and women in conversation.* New York, NY: Morrow.

Tannenbaum, S. I. (1997). Enhancing continuous learning: Diagnostic findings from multiple companies. *Human Resource Management*, *36*, 437–452. http://dx.doi.org/10.1002/(SICI)1099-050X(199724)36:4<437::AID-HRM7>3.0.CO;2-W

Taylor, M., Esbensen, B. M., & Bennett, R. T. (1994). Children's understanding of knowledge acquisition: The tendency for children to report that they have always known what they have just learned. *Child Development*, *65*, 1581–1604. http://dx.doi.org/10.2307/1131282

Taylor, P. J., Russ-Eft, D. F., & Chan, D. W. L. (2005). A meta-analytic review of behavior modeling training. *Journal of Applied Psychology*, *90*, 692–709. http://dx.doi.org/10.1037/0021-9010.90.4.692

Teoh, Y. S., & Lamb, M. (2013). Interviewer demeanor in forensic interviews of children. *Psychology, Crime & Law*, *19*, 145–159. http://dx.doi.org/10.1080/1068316X.2011.614610

Thierry, K. L., Lamb, M. E., Orbach, Y., & Pipe, M.-E. (2005). Developmental differences in the function and use of anatomical dolls during interviews with alleged sexual abuse victims. *Journal of Consulting and Clinical Psychology*, *73*, 1125–1134. http://dx.doi.org/10.1037/0022-006X.73.6.1125

Tickle-Degnen, L., & Rosenthal, R. (1990). The nature of rapport and its nonverbal correlates. *Psychological Inquiry*, *1*, 285–293. http://dx.doi.org/10.1207/s15327965pli0104_1

Tomasello, M. (2014). The ultrasocial animal. *European Journal of Social Psychology*, *44*, 187–194. http://dx.doi.org/10.1002/ejsp.2015

Trankell, A. (1972). *Reliability of evidence: Methods for analyzing and assessing witness statements*. Stockholm, Sweden: Beckmans.

Trocmé, N., Fallon, B., MacLaurin, B., Sinha, V., Black, T., Fast, E., . . . Holryod, J. (2010). *Canadian incidence study of reported child abuse and neglect—2008: Executive summary & chapters 1–5*. Ottawa, Canada: Public Health Agency of Canada.

Undeutsch, U. (1982). Statement reality analysis. In A. Trankell (Ed.), *Reconstructing the past: The role of psychologists in criminal trials* (pp. 27–56). Deventer, Netherlands: Kluwer.

U.S. Department of Education. (2015). *Building the legacy: IDEA 2004*. Retrieved from http://idea.ed.gov/explore/home

U.S. National Institutes of Health. (2007). *Understanding clinical trials*. Retrieved from http://clinicaltrials.gov/ct2/info/understand

Valenti-Hein, D. (2002). Use of visual tools to report sexual abuse for adults with mental retardation. *Mental Retardation*, *40*, 297–303. http://dx.doi.org/10.1352/0047-6765(2002)040<0297:UOVTTR>2.0.CO;2

Vallano, J. P., & Schreiber Compo, N. (2015). Rapport-building with cooperative witnesses and criminal suspects: A theoretical and empirical review. *Psychology, Public Policy, and Law*, *21*, 85–99. http://dx.doi.org/10.1037/law0000035

van Schaik, J. E., van Baaren, R., Bekkering, H., & Hunnius, S. (2013). *Evidence for nonconscious behavior-copying in young children.* Retrieved from http://mindmodeling.org/cogsci2013/papers/0284/paper0284.pdf

Verkampt, F., & Ginet, M. (2010). Variations of the cognitive interview: Which one is the most effective in enhancing children's testimonies? *Applied Cognitive Psychology, 24,* 1279–1296. http://dx.doi.org/10.1002/acp.1631

Verkampt, F., Ginet, M., & Colomb, C. (2014). The influence of social instructions on the effectiveness of a cognitive interview used with very young child witnesses. *European Review of Applied Psychology/Revue Européenne de Psychologie Appliquée, 64,* 323–333. http://dx.doi.org/10.1016/j.erap.2014.09.003

Walker, A. G. (1993). Questioning young children in court: A linguistic case study. *Law and Human Behavior, 17,* 59–81. http://dx.doi.org/10.1007/BF01044537

Walker, A. G. (with Kenniston, J., Inada, S. S., & Caldwell, C.). (2013). *Handbook on questioning children* (3rd ed.). Washington, DC: American Bar Association Center on Children and the Law.

Walker, S. (2009). Sociometric stability and the behavioral correlates of peer acceptance in early childhood. *The Journal of Genetic Psychology: Research and Theory on Human Development, 170,* 339–358. http://dx.doi.org/10.1080/00221320903218364

Walsh, W. A., Jones, L. M., Cross, T. P., & Lippert, T. (2010). Prosecuting child sexual abuse: The importance of evidence type. *Crime & Delinquency, 56,* 436–454. http://dx.doi.org/10.1177/0011128708320484

Wandrey, L., Lyon, T. D., Quas, J. A., & Friedman, W. J. (2012). Maltreated children's ability to estimate temporal location and numerosity of placement changes and court visits. *Psychology, Public Policy, and Law, 18,* 79–104. http://dx.doi.org/10.1037/a0024812

Wang, Q. (2013). *The autobiographical self in time and culture.* http://dx.doi.org/10.1093/acprof:oso/9780199737833.001.0001

Warren, A. R., & Woodall, C. E. (1999). The reliability of hearsay testimony: How well do interviewers recall their interviews with children? *Psychology, Public Policy, and Law, 5,* 355–371. http://dx.doi.org/10.1037/1076-8971.5.2.355

Warren, A. R., Woodall, C. E., Hunt, J. S., & Perry, N. W. (1996). "It sounds good in theory, but . . .": Do investigative interviewers follow guidelines based on memory research? *Child Maltreatment, 1,* 231–245. http://dx.doi.org/10.1177/1077559596001003006

Warren, A. R., Woodall, C. E., Thomas, M., Nunno, M., Keeney, J. M., Larson, S. M., & Stadfeld, J. A. (1999). Assessing the effectiveness of a training program for interviewing child witnesses. *Applied Developmental Science, 3,* 128–135. http://dx.doi.org/10.1207/s1532480xads0302_6

Warren-Leubecker, A., Tate, C. S., Hinton, I. D., & Ozbek, I. N. (1989). What do children know about the legal system and when do they know it? First steps down a less traveled path in child witness research. In S. J. Ceci, D. F. Ross,

& M. P. Toglia (Eds.), *Perspectives on children's testimony* (pp. 158–183). http://dx.doi.org/10.1007/978-1-4613-8832-6_8

Wason, P. C., & Johnson-Laird, P. N. (1972). *Psychology of reasoning: Structure and content*. Cambridge, MA: Harvard University Press.

Wason, P. C., & Shapiro, D. (1971). Natural and contrived experience in a reasoning problem. *The Quarterly Journal of Experimental Psychology, 23*, 63–71. http://dx.doi.org/10.1080/00335557143000068

Waterman, A. H., & Blades, M. (2011). Helping children correctly say "I don't know" to unanswerable questions. *Journal of Experimental Psychology: Applied, 17*, 396–405. http://dx.doi.org/10.1037/a0026150

White, T. L., Leichtman, M. D., & Ceci, S. J. (1997). The good, the bad, and the ugly: Accuracy, inaccuracy, and elaboration in preschoolers' reports about a past event. *Applied Cognitive Psychology, 11*, S37–S54. http://dx.doi.org/10.1002/(SICI)1099-0720(199712)11:7<S37::AID-ACP546>3.0.CO;2-4

Wood, J. M., McClure, K. A., & Birch, R. A. (1996). Suggestions for improving interviews in child protection agencies. *Child Maltreatment, 1*, 223–230. http://dx.doi.org/10.1177/1077559596001003005

Wood, J. M., Nathan, D., Nezworski, M. T., & Uhl, E. (2009). Child sexual abuse investigations: Lessons learned from the McMartin and other daycare cases. In B. L. Bottoms, C. J. Najdowski, & G. S. Goodman (Eds.), *Children as victims, witnesses, and offenders: Psychological science and the law* (pp. 81–101). New York, NY: Guilford Press.

Woolford, J., Patterson, T., Macleod, E., Hobbs, L., & Hayne, H. (2015). Drawing helps children to talk about their presenting problems during a mental health assessment. *Clinical Child Psychology and Psychiatry, 20*, 68–83. http://dx.doi.org/10.1177/1359104513496261

World Health Organization. (2014). *Classifications: International classification of functioning, disability and health (ICF)*. Retrieved from http://www.who.int/classifications/icf/en/

Yuille, J. C. (1988). The systematic assessment of children's testimony. *Canadian Psychology/Psychologie Canadienne, 29*, 247–262. http://dx.doi.org/10.1037/h0079769

Yuille, J. C., Cooper, B. S., & Hervé, H. F. (2009). The Step-Wise Guidelines for Child Interviews: The new generation. In M. Casonato & F. Pfafflin (Eds.), *Pedoparafile: Psychological perspectives, forensic psychiatric* (Giulia Cordano, Trans., pp. 120–141). Milan, Italy: Franco Angeli.

Yuille, J. C., Hunter, R., Joffe, R., & Zaparniuk, J. (1993). Interviewing children in sexual abuse cases. In G. S. Goodman & B. L. Bottoms (Eds.), *Child victims, child witnesses: Understanding and improving testimony* (pp. 95–115). New York, NY: Guilford Press.

Zajonc, R. B. (2001). Mere exposure: A gateway to the subliminal. *Current Directions in Psychological Science, 10*, 224–228. http://dx.doi.org/10.1111/1467-8721.00154

INDEX

AAC (augmentative and alternative communication), 156–157

Abuse investigations. *See also* Sexual abuse interviews
  alternative hypotheses in, 82
  physical evidence in, 163
  practice narratives for, 103

Abuse prevention books, 41

Accuracy of responses
  from child eyewitnesses, 14–19
  in cognitive interviews, 176
  to focused questions, 66
  to open-ended prompts, 62, 65
  and understanding of *truth*, 93–94

Accusatory questions, 127

Achieving Best Evidence in Criminal Proceedings (Ministry of Justice), 174

Additional information
  open-ended prompts to elicit, 63–65, 117
  in repeated interviews, 162

Addition of sounds (pronunciation error), 70

Adolescents. *See also* Teenagers
  forensic interviews with, 5
  language development of, 68–69
  repeating referents in questions for, 125

Affordances, of objects, 148

After, as confusing word, 72

Age, questions about, 132

Age-appropriate interview spaces, 84

Age of acquisition (AoA), 25, 167–168

Aggression, 158

Allegations
  bizarre, 4

Alleged disclosures, 34

Alleged offense information, 81

Alternative hypotheses, 31, 82, 139

Ambiguous communication, 3–4

Ambiguous information
  clarifying, 19, 134–135
  hypothesis testing for, 33–34
  question frames for, 130

Ambiguous questions, 124–125, 131

American Professional Society on the Abuse of Children, 112, 178–179

Analog research, 26–27, 116

Anatomically detailed dolls, 147

Anxiety-related behavior, 158

Any, as confusing word, 71–72, 78, 134

Anything, questions containing, 21

AoA (age of acquisition), 25, 167–168

Appearance
  questions about, 132
  similarity of, 51–52

Arson investigations, 19, 22, 31

Assessments
  developmental, 35–36, 146, 160–161
  prop-based techniques for, 144, 146

Assumptions, about events, 29n1

Assurance, in absence of knowledge, 12

Attention, nonthreatening, 53–54

Attention-deficit disorder, 152

Attention problems, 157

Attorneys. *See also* Defense attorneys
  on cognitive abilities of children, 167–168
  confusing questioning styles of, 69n4
  leading questions for, 14

Atypical behaviors, 153

Atypical events, free narratives about, 118

Augmentative and alternative communication (AAC), 156–157

Authority cues, 52

Autism, 150

Autism spectrum disorder, 150, 152, 153, 158

Automaticity, 50–51

Baby talk, 71

Background information
  building rapport with, 87
  compiling, 80–81
  discussing, 103–104

Basic research, 24–25

Before, as confusing word, 72

Behavior(s). *See also* Cooperative
    behavior
  anxiety-related, 158
  atypical, 153
  of children, 14–15
  conversational style and, 49–50
  in developmentally neutral
    interviews, 153
  in-sync, 54–55
  of interviewers, 54–55, 98
  nonverbal, 55, 56
  oppositional, 158
  researchers' predictions of, 4
Behavioral challenges, 158
Behavioral inhibition, 20
Behavioral modeling, in training,
  180–181
Bennett, R. T., 17
Biases
  confirmation (myside), 32–33
  in confirmatory interviewing, 42–43
  and prior knowledge, 46–47
Biggs, Marleen, 66
Birch, Di, 174
Birch, Rebecca, 23n7
Bizarre allegations, 4
Bizarre questions, 15
Blind interviewing, 41–43, 47
Blocked practice, 181
Body diagrams, 146–149
Body part labeling, 146
Botkin, P. T., 3
Bottoms, Bette, 57
Bouquard, T. L., 19
Bradley Johnson, Sharon, 156n4
Breadth questions, open-ended, 12, 60,
  61, 115, 116
Breaks
  conversational, 130
  interview, 114, 136
Brevity, of checklists, 164–165
Briefing interviewers, 41–45
Broad questions, open-ended, 12, 60, 61
Brown, D. A., 103
Brubacher, Sonja P., 18, 70, 117–118,
  119–120, 182
Bruck, M., 42
Bull, Ray, 174

Caldwell, C., 72
Camparo, Lorinda B., 92, 127, 137, 178
Cantlon, J., 45
Caregivers, communication with, 151
CARES Northwest, 151, 154
Case issues phases, 109–139
  after unexpected disclosures, 106–107
  closing interview phase, 137
  encouraging reticent children in,
    138–139
  free narrative phase, 115–121
  ground rules phase, 96
  guidelines for, 109–110
  interview breaks in, 136
  interviewer behavior in, 54
  questioning and clarifying phase,
    122–136
  topic-raising phase, 110–114
Case-specific decisions and exploration,
  141–168
  about cognitive abilities of children,
    167–168
  about developmental assessments,
    160–161
  about physical evidence, 163
  about repeated interviews, 162–163
  about support people in interview
    spaces, 161–162
  about using checklists, 164–166
  about using prop-based techniques,
    144–149
  for children with disabilities,
    149–160
  for young children, 142–144
Case timelines, 47
Cauffman, Elizabeth, 25–26
Ceci, S. J., 42
Centers for Disease Control and
  Prevention (CDC), 149–151
Cerebral palsy, 157, 159
Change, openness to, 186–188
Chapman, J. P., 23n6
Chapman, L. J., 23n6
Checklists, 155, 164–166
Child Advocacy Center protocol, 31
Child-centered approach to forensic
  interviews, 34–36
Child-friendly interview spaces, 83–84
Child information, background, 81

Child protective services
    breadth of interviews by, 110
    commander's intent for interviews
        by, 37–38, 82
    expected topics in interviews by, 164
    ground rules phase for repeated
        meetings with, 97
    interviewing by, 10
    unexpected disclosures to, 106–107
Child-specific approach to interview
        planning, 154–156
Chronic health problems, 149
Churchland, Patricia, 55
CI. See Commander's intent
Clarification, 19. See also Questioning
        and clarifying phase
    in free narrative phase, 120
    in informed interviewing, 44
    prompting for, 61
    prop-based techniques for, 144,
        146–149
    question frames for, 130
    of unclear speech, 71
Clark, C. R., 40
Clinical activities, goals of, 40
Closing interview phase, 137
Coercive interrogations, 26
Cognitive abilities, of children, 167–168
Cognitive challenges
    children with, 157–158
    during interviewer training, 181
Cognitive disabilities, 149, 157–158
Cognitive interviews, 171, 175–177
Comfort techniques, prop-based, 144–146
Commander's intent (CI)
    articulating, 81–82
    of forensic interviews, 37–39
Communication
    about disabilities, 151
    ambiguous, 3–4
    augmentative and alternative,
        156–157
    with caregivers, 151
    prop-based techniques, 144, 146–149
Comprehension, 68, 91–92
Concept checks, 35
Conceptual understanding, by experts,
        183
Concrete questions, 94, 153
Conditionalized knowledge, 183

Conduct disorders, 158
Confabulation
    and accuracy of eyewitnesses, 17–19
    with DYK questions, 127
    and nonsuggestive topic prompts,
        110, 111
    by young children, 148
Confessions, false, 26
Confirmation bias, 32–33
Confirmatory interviewing, 42
Confusing answers, from young
        children, 143
Confusing questioning styles, 69n4
Confusing words, 71–73
Confusions, language, 15
Connell, M. W., 183
Connell, Mary, 40–41
Contact cultures, 53
Content, interview. See Case issues
        phases; Early interview phases
Content planning, 82–83
Contextual information
    in free narrative phase, 116
    and source-monitoring errors, 16
    and temporal memory, 132–133
    testing hypotheses with, 31, 82
Contradictions
    in blind interviewing, 44
    clarifying, 134–135
    and difficult words/question forms, 71
    in repeated interviews, 162
    in repeated questions, 135
    from young children, 143
Control
    of interview pacing and direction,
        36–37
    of storytelling process, 10
Conventional content. See Case issues
        phases; Early interview phases
Conventional interview protocols,
        170–171
Conversational habits, 49–78
    feedback on, 185
    related questions, inconsistent
        answers to, 77–78
    and role of habits in expert perfor-
        mance, 50–51
    of successful interviewers, 49–50
    in supportive conversational style,
        51–60

Conversational habits, *continued*
  using developmentally appropriate
    language, 67–76
  using open-ended prompts, 60–67
Conversational style
  of adults with children, 8–19
  and children's behavior, 49–50
  directive, 8–10, 66
  supportive, 51–60
Conversations
  with children, 169–170
  documented, 113
  neutral, 114
  silence in, 55–56
Cooperative behavior
  by children with disabilities, 152, 154
  and eyewitness accuracy, 14–15
  and hypothesis testing, 34
  interviewer behaviors that foster,
    54–55
Correlation, illusory, 23n6
Corroborative evidence, 36–37
Criminal investigations
  breadth of interviews conducted for,
    110
  commander's intent in, 39
  repeated interviews in, 162–163
  testimony of children in, 4
Criminal Justice Act of 1991 (Great
    Britain), 174
Critical incident stress debriefing, 23
Culturally-inclusive interview spaces, 84
Culture(s)
  and conversational habits, 60
  eye contact in, 53–54
  and language, 75–76

Dai, X., 167
Danby, Meaghan, 91–92
Day care abuse cases (1980s), 4, 42
Debriefing, critical incident stress, 23
Debriefing sessions, 184–186
Decisions, case-specific. *See* Case-
    specific decisions and exploration
Defense attorneys
  complex questions asked by, 69n4
  on flexibility of interview protocols,
    80
  on informed interviewing, 46–47
  on interview spaces, 83

Deletion of sounds (pronunciation error),
    70
Demonstrations, in training programs, 180
Depth questions, open-ended, 12, 60,
    61, 115
Descriptions of events, training children
    to provide, 98–102
Developmental assessments, 35–36, 146,
    160–161
Developmental delays, 96
Developmental disabilities, 69, 149–150
Developmentally appropriate language,
    59, 67–76
  cultural differences in, 75–76
  difficult words, 71–73
  overestimation and underestimation
    of, 68–69
  for question forms, 73–75
  and unclear speech by children, 69–71
Developmentally neutral interviews,
    152–154
Developmental psychology, 3, 4
*Diagnostic and Statistical Manual of
    Mental Disorders, Fifth Edition
    (DSM–5)*, 150, 151
Dickinson, Jason J., 18, 90, 96, 145
Difficulties, gathering information
    about, 153–155
Direction, of interview, 36–37
Directive prompts, 112–113
Directive style of conversation, 8–10, 66
Direct questions, about allegations, 111
Disabilities, children with, 149–160
  accommodating, 151–156
  cognitive disabilities, 149, 157–158
  developmental assessments for,
    160–161
  emotional and behavioral challenges,
    149, 158
  health problems, 149, 158–159
  movement disorders, 149, 159–160
  perceptual disorders, 149, 159
  talking about differences with, 151
  terminology associated with
    disabilities, 150–151
Disambiguation, 33–34
Disclosures
  after long silences, 56
  alleged, 34
  discussing prior, 112–114

new, 120, 136, 165
in repeated interviews, 163n5
during therapy, 40–41
unexpected, 106–107
in unrecorded reports, 34
Discrepancies, 77–78. *See also*
Contradictions; Inconsistencies
Distractions, 83–84, 152
Do-confirm lists, 165
Documentation techniques, prop-based,
144, 146–149
Dolls, anatomically detailed, 147
Don't-guess instructions, 91
Double-checking information, 65–66,
117, 153–154
Do-you-know (DYK) questions, 127
Do-you-remember-X questions, 74
Draw-and-talk technique, 146–147
Drawing, free, 145–146
DSM–5 (*Diagnostic and Statistical Manual
of Mental Disorders, Fifth Edition*),
150, 151
Dual representation, 148
Dual roles, for mental health professionals,
37–38
DYK (do-you-know) questions, 127

Early interview phases, 79–107
after unexpected disclosures, 106–107
conducting practice narratives, 97–103
discussing background information,
103–104
ground rules phase, 89–97
interviewer behavior in, 54
interview planning phase, 80–83
interview space preparation, 83–84
introduction phase, 85–89
rapport building in, 85–88
Echolalia, 158
Effort, insufficient, 21–22
Effortful control, 7–8
Elaboration, question frames for, 130
Embarrassed pauses, 130
Emotional comments, by interviewers, 41
Emotional disturbances, 149, 158
Encouragement
in free narrative phase, 115
in practice narrative phase, 98, 102
question frames for, 130
for reticent children, 138–139

Environmental stimuli, sensitivity to, 159
Epilepsy, 158
Episodic language, 119
Episodic recall training. *See* Practice
narrative phase
Erbaugh, C., 45
Errors
internal intrusion, 17, 121
pronunciation, 70–71
with prop-based techniques, 145–147
source-monitoring, 16–17, 110
in training activities, 181
Esbensen, B. M., 17
Esplin, P. W., 86, 112
Euro American cultures, pacing in, 55–56
Evans, Angela D., 127
Event triggers, 165
Evidence-based practice, 27, 178
Expansion paraphrasing, 56, 57
Expert performance
habits in, 50–51
novice vs., 183
training and, 179–182
Explanations
from children, 3
for questions, 135
Explicit learning, 179
Explicit memory, 20–21, 50
Exploration
case-specific. *See* Case-specific
decisions and exploration
in support of investigations, 36–37
Expressive language, 68
Extended Forensic Evaluation, 163n5
Eye contact, 53–54, 158
Eyewitness accuracy, 14–19
and confabulation, 17–19
and cooperative behavior, 14–15
and language confusions, 15
and memory intrusions, 15–16
source-monitoring errors, 16–17

Facilitators, 12
and open-ended prompts, 13, 60
in practice narrative phase, 98, 102
in still-your-turn feedback, 56
Fact-Finding Child Interview (State of
Maine Child and Family Services).
See State of Maine Child and
Family Services protocol

False confessions, 26
False memories, 16
False narratives, 111
False promises, 137
Family members, background information
    about, 103–104
Fatal funnels, 7–8
Fear, 19, 86
Feedback
    in interviewer training, 180, 182–186
    still-your-turn, 56–57, 61, 63
Feelings, questions about, 127–128, 130
Fetal alcohol effect, 150
Fetal alcohol spectrum disorder, 150
Fetal alcohol syndrome, 150
Field research, 25–27, 58
Fischer, K. W., 183
Fisher, Ron, 175–176
Flavell, J. H., 3
Flexible question frames, 66
Focused questions
    benefits of, 65–66
    defined, 61
    effort of children in response to, 21–22
    and eyewitness accuracy, 15, 17–19
    and inconsistent testimony, 21
    in interviews with children, 8–19
    moving from open-ended prompts to,
        63–65
    as prompts, 13, 14
    in questioning cycle, 67
Forensic interviewing, 8
*Forensic Interviewing in Cases of
    Suspected Child Abuse* (American
    Professional Society on the Abuse
    of Children), 178–179
Forensic interviews, 29–47
    with adolescents, 5
    briefing interviewers for, 41–45
    characteristics of, 30–39
    child-centered approach in, 34–36
    commander's intent of, 37–39
    exploration in support of investiga-
        tions in, 36–37
    goals of, 5, 37–39
    hypothesis testing in, 30–34
    by mental health professionals, 39–41
    planning, 80–83
    prior knowledge and bias in, 46–47
    story interviews vs., 29–30

Formatting, checklist, 165
Four-card task, 32–33
Free drawing, 145–146
Free narrative phase, 115–121
    discussing repeated events in, 117–121
    question frames for, 130
    requests to repeat information in,
        117
    structure of, 115–117
    successful, 121
Free recall, 14
Friedman, William J., 133, 167
Friends, background information about,
    103–104
Fry, C. L., Jr., 3
Functional interview spaces, 84

Gawande, Atul, 164
Gaze, 53–54
Geiselman, Ed, 175–176
Gender, eye contact and, 53
Generic interview protocols, 174
Generic language, 118, 119
Goals
    of clinical activities, 40
    of forensic interviews, 5, 37–40. *See
        also* Commander's intent [CI]
    of practice narrative phase, 98
Goodman, Gail, 42–43
Gross, Julien, 145
Ground rules
    delivering, 89–90
    in questioning and clarifying phase,
        131
    selection and placement of, 96
Ground rules phase, 89–97
    delivering rules, 89–90
    don't-guess instructions, 91
    ignorant interviewer instructions,
        95–96
    instructions about false statements
        by interviewers, 92–93
    instructions about telling the truth,
        93–95
    for repeated interviews, 97
    selection and placement of rules, 96
    successful, 97
    tell-me-when-you-don't-understand
        instructions, 91–92
    transition to, 90–91

Guess, as confusing word, 72
Guessing
    by children, 11–12
    at unclear speech, 71

Habits. *See also* Conversational habits
    defined, 50
    expert performance and, 50–51
Hayne, Harlene, 145
Health problems, 149, 158–159
Hearing impairments, 157, 159
Heath, Chip, 38
Heath, Dan, 38
Hershkowitz, I., 59, 86, 112
Highly-structured interview protocols,
    172–173
Honesty, 93–95
Hulse, Debby, 73n6
Human figure diagrams, 147
Hunt, J. S., 10, 69
Hybrid interviewing models, 42, 45
Hypotheses, alternative, 31, 82, 139
Hypothesis testing
    disambiguation in, 33–34
    in forensic interviews, 30–34
    and informed interviewing, 44
    in interview planning, 82
    primary-issues, 31–33

Identity-first language, 151
I don't know responses. *See also* Reticent
        children
    clarifying, 130–132
    interview ground rules on, 89–91
    in topic-raising phase, 112
Ignorant interviewer instructions,
    95–96
Illusory correlation, 23n6
Implicit learning, 179–180
Implicit memory, 20, 50
Impossible questions, 89
Impulsive responding, 131–132
In, as confusing word, 72, 153
Inada, S. S., 72
Incident-labeling process, 118–120
Incidents, descriptions of, 100
Inconsistencies, 4
    and focused questions, 21
    question frames to resolve, 130

in questioning and clarifying phase,
        134–135
    and related questions, 77–78
    and repeated questions, 135
Indirect questions, 127
Individuals with Disabilities Education
        Act, 150
Influence, interviewer, 47
Information. *See also* Ambiguous
        information; Contextual
        information
    about child's strengths and difficul-
        ties, 153–155
    additional, 63–65, 117, 162
    background, 80–81, 87, 103–104
    conceptual understanding of, 183
    discussing background, 103–104
    double-checking, 65–66, 117,
        153–154
    question frames for eliciting,
        129–130
    requesting children repeat, 117
    retrieval of, by experts, 183
    in training programs, 180
Informed interviewing, 43–47, 81
Inhibited temperament, 20
Initial narratives, 61
Inside, as confusing word, 72
In-sync behavior, 54–55
Intellectual disabilities, 148, 157–158
Intellectual impairments, 154
Internal intrusion errors, 17, 121
International Classification of Diseases,
        150
Interpreters, 156–157
Interrupting, in interviews, 76
Intervention testing, 24–27
    basic research findings in, 24–25
    later phases of, 26–27
    preliminary field and analog research
        in, 25–26
Interview content. *See* Case issues
        phases; Early interview phases
Interviewer-provided social support,
        57–59
Interviewers. *See also* Training for
        interviewers
    behavior of, 98
    briefing, 41–45

Interviewers, *continued*
    conversational habits of successful,
        49–50
    emotional comments by, 41
    influence of, 47
    introducing, 85–89
    memory of, 33–34
    objectivity and neutrality of, 40
Interview instructions, 89. *See also*
    Ground rules phase
Interview planning, 80–83
    articulating commander's intent in,
        81–82
    child-specific approach to, 154–156
    compiling background information
        in, 80–81
    constructing alternative hypotheses,
        82
    content planning, 82–83
    creating hypothesis testing strategies,
        82
    successful, 83
Interview protocols, 169–179. *See also*
    specific organizations
    characteristics of, 170–174
    for cognitive interviews, 175–177
    defined, 170
    explicit vs. implicit learning of,
        179–180
    flexibility in, 80
    interview phases in, 79, 80
    narrative elaboration technique in,
        178
    of professional organizations and
        policy committees, 178–179
Interview spaces, 83–84, 161–162
Interviews with children, 7–27
    directive style of conversation in, 8–10
    effortful control in conducting, 7–8
    evolution of practice guidelines on,
        22–27
    factors in eyewitness accuracy of,
        14–19
    focused questions in, 8–19
    forensic. *See* Forensic interviews
    open-ended recall prompts in, 12–14
    overcoming reticence in, 19–22
    story, 29–30
    unanswerable questions in, 11–12

Introduction phase, 85–89
    rapport building in, 86–88
    for repeated interviews, 87–88
    starting interviews, 85–86
    successful, 88–89
Intrusions
    internal intrusion errors, 17, 121
    memory, 15–16
Intuition, professional, 22–24
Investigations
    abuse. *See* Abuse investigations
    criminal. *See* Criminal investigations
    exploration in support of, 36–37
    neglect, 82, 163
Irritability, 158

Jarvis, P. E., 3
Jones, David, 174
Jurisdiction-specific interview protocols,
    174

Kaake, A. M., 18
Katz, C., 59
Kenniston, J., 72
Kinship terms, 73
Know, as confusing word, 72
Knowledge, 16–17, 50, 183
Kolditz, Tom, 38
Kuehnle, Kathryn, 40–41

Lamb, Michael E., 12, 22, 26, 36, 44, 58,
    59, 86, 92, 112, 117, 167, 177
Language
    developmentally appropriate, 59,
        67–76
    in developmentally neutral interviews,
        153
    episodic, 119
    expressive, 68
    general, 118, 119
    identity-first, 151
    in opening introductions, 85
    person-first (people-first), 151
    productive, 68
    receptive, 68
Language confusions, 15
Language development, 24–25, 167–168
Language impairments, 149, 153, 154,
    156–157

Law enforcement. *See also* Police officers
    effortful control in, 7–8
    openness to change in, 186–188
Leading questions, 14
Learning
    advanced interviewing skills, 141–142
    explicit, 179
    implicit, 179–180
    slow and hard, 183–184
Lee, K., 127
Left-branching sentences, 73–74
Less-structured interview protocols,
    172–173
Liberty, A. E., 18
Lie, understanding of, 94, 95
Lindsay, D. S., 116
Los Angeles Police Department
    (LAPD), 176
Lyon, Thomas D., 21, 94, 96, 112, 113,
    127, 128, 177
Lytle, Nicole, 148

Macleod, Emily, 145
Made to Stick (Heath and Heath), 38
Malloy, Lindsay, 25–26, 59
McClure, Kimberley, 23n7
Medical conditions, 69. *See also* Health
    problems
Memorandum of Good Practice protocol,
    171, 174–175
Memory(-ies)
    and confabulation, 17–18
    explicit, 20–21, 50
    false, 16
    implicit, 20, 50
    of interviewers, 33–34
    normal lapses in, 20–21
    retrieval of, by young children, 14
    scripted, 100, 117–118
    temporal, 132–133
    working, 33, 50
Memory intrusions, 15–16
Mental health professionals, dual roles
    of, 39–41
Mental retardation. *See* Intellectual
    disabilities
Metacognitions, 181
Michaels, Kelly, 42
Miller, G., 15

Milne, R., 80
Milne, Rebecca, 43
Mimicry, 54–55
Minimal alleged offence information
    approach, 43
Minimal encouragers. *See* Facilitators
Mirror neurons, 55
Misconceptions, by parents, 43n4
Misinformation, exposure to, 110
Misunderstandings, 15, 69–70
Morgan, M., 44
Movement disorders, 149, 159–160
Multiple interviews. *See* Repeated
    interviews
Multiple questions, in single utterance, 74
Muscular dystrophy, 159
My, appropriate use of, 25
Myside bias, 32–33

Narrative elaboration technique, 178
Narratives. *See also* Free narrative phase;
    Practice narrative phase
    about atypical events, 118
    distinguishing false and true, 111
    encouraging interviewers to explore,
        189–190
    initial, 61
    of repeated experiences, 17
Narrative training, 98
National Association of Certified Child
    Forensic Interviewers protocol, 35
National Center for Prosecution of
    Child Abuse, 44
National Children's Advocacy Center,
    149
    Child Forensic Interview Structure,
        87, 96, 112, 179
    Extended Forensic Interview Protocol,
        163n5
National Institute of Child Health and
    Human Development (NICHD)
    Investigative Interview Protocol,
        26, 33, 116, 177
Negatives, in questions, 75
Neglect investigations, 82, 163
Neutral conversation, 114
Neutral interview spaces, 84
Neutrality, interviewer, 40
New disclosures, 120, 136, 165

NICHD Investigative Interview
    Protocol. *See* National Institute
    of Child Health and Human
    Development Investigative
    Interview Protocol
No, as default answer, 143
Noncontact cultures, 53–54
Nonsuggestive topic prompts, 110–111
Nonthreatening attention, 53–54
Nonverbal behavior, 55, 56
Nonverbal cues, of positivity, 53
Note taking, 33–34, 56
Novel environments, 179–180
Novice performance, 183
Number, questions about, 132–134, 168

Objectivity, interviewer, 40
Off-topic talk, 122–123
Open-ended breadth questions, 12, 60,
    61, 115, 116
Open-ended broad questions, 12, 60, 61
Open-ended depth questions, 12, 60, 61,
    115
Open-ended prompts (open-ended
    questions)
    benefits of, 62–65
    building rapport with, 86–87
    in child-centered approach, 35
    defined, 60
    in developmentally neutral interviews,
        153
    in free narrative phase, 115, 120
    minimal encouragers vs., 61
    other prompts vs., 12–14, 61
    in practice narrative phase, 98, 102
    privileging, 59–67
    in questioning and clarifying phase,
        129–130
    in questioning cycle, 67, 126
    as topic prompts, 111
    in topic-raising phase, 112–113
Opening introductions, 85–86
Openness to change, 186–188
Opposites game, 11–12
Oppositional behavior, 158
Option-posing questions, 13, 14, 61
Orbach, Y., 86, 112
Oregon Interviewing Guidelines
    Workgroup, 161

Oregon's Children's Justice Act Task
    Force, 151
Orienting comments, 88
Oxytocin, 55

Pacing, interview, 36–37, 55–56
Paraphrasing techniques, 56–57
Parents, misconceptions by, 43n4
Passive sentences, 74
Pattern recognition, by experts, 183
Pause points, 165
Pauses
    embarrassed, 130
    in interviews, 55–56
    in topic-raising phase, 114
Payne, G., 45
Penetration, words describing, 72
Perceptual disorders, 149, 159
Perry, N. W., 10, 69
Perseveration, 148, 158
Person-first language (people-first
    language), 151
Peterson, Carole, 66
Phonemes, 70
Phonology, 69
Physical evidence, 113, 163
Piaget, Jean, 12
Play therapy rooms, 83
Pointing words, 73. *See also* Referents
Police officers. *See also* Law enforcement
    authority cues of, 52
    directive style of interviewing by, 10
    opening introductions for, 85–86
Policy committees, protocols of, 178–179
Poole, D. A., 12, 18, 22, 116, 167
Positivity, 52–53
Posttraumatic stress disorder, 23
Powell, Martine B., 12, 44, 112, 117–118,
    119–120
Practice-based interview protocols, 171
Practice guidelines, 22–27
Practice narrative phase, 97–103
    goals of, 98
    structure of, 101–103
    successful, 103
    training children to describe events
        in, 98–101
Practice questions, in ground rules phase,
    90, 92

Practicing, in training programs, 180, 181
Pragmatics, 69
Pratt, C., 15
Preschoolers, 101n2, 142–144
Price, Heather L., 43, 103
Primary-issues hypothesis testing, 31–33
Prior disclosures, discussing, 112–114
Problem-solving tasks, 37–38, 50n1
Productive language, 68
Professional organizations, protocols of,
        178–179
Project Ability (Shelton, et al.), 152
Prompts. *See also* Open-ended prompts
        (open-ended questions)
    defined, 12
    directive, 112–113
    nonsuggestive topic, 110–111
    suggestive, 13, 14, 153
Pronunciation errors, 70–71
Prop-based techniques, 25, 144–149
Proprietary interview protocols,
        171–172
Publicly-available interview protocols,
        171–172

Question forms, 73–75
Question frames (question stems),
        66, 128–131
Question hierarchy, 174
Questioning and clarifying phase,
        122–136
    age, size, and appearance in, 132
    ambiguities and inconsistencies in,
        134–135
    encouraging interviewers to explore
        narratives in, 189–190
    I don't know responses in, 131–132
    number and time in, 132–134
    question frames in, 128–131
    questioning cycle in, 125–126
    recall-detail questions in, 126–128
    repeating questions in, 135
    revisiting ground rules in, 131
    rushing into, 116–117
    successful, 136
    topic drift in, 122–125
    topic markers in, 122–125
    topic shifters for, 122–123
Questioning cycle, 62, 67, 125–126

Questions. *See also* Open-ended prompts
        (open-ended questions)
    accusatory, 127
    ambiguous, 124–125, 131
    bizarre, 15
    concrete, 94, 153
    direct, about allegations, 111
    discrepancies/inconsistencies in
        answers to, 77–78
    do-you-know, 127
    do-you-remember-X, 74
    focused, 8–19, 21–22, 61, 63–67
    forms of, 60
    impossible, 89
    indirect, 127
    leading, 14
    multiple, in single utterance, 74
    option-posing, 13, 14, 61
    practice, 90, 92
    recall-detail, 13, 14, 61, 66, 67,
        125–128, 153
    related, 77–78
    repeating of, 135
    suggestive, 13, 14, 61
    tag, 126
    unanswerable, 11–12
    yes/no, 10, 66, 110–112, 134, 153, 158
Quiet interview spaces, 83–84

Randomized controlled field trials, 26
Rapport building
    in developmentally neutral interviews,
        153
    discussing background information
        for, 103
    in early interview phases, 85–88
    with inhibited children, 20
    and open-ended prompts, 62–63
    in practice narrative phase, 98
    smiling during, 54
Reactions, question frames about, 130
Read-do lists, 165
Reality monitoring, 18
Reasons, question frames about, 130
Recall, free, 14
Recall-detail questions, 14, 61
    accuracy of responses to, 66
    in developmentally neutral interviews,
        153

Recall-detail questions, *continued*
  phrasing for, 126–128
  as prompts, 13
  in questioning and clarifying phase, 125–128
  in questioning cycle, 67, 125–126
Receptive language, 68
Reconsolidation, memory, 15–16
Recording, during breaks, 136
Reese, E., 167
Referents, 73, 125
Refresher training, 182
Reich, P. A., 72
Rejection, social, 52
Related questions, 77–78
Reluctance to answer, 131
Remember, as confusing word, 72
Reminiscence, 117, 162
Repeated events, 17, 100–102, 117–121
Repeated interviews (multiple interviews)
  case-specific decisions about, 162–163
  developmental assessments in, 35–36
  ground rules phase in, 97
  introductory comments and rapport building in, 87–88
Repetition
  of questions, 135
  as response to confusing questions, 75
  of unclear speech, 117
Research
  analog, 26–27, 116
  basic, 24–25
  field, 25–27, 58
Response time, 154
Reticent children, 19–22
  conditions and histories of, 22
  encouraging, in case issues phases, 138–139
  fear of getting in trouble for, 19
  with inhibited temperament, 20
  insufficient effort by, 21–22
  normal memory lapses of, 20–21
  rapport building with, 103
Reversal of sounds (pronunciation error), 71
Revised National Institute of Child Health and Human Development Investigative Interview Protocol, 58–59
Right-branching sentences, 73

Roberts, Kim, 117–118, 119–120
Rotenberg, Ken, 53
Rule codes, 180

Safe interview spaces, 84
Salas, Eduardo, 180, 181
Sanitization, of physical evidence, 163
Saywitz, Karen J., 75, 92, 127, 137, 178
Schofield, Thomas, 54
School-age children
  comfort techniques for, 145
  ground rules phase for, 90
  interviewer-provided social support for, 58
  language competency of, 68
  note taking in interviews with, 56
  positivity for, 53
  practice narratives with, 102
  questions about time for, 133
Schwartz, M., 183
Scope, of forensic interviews, 82
Scripted events, 100, 117–118
Scripts
  for ground rules instruction, 90
  in interview protocols, 166, 172
  organization of memories in, 117–118
Seizure disorders, 158
Selective note taking, 56
Self-reflection, 181
Semantics, 69
Sensory details, question frames about, 130
Sequences of activities, prompting about, 61
Sex, comprehension and usage of, 153
Sexual abuse interviews
  Commander's intent in, 39
  confusing words in, 72
  encouraging reticent children in, 139
  expected topics in, 164
  hybrid interviewing model for, 45
  hypothesis testing in, 31, 33–34
  inconsistencies/discrepancies in, 77–78
  interviewer-provided social support in, 58
  questioning cycle in, 125–126
  reticence of children in, 19, 22
  support of broader investigation in, 36, 37
  topic-raising phase in, 112
  unclear speech in, 69–70

Sexual play, 113–114
Shelton, K., 152
Shulman, Elizabeth, 25–26
Silence, 55–56
Similarity of appearance, 51–52
Simple paraphrasing, 56
Simulations, training, 182, 186–187
Size, questions about, 132
Skepticism, 29n1, 30, 33
Sketch reinstatement of context
        technique, 147n2
Skill mastery, 167–168
Smiling, 53, 54
Smith, Jim, 156n4
Smith, Kevin, 43, 80
Social interactions, rejection in, 52
Social support, interviewer-provided,
        57–59
Sound substitution, 70–71
Source-monitoring errors, 16–17, 110
Source monitoring process, 16
Specific episodes
    labeling of, 118–120
    prompting free narratives about, 118,
        119
    question frames about, 130
Speculation, by children, 12, 15, 91
Speech
    atypical, 156–157
    unclear, 69–71, 157
Speech impairments, 149
Stamina, children with limited, 159
Statement validity analysis, 175
State of Maine Child and Family Services
        protocol, 35, 36, 88, 165, 173
State of Michigan Governor's Task
        Force on Child Abuse and
        Neglect and Department of
        Human Services protocol, 31, 40,
        85, 91, 114, 156n4, 163
Step-Wise Guidelines, 174, 175
Step-Wise Interview, 171, 175
Still-your-turn feedback, 56–57, 61, 63
Stolzenberg, S. N., 127
Story interviews, 29–30
Storytelling process, control of, 10
Strengths, gathering information about,
        153–155
Substitution, sound, 70–71
Suggestive prompts, 13, 14, 153

Suggestive questions, 61
Suggestive techniques, 57–58
Summary paraphrasing, 56–57
Supervision, interviewer, 182–186
Supportive conversational style, 51–60
    gentle entry in, 52
    impact on children's testimony of,
        57–59
    in-sync behavior in, 54–55
    nonthreatening attention in, 53–54
    pacing in, 55–56
    positivity in, 52–53
    rapport building with, 87
    similarity of appearance in, 51–52
    still-your-turn feedback in, 56–57
Support people, in interview spaces,
        161–162
Suspects, in topic-raising phase, 113
Syntax, 69

Tag questions, 126
Target events, 21, 123–124
Taylor, M., 17
Technology-based training, 182
Teenagers. See also Adolescents
    free narrative phase for, 115
    language development of, 68–69
    reticence of, 19
Tell-me-when-you-don't-understand
        instructions, 91–92
Temporal memory, 132–133
Ten Step Investigative Interview
        protocol, 177–178
Teoh, Y. S., 58
Testing, intervention, 24–27
That, in forensic interviews, 124
The Checklist Manifesto (Gawande), 164
Therapy, disclosures during, 39–41
There, as confusing word, 73
Think, as confusing word, 72
Throwing (in training), 189–190
Time
    questions about, 132–134
    word related to, 72–73, 93
Timelines, case, 47
Timing, of ground rules phase, 96
Toddlers, 21, 55, 68
Tomorrow, as confusing word, 72–73
Topic drift, 65
Topic-drift checks, 122–125, 130

Topic management, 129
Topic markers
    in developmentally neutral interviews,
        153
    in open-ended questions, 65
    question frames with, 130
    in questioning and clarifying phase,
        122–125
Topic openers, 130
Topic-raising phase, 110–114
    nonsuggestive prompts for, 110–111
    structure of, 111–114
    successful, 114
Topic shifters, 86–87
    in developmentally neutral interviews,
        153
    to ground rules phase, 90
    to practice narrative phase, 101–102
    question frames for, 130
    to questioning and clarifying phase,
        122–123
    to topic-raising phase, 111
Touch, as confusing word, 72
Touching, prop-based questions about,
    147–148
Tourette's disorder, 159–160
Training for interviewers, 179–186
    and blind vs. informed interviewing,
        44–45
    effective, 180–182
    encouraging interviewers to explore
        narratives, 189–190
    ongoing supervision and feedback in,
        182–186
    and openness to change, 186–188
    technology-based, 182
Training-to-describe, 98–102
Transition comments, 86
Trouble, fear of getting in, 19
True narratives, distinguishing false and,
    111
Trust, 52, 55
Trustworthiness, 53
Truth, instructions about telling, 93–95

Unanswerable questions, 11–12
Unclear speech, 69–71, 157
Unexpected comments, 37–38, 136
Unexpected disclosures, 106–107
Uniforms, 52

Vision loss, children with, 159

Walker, Anne Graffam, 72, 127, 132
Wandrey, Lindsay, 132, 133
Warren, Amye R., 10, 69, 180
White, L. T., 12
Why, in recall-detail questions, 127
Wood, Jim, 23n7
Woodall, C. E., 10, 69
Wording, of checklist items, 165
Word usage
    in conversational habits, 59–60,
        71–73
    in ground rules phase, 90, 91
    inconsistencies due to, 135
Working memory, 33, 50
World Health Organization, 164
Wright, J. W., 3
Writing, atypical, 156–157

Yes/no paraphrasing, 56, 57
Yes/no questions, 10
    accuracy of responses to, 66
    for children with autism spectrum
        disorder, 158
    in developmentally neutral interviews,
        153
    inconsistencies in answers to, 134
    as topic prompts, 110–112
Yesterday, as confusing word, 72–73,
    101n2, 160–161, 167–168
Young children
    case-specific decisions for, 142–144
    clarifying ambiguities with, 134
    confabulation by, 18
    developmental assessments for,
        160–161
    free narrative phase for, 116
    ground rules phase for, 89, 96
    hypothesis testing with, 34
    memory retrieval by, 14
    mispronunciations by, 70
    narrative elaboration technique
        with, 178
    prop-based techniques with, 147, 148
    questioning and clarifying with, 122
    questions about numbers for, 132
    repeating questions for, 135
    still-your-turn feedback for, 57
Yuille, John, 178

ABOUT THE AUTHOR

Debra A. Poole, PhD, is a professor of psychology at Central Michigan University. Since receiving a doctorate in developmental psychology from the University of Iowa, she has conducted studies on children's eyewitness testimony and interviewing techniques. Her research, funded by grants from the National Institute of Mental Health and the National Science Foundation, has explored the effects of repeated questioning, how children respond to different question forms, the influence of misinformation from parents on children's event narratives, children's ability to report the sources of their knowledge, and the risks and benefits of interview props. Dr. Poole has worked with policy groups in Michigan and Maine to craft interview protocols and is on the editorial boards of the journals *Law and Human Behavior* and *Psychology, Public Policy, and Law*.